GENESIS

A Biography

DAVE BOWLER AND BRYAN DRAY

GENESIS

A Biography

SIDGWICK & JACKSON
LONDON

To Mom and Dad
for years of love and understanding – I could not have asked for more.
And for Denise
for providing the key that opened my heart, my eyes and my world.
Always
David

To Trisha, Emma and Rebecca
for love and support.
And to Mum, Dad, Gran, Joyce and Wal
for having wallets larger than their doubts.
Bryan

First published 1992 by Sidgwick & Jackson Limited
a division of Pan Macmillan Publishers Limited
Cavaye Place London SW10 9PG
and Basingstoke

Associated companies throughout the world

ISBN 0 283 061324

3 5 7 9 8 6 4 2

A CIP catalogue record for this book is available from
the British Library

Typeset by Intype, London
Printed and bound in Great Britain by
Mackays of Chatham PLC, Chatham, Kent

Acknowledgements

There have been a number of people without whose contributions this book would have been impossible. Prime amongst these are the individual members of Genesis themselves to whom we pay suitable homage for their inspirational music. In particular we would like to thank Anthony Phillips, Steve Hackett and Mike Rutherford for giving their time so generously and Phil Collins and his personal assistant Annie Callingham for their intervention at a time when all appeared lost. Similarly we would like to thank Tony Smith and Carole Willis Impey at Hit & Run, Billy Budis at Kudos, Carole Broughton at Jonathan King Enterprises Ltd, Hugh Padgham and Dennis Muirhead at Muirhead Management and Fizle Sagar at Probond for dealing with our numerous requests for assistance so helpfully. Much of the basic information and research for the book came from the Best of British and BBC co-production, *The Story Of Genesis*, on which we acted as researchers. For the provision of additional material we are indebted to Mae Miller and Jonathan Masters at the Beeb. Geoff Parkyn at Genesis Information has been a mine of information for many years and all Genesis devotees should immediately send an SAE for details to PO Box 107, London N6 5RU. That wit, bon viveur and generally suave man-about-town Mark Ellen has also been a tower of strength and did supremely well to hide what must have been mounting irritation at our regular requests for advice.

Press and radio have also served us well in allowing us to use quotes from their publications and programmes and in that regard we would like to thank Chantal Kershaw (*Q* and *Sounds*), Karen Walter and Danny Kelly (*New Musical Express*), Allan Jones (*Melody Maker*), Paul Ashford (*International Musician*), Martin Townsend

(*Vox*), Andrew King (Omnibus Press), Alan Carruthers (BRMB-FM), Allison Martin (BBC Radio), Steve King (Hallam FM), John MacCalman (Radio Clyde), Paul Colbert (*Making Music*), Ian Woodward (*Me*), Maureen Dowdeswell, Penny Vincenzi (*Options*), Sandra Brind (*Times* Newspapers), Brendan Quayle, *Kerrang*, *Rolling Stone*, Piccadilly Radio, Capital Radio and Granada Television. The files of certain journalists have been ransacked particularly thoroughly and we would like to single out Chris Welch, Barbara Charone, Armando Gallo and Hugh Fielder for special mention. Despite diligent research, some of the magazines and writers have been impossible to trace, mainly as they have ceased trading, so we would also like to express our gratitude to them. Radio material was thoroughly, and only very occasionally illegibly, transcribed by Denise Dean, to whom a huge debt is owed.

In compiling a tome of this size, some light relief is required and for that we are very grateful to Reeves and Mortimer, Spinal Tap and also to Mr Chris Patten who brightened 'Black Thursday' with his misadventures in Bath. Musical accompaniment was provided by Lush, the Cure, Prefab Sprout, REM and Lou Reed, without whose sterling work, sanity might have slipped away. The biggest thanks of all goes to our families who were there when we needed them and not when we didn't – apologies for our accompanying miserable behaviour in the throes of journalistic chaos. Finally, to all those who over the last few years have been unhelpful, rude or downright dismissive of our efforts and who have told us that we could never write this book and get it published, we have no intention of saying, 'We told you so', but we would just like to point out how bloody stupid you look.

Note 'In The Beginning', 'Where The Sour Turns To Sweet', 'Silent Sun' and 'Am I Very Wrong': Composer Genesis, Publisher Jonjo Music Co. Ltd. 'Everyone's Gone To The Moon': Composer Jonathan King, Publisher Marquis Music Co. Ltd.

Contents

Introduction

As the world trudges into the 1990s, one of the cornerstones of popular culture, rock and roll, heads for its fortieth birthday in a state of considerable disarray, undergoing a mid-life crisis. The tell-tale signs have been there for many years – indeed in 1987 one of pop's key figures, Morrissey, expounded the view that it was on the brink of death, the evidence of its impending demise clear to see. Suffocated by its self-imposed limitations, 'rock' has become largely the preserve of the record companies and their bloated corporate rock bands crossing the globe, 'pop' dominated more than ever by the image-obsessed and the one-hit wonder. 'T'was ever thus' is a sentiment that has some truth in it, for if the history of rock is littered with legendary figures, there are few who have achieved their exalted status for musical reasons alone – take the Sex Pistols, Elton John and more recently Guns 'N' Roses, for instance. The memories that come flooding back of all of these are not necessarily of 'Anarchy In The UK', 'Candle In The Wind' or 'Sweet Child O'Mine' but pictures of angry youths, ludicrous wigs and spectacles, or wanton excess. Iconic? Certainly. Musically exciting? Sometimes. Legendary? Definitely.

A far harder road to immortality is through consistently high artistic achievement, flying the musical flag rather than that of the trends of the day. The criteria here are inevitably more subjective, but the cornerstone qualification must be the ability to put raw emotion and soul on to tape, while still maintaining a high level of innovation and experimentation. The legacy that artists of the calibre of the Beatles, U2 and Lou Reed will leave behind is a body of work of imagination, excitement and songwriting excellence fuelled by an integrity, commitment and passion that sets them apart. Soul music in the truest sense of the term. And that's where Genesis come into the picture.

Many will no doubt balk at the idea of Genesis being described as a soul group. Genesis? Arch-purveyors of that much despised early seventies phenomenon 'progressive rock'? The archetypal reserved, white, English band? The last bastions of art-rock, the school of thought where technique was all and songs were sacrificed on the high altar of the virtuoso player? Those simple, superficial views of Genesis have been put forward by lazy pop pundits for two decades now but such claims do not hold water. Genesis never were part of that crowd, which embraced the likes of Emerson, Lake and Palmer and King Crimson, where the blind concentration on technique often relegated the songs to a secondary role, an attitude that existed into and beyond punk despite the protestations of journalist Charles Shaar Murray who pointed out that judging a guitarist by how fast he plays is like judging a novel by how quickly it was typed. This 'everything including the kitchen sink' mentality rarely, if ever, afflicted Genesis. At the heart of all their recordings, from the earliest days of *From Genesis To Revelation* through to the enormous international success of *We Can't Dance*, they have been first and foremost a collective of songwriters, not musicians, talented players though they are. Each musical device employed has been used purely to serve the song that they are working on, to increase its emotional impact rather than to enhance the reputation of the musician. As Mike Rutherford has said, 'We've never been worried about technique. We're much more concerned with feel.'[1]

Despite strenuous efforts by the band over the years to set the record straight, Genesis are still perceived by many to be art-rockers: cold, clinical technicians with university degrees in music and mathematics, churning out inaccessible, monotonous epics. It's time that view was changed and the group's place in the scheme of things reassessed. As well as telling the story of Genesis from formation to the present day, this book will aim to illustrate just how important their contribution to the world of popular music has been and to offer the opportunity to look again, in a new light, at their recording work. Sweet soul music . . . ?

CHAPTER ONE

'You're in the hands of destiny'

The Genesis phenomenon began at Charterhouse public school in the mid–1960s, where the two initial songwriting teams of Tony Banks and Peter Gabriel, and Michael Rutherford and Anthony Phillips met and began working together. This particular snippet of information has been worked to death over the years, either baldly stated as background detail or used by critics less disposed to their work (with typical British inverted snobbery) as yet another stick with which to beat them. Charterhouse, however, has rarely been looked upon as anything other than the place where the band happened to meet.

This viewpoint is entirely fallacious. Just as Elvis Presley could have been a product only of America's Deep South in the mid-fifties, as the Beatles could have come only from Liverpool in the early sixties and as U2 could have graduated only from mid-seventies punk-inspired activity in Dublin, Genesis was very much a product of its environment – a 1960s English public school.

Think about these examples for a few moments. Elvis Presley was the first real rock and roll singer to make the breakthrough to a national and then international audience. Look at his earliest hits, such as 'That's All Right (Mama)', 'Blue Suede Shoes', 'Heartbreak Hotel' or 'Hound Dog', and you'll find they are just one small step removed from the songs played by the black jazz, gospel or rhythm and blues players of the American South – men like John Lee Hooker, Howlin' Wolf, Muddy Waters. Opportunities for black musicians in those fiercely racist times were inevitably at a premium – the likelihood of one of their number becoming a major international star was so remote that it was never even considered and the music was destined to remain the preserve of a select few.

However, a handsome truck driver from Tupelo changed all that. He had a deep love of the R. & B. songs which he heard as he drove across the South, a thorough grounding in church and gospel music and was steeped in the traditions of white radio music as purveyed by the likes of Crosby and Sinatra. Elvis drew on all these myriad influences to come up with what was, to the majority of white America, an incredibly innovative, exciting and undeniably sexual music that struck a chord with youngsters throughout the nation. The exciting, pounding rhythms of R. & B., coupled with his raucous yet melodic delivery, was complemented by his good looks and pelvic gyrations, which scandalized the guardians of American morals but captured the hearts of millions of young American girls. Boyfriends could only look on in a mixture of envy and admiration for this young man who embodied every adolescent's idea of the American Dream.

Fortunately for Elvis and for the future of rock and roll, these teenagers were the first generation to reap the benefits of a booming world economy which followed hard on the heels of World War Two. Parents who had had to suffer the hardships of the Depression and then the war were determined that their offspring would not go without in the same way. So a whole generation of young people found themselves with a reasonable level of disposable income, courtesy of good old dad. And what better way to dispose of it than on the latest Elvis record?

Essentially Elvis was the sum total of his various musical roots, bringing them together in such a way that they were palatable to the majority. Had he not been white then such global success would have been unthinkable, but effectively he was singing black music, albeit in a manner more restrained and accessible to the general public. The music he heard as he travelled through the Deep South, coupled with the wealth of indigenous talent both behind and in front of the microphone, moulded his tastes and abilities to the point where this naturally gifted entertainer could bring R. & B. to the masses.

Just as Presley was beginning his reign, across the Atlantic in Liverpool youngsters were piecing together their own groups, excited by the songs they heard on late-night Radio Luxembourg, by the likes of Presley, Buddy Holly and Bill Haley. As they became involved in the local music scene, they took full advantage of Liverpool's position as one of the major sea-port links with America. Merchant seamen returning from voyages would bring with them obscure records by the bluesmen of Chicago and the South, the very same musicians from whom Elvis had drawn his inspiration. These would immediately be seized by players and DJs, desperate to hear the weird and wonderful noises so redolent of a far-off country and a different way of life. Bands would often play cover versions of these songs, easily passing them off as their own since none but a select circle had ever heard the originals. The enthusiasm and energy given off by these records also drove bands to write their own songs. One such group was led by John Lennon and included Paul McCartney and George Harrison. After a host of different names, such as the Quarrymen and Johnny and the Moondogs, they eventually settled on the Beatles.

The Beatles' musical passions were the rock and roll sounds of America, but they interpreted them in a very English manner. Their songs were a little more studied, with less of the wild abandon of their American heroes, and with more regard to harmonies and melody, an attribute brought to the group largely by Paul McCartney and his abiding love affair with the traditions of music hall. As much as their musical ability though, the Beatles' own personalities played a huge part in their transformation into the world's biggest group. Their roots in the hard sea-port of Liverpool gave rise to a sharp, acerbic wit, which was to be found both musically and lyrically in their songs and which was later to charm the world's newspapermen in press conference after press conference. That typically schizophrenic scouser personality – which can have you in stitches from hilarious one-liners, then in stitches from a knife wound – seeped into their songs, the powerful contrasts adding new, exciting dimensions to the music.

Perhaps the crucial experience in the Beatles' development was their time in Hamburg in the early sixties, where they were forced to play through the night to hoards of German seamen, all hungry for a spectacular rock show. Here they not only honed their skills as live performers before critical and often aggressive crowds but also, because of the long sets, began to experiment with songwriting, in earnest, turning potential into reality with material penned by Lennon and McCartney, some of which found its way on to their early LP and single releases. Had they not been a Liverpool group this opportunity might never have arisen as it was Merseyside entrepreneur Allan Williams who organized these trips to the Reeperbahn, with groups such as Derry and the Seniors and Gerry and the Pacemakers also benefiting from the experience. This was a turning point for the nascent Fabs. Prior to their first visit they were considered no-hopers – Williams sending them as a last resort when another group cancelled, much to the fury of Howie Casey, playing with Derry and the Seniors, who told Williams that if he sent over such a lousy band he'd mess up for everyone a profitable scene. History shows just what immense strides the group made during their time in Germany, and just how much a product they were of their initial surroundings and experiences.

A little more than a decade after the explosion of Beatlemania, a new musical phenomenon swept the land in the form of punk rock, a force which tore down established guidelines of musical taste and fashion, and which had far-reaching repercussions throughout the world. Teenagers seized on the fact that you no longer needed any ability to play in a band, just the desire to do so – a real tonic after years of professorial musicians and jazz-rock virtuosos such as John McLoughlin, Pink Floyd, ELP and Carlos Santana. You no longer had to be a genius to be in a rock group – fierce energy and aggression, however unfocused, were the vital ingredients, qualities which the likes of the Sex Pistols, the Clash and Siouxsie and the Banshees possessed in abundance. Music was just a part of the overall scheme of things; fashion and the desire to tear down the establishment now being every bit as important.

'New-wave', as it was sometimes termed, also took hold in Dublin. It was, however, rather different to its British equivalent. While for British punk it was vital that the end product reflected anger and the rejection of everything that had gone before, the Irish bands were more concerned with punk's initial premise that the desire to communicate, not immense technical proficiency, was the important criterion, echoing the American 'garage band' philosophy of Iggy and the Stooges. While the Pistols and the Banshees flaunted their lack of ability, bands like the Boomtown Rats saw that as just a constituent element of their whole ethos. These bands were excited by the new opportunities they had been given to make music, but were not so foolish as to ignore their forebears and drew on the influences of the past whenever it served their purpose.

U2 were very much a part of the new-wave movement in late-seventies Dublin and were of the same social group that spawned the Virgin Prunes. Originally inspired by the *idea* of the Sex Pistols as much as the music, they formed a group – indeed they were a band before any of them could really play. If the concepts of anger and rebellion were an integral part of the original U2 ideal, they were tempered by the gentler sides of their backgrounds: their grounding in traditional Irish folk music, their interest in the American school of new-wave as purveyed by Patti Smith, Television and Talking Heads, and also their deep religious beliefs.

The prevailing Dublin attitude of encouraging rather than scorning artistic endeavour also acted in their favour, with teachers offering them the use of school facilities for practice – very different to the masters at Charterhouse! Evidence of the effects of this swamp of influences can be found in abundance on U2's first records, *Boy* and *October*, with the anger of 'Out Of Control' or 'Electric Co.', the religious message behind 'Gloria', the passion of 'I Will Follow' or the pastoral 'October'. These were songs that could have come only from a band with their background at that period in time.

All these great artists were very much products of their own particular surroundings and times, which when harnessed to their own natural talents gave rise to an explosion of music so powerful that it won them their places in the history of popular culture, setting them apart from those who came later. This applies every bit as much to the story of Genesis. The initial nucleus of the band, Tony Banks, Peter Gabriel, Michael Rutherford and Anthony Phillips, were pupils at Charterhouse, an established public school in the mid–1960s. Social revolution was in the air – with the advent of the Beatles and the Rolling Stones, the rise of flower-power, aggressive student unrest on the Continent, protests against American involvement in Vietnam, greater political awareness and an expanding drug culture – and the world would never be quite the same again. England was at the heart of this dramatic period, its music both reflecting and inspiring the changes.

Inevitably, a group of adolescent boys housed in the repressive atmosphere of an English public school, one of the last great repositories of Victorian values and the spirit of Empire, would find concepts such as revolution, freedom and the overthrow of the old guard in favour of a more creative way of life very attractive. However, as boarders, reality meant that uniforms still had to be worn, hair kept short, lessons attended and standards upheld – failure to do so would mean punishment. Discipline was so strong that Peter Gabriel was later to observe that 'they say you can tell an ex-public schoolboy in prison because he takes to it like a duck to water.'[2]

Weekends were a little more relaxed and, inspired by the hits of the day, groups of boys would gather to attempt to recreate these songs and write their own. The very fact that the members of the fledgling Genesis were virtually forced to stay within the confines of the school grounds enabled them to apply the fullest concentration to their music. In the 'outside world' people of their own age had any number of leisure activities with which they could fill their spare time, but Banks, Gabriel, et al, had little choice –

sport or music being the only real options available to them. They decided to channel their energies into songwriting and performing, thereby forging a link, however tenuous, with their peers in the outside world. Being in a pop group was certainly not *de rigueur* for public schoolboys at that time and was looked on as a major rebellion against authority of the school, despite the success in the pop world of Charterhouse old-boy Jonathan King, who was to help them make the first tentative steps towards fame and fortune.

Circumstances therefore gave them the chance to concentrate their endeavours on music, which provided a tremendous mental and emotional release from the enforced discipline of day-to-day life at Charterhouse. However, not only did the school actually give them the time and means to play music, it also offered them a wide-ranging catholic musical background from which they would regularly draw inspiration over the years. Inevitably, classical music was the preferred style at Charterhouse and music lessons would centre around the lives and works of the great composers. Those wishing to learn an instrument would be taught classical pieces – electric guitar lessons certainly did not feature on the school's curriculum! The sweeping, majestic movements, combined with themes on a grand, epic scale found in these works would often be echoed in Genesis' music, particularly in early songs like 'Fountain of Salmacis' or 'Supper's Ready'.

Church music was also to influence their attitudes to writing and performing, shaping the belief that the most important aspect of their music was its emotional content. Peter Gabriel has often stated that he found singing hymns an incredibly powerful emotional experience, and recalls coming out of school assemblies in the Chapel, having screamed his head off, feeling on top of the world. 'On the few good hymns, which were anthem-like in some ways, I think it's the closest that the white man gets to soul music.'[3] Mike Rutherford and Anthony Phillips were equally moved, later writing a hymn together which finally found a home on Charisma's *Beyond An Empty Dream* collection. This innate feel for music of passion and commitment, and for the sanctity of the song over the technical performance, stood the band in good stead and is perhaps the central most important factor in their success. Contemporaries of the so-called 'classical rock' school, such as Pink Floyd, the Moody Blues or Emerson, Lake and Palmer, were all highly gifted technicians but they often produced stark, even clinical music. It is clear even to the most casual listener that, if nothing else, Genesis have always instilled a real and rare passion into what they do. Essentially they write soul music in its widest sense, a compulsion which can be readily traced back to their realization of the power music has to unleash a whole sea of emotions, a realization they made when singing hymns at Charterhouse.

The third musical influence to which they were exposed was, of course, the rock music of the day, be it by the Beatles, Stones, Beach Boys, Motown or any number of other exciting and innovative acts – surely the sixties will be remembered as the most fertile and important period in the history of pop music. At Charterhouse, with little freedom or inclination to do much else, the boys would spend an hour each evening listening to the pop classics of the day. Peter Gabriel remembers it as 'a very important hour.'[3] During this time they assimilated the rudiments of songwriting – and there could not have been better teachers of that than the likes of Lennon and McCartney.

It is apparent, then, that the founder members of Genesis were in the right place at the right time, soaking up a whole range of ideas and influences that they would be able to use to the full in their future songwriting careers. Also their initial tastes and the original ethos of the group would not have been quite the same had they got together elsewhere. They were, in part, a product of their surroundings.

However, all this is not nearly enough on which to base an explanation for their success. The essential element was the individual talents of Banks, Gabriel, Phillips and Rutherford – and later the injection of new experiences, tastes and backgrounds in the forms of Steve Hackett and Phil Collins – their ability to absorb the lessons and eventually to combine them with their own ideas, translating this into an exciting, iconoclastic musical synthesis. Not only were they each blessed with musical skills, but in some way the chemistry which existed between them, and which has remained intact throughout their various changes in personnel, served to create a group which was greater than the sum of its constituent parts, an ever-evolving entity which seemingly has its own life beyond the individual group members.

Peter Gabriel was, along with Tony Banks, the first to arrive at Charterhouse in September 1963. He was born on 13 February 1950 into a background that gave a number of hints as to his future. His father was a respected electrical engineer and inventor, a path that Peter was to follow through his fascination with the relationship between technology and music. It also goes some way to explaining the experimental nature of much of his work, both inside and outside music. His mother was one of five sisters, all of whom played a musical instrument, and his father's sister was an opera singer, which meant that he grew up on a steady diet of classical and church music. Inevitably this led to piano lessons for the young Gabriel until, at the age of nine, he rebelled and decided he'd rather watch TV instead. Although the music around him must have seeped into his sub-conscious, Peter never felt any particular enthusiasm for it until he first heard pop music. He recollects a song by Johnny and the Hurricanes, 'Red Rock River', and the excitement the roughness of the recording stirred in him. 'I was always drawn to things that had an interesting sound – I can still remember the exact circumstances when I first heard the Beatles, Jimi Hendrix and Nina Simone. The sounds made a great impression on me.'[3] Peter recalls a very happy childhood in the midst of a normal upper-middle class family, living in a farm cottage with plenty of adjoining space to play and explore. His only regret was that, with typical English reserve, the family were rarely open with one another in any emotional way, a preoccupation which was to find its way into many of his later lyrics.

Tony Banks was born on 27 March 1950, in East Hoathly, the youngest of five children. He took to the piano at an early age until the regimentation of regular lessons and learning set pieces dissipated its appeal. This distaste for rules and regulations has been a catalyst for the highly original writing style that he has employed both as an individual and with Genesis. Nevertheless, he persisted with his studies when he was sent as a boarder to Boarzell prep school in Hurst Green at the age of seven, his mother, also a pianist, having arranged lessons with the headmaster's wife. As a consequence Tony was a more than competent player by the time he went on to Charterhouse, where he continued to study classical piano as an extracurricular subject.

Banks' and Gabriel's reactions to Charterhouse's forbidding strictures were very similar, Banks remembering that 'I went through periods of being extremely unhappy. I was shy and liked to be on my own a lot and the Charterhouse system is not good for people like that'[4] – having already spent six years at boarding school, that says much for the intimidating atmosphere that Charterhouse could inspire in some of the boys. Gabriel was equally negative in his reaction, suffering a greater culture shock than Tony since this was his first time as a boarder, though he had been a weekday boarder during his final year at prep school, in order to get acclimatized to that way of life: 'I hated Charterhouse, it was terrible.'[3]

The existing regime was not altogether different from that portrayed in the novel *Tom Brown's Schooldays*, set in a public school more than a century earlier. The same power structure was in place with the older boys using the younger ones as their 'fags', dogsbodies to perform menial duties. Charterhouse saw itself as a schooling ground for the future captains of commerce and industry, for politicians and military officers. It suited the strong, outgoing types but had little time or tolerance for the introverted boys. Both Tony and Peter realized that their time there was going to be difficult but found in each other kindred spirits and a shared interest in pop music, so they stuck together in adversity in order to 'survive with the least pain'.[5]

The problems that were constantly thrown at them in the form of the school's rules and regulations only strengthened their passion for music. Peter points out the contrast between the school and the sounds they were hearing on the radio: 'It was a very repressive atmosphere and so to hear things like Otis Redding and the Stax and Motown artists, they seemed very free and open and liberating in comparison. I think these were pivotal experiences that made us want to get involved with music.'[3] Tony particularly noted the differences between school life and that of the outside world. 'From what we read, the rest of the country was becoming more liberal but the schools took so long to go that way. I found it very restrictive – rock music was our escape, it really helped me through the last year or so. We used to go out to the local record shops and get them to play us the latest Beatles album in the listening booths and then not buy them! That was a lot of fun!'[4]

One of the very few and consequently very precious freedoms allowed the boys was the chance to play the piano in the dining hall. Every day, following classes, there was a great rush to get there first – Gabriel often trying to beat the others by crawling through serving hatches! Banks generally claimed the piano, though, so Peter would sing along with him, although at that time he had no pretensions towards singing, being far more interested in playing the drums. His drum-kit was his prized possession and he had his first taste of live performance at fifteen, drumming with a short-lived rhythm and blues outfit called the Spoken Word. Initially, Tony and Peter merely recreated tunes such as 'Try A Little Tenderness' and 'You Put A Spell On Me' – Banks was particularly impressed with Gabriel's performance of soul music. Soon they were writing their own songs, generally putting them together by improvising around the piano: Peter singing along to Tony's chord progressions, the songs continually changing and evolving.

As Tony and Peter were beginning to come to terms with Charterhouse, returning for their second year there, the new intake brought Michael Rutherford to the school. Slightly younger than the others, he was born on 2 October 1950, numbering the poet Shelley and the composer Lord Berners among his forebears – a clear portent for his future! His earliest years were spent in Portsmouth, but in 1956 his father retired from his position as a captain in the Navy and the family moved to Cheshire. Like Tony, Mike found himself at boarding school – The Leas in Hoylake – at the age of seven, where he remained until he left for Charterhouse. Naturally enough, he found living away from home at such a tender age a little strange, but generally enjoyed the experience. Mike had been playing the guitar from the age of seven, for no reason other than its shape – 'I liked the symmetry of it, it pleased my eye.'[5] Early on he was exposed to his sister's record collection, featuring Elvis and the Everley Brothers, later moving on to Cliff Richard and the Shadows. He entered Charterhouse just before his fourteenth birthday in September 1964 and admits to being terrified by the place. 'It wasn't a good place for any of us. We weren't right for it – they're easier if you're into sport and activities which we weren't,'[4] he says.

Just as Tony and Peter had found an escape in their music and friendship, Mike did likewise when, in April 1965, Anthony Phillips arrived. 'Without playing and writing I'd have gone crazy.'[4]

Phillips, born in December 1951, came to Charterhouse an accomplished and inventive guitarist. He had a friend at the school, Rivers Job, the two having already formed a group in the early sixties called the Spiders, named after a little known combo from Merseyside. Quite naturally, they soon put together a new group, Anon, featuring Richard MacPhail on vocals and Rob Tyrell on drums. This was to be Rutherford's salvation for they began to look for a rhythm guitarist. Mike fitted the bill perfectly, and went on to become their lead singer when MacPhail left following parental pressure. They specialized in Rolling Stones covers, 'because they had that rebellious edge to them,'[4] Ant says. He recalls:'We used to sleep, eat and drink music, it was an absolute passion. It was very worrying for the school, because obviously they thought we were going to bring down the establishment. It was regarded as dangerous and subversive.'[4]

Mike's tenure as lead singer was short-lived, Ant admitting, 'I gave him a hard time! I goaded him into singing "Mercy Mercy" by the Stones and he couldn't make the high notes! He dropped out of the group for a while and a music scholar called Mick Coleman joined us.' Having left Anon, Mike formed another group. Ant recalls that 'it was a less intense thing that didn't really happen – they kept blowing up their equipment!' Unfortunately, Mike then fell foul of a particularly strict House Master who took action against him: 'I was banned from playing the guitar through my whole career there. I guess pop music was the symbol for the revolution about to overthrow the establishment and bring the country down. My House Master thought I was going to start the revolution and so the guitar was banned which probably made me even keener. I had to sneak into classrooms and dark cellars to practise!'[4]

Ironically, just as Anon's future was in some doubt, Banks and Gabriel had formed a group called the Garden Wall. That the school now had two putative bands was seized upon by Richard MacPhail, who wanted to mark his departure from Charterhouse in the summer of 1966 by staging an end-of-term concert. Having used much of his free time on trips to London to see bands at clubs such as the Marquee, he wanted to recreate that kind of atmosphere at Charterhouse and so lined up both groups for the July concert.

The initial reaction of the school establishment was fairly pre-dictable – initially bemused by it, the more hard-line members of staff were horrified and attempted to quosh the event or at least minimize its impact. The principles of Charterhouse were founded on the idea of team spirit and the community – team sports such as rugby and cricket were actively encouraged, whereas individual pursuits like tennis and golf were less acceptable. The idea of forming a pop group was far worse than that! Mike Rutherford feels that, threatened by the social change going on in the outside world over which they had no control, the masters became ever keener to maintain the accepted order at the school. 'They just saw pop music as the revolution that was going to bring everything down and so they tried to stop it.'[4] Ultimately thanks to MacPhail's persuasive powers, allied to the fact that it was at the end of the school term (thus leaving no time for any pupil unrest in its aftermath), the establishment relented and allowed the concert to go ahead. The sting in the tail of this concession was that it had to take place in the school hall starting in the late afternoon, which meant that the groups played in broad daylight, thus making it difficult to create any sort of atmosphere. It was also made clear that there would be no announcements from the stage.

MacPhail was sufficiently delighted with this news to throw

himself into arrangements for the show. He found another school
group to open the concert, before the Garden Wall took to the
stage. Tony and Peter had found themselves a drummer, Chris
Stewart, since it was physically impossible for Peter to fill both
roles, but were still short of guitar and bass and were forced to
rope in Rivers Job and Anthony Phillips to help them out before
they played their set with Anon. Tony remembers the show quite
vividly: 'I was playing piano and I wasn't actually on the stage
because we couldn't lift it up, so no one knew I was playing
until the fourth number which I started, "When A Man Loves A
Woman". We did a few improvised things, a soul version of "I
Am A Rock", "You Really Got A Hold On Me", it was pretty
terrible.'[4] The act also featured a twelve-bar number where Peter
had to give the signal to stop. Ant remembers that 'Peter would
give the signal but Chris wouldn't stop, he was just flailing away
not looking at anyone! It went on and on, Peter was signalling
more and more exaggeratedly, the audience was going to sleep
and in the end I just stopped playing!' Signalling aside, Peter made
his particular bid for attention by wearing a kaftan and beads,
crawling around the stage and throwing rose petals into the air.

Anon followed them, though Ant remembers their music
master, Geoffrey Ford, insisted on calling them The Anon. During
the change over of instruments between songs, Richard MacPhail
decided to puncture the deafening silence by announcing the next
song. According to Ant, 'Suddenly this music master was at the
stage, red and Vesuvian, shouting, "No announcements!" He
stopped the concert and there was nearly a riot – they were rocking
this big clock in the main hall!' Despite the abrupt ending, Ant
still remembers it as being a 'great, great evening,'[5] an evening
which convinced him that this was what he wanted to do in
the future. Anon soon disbanded, but, far from dampening his
ambition, this gave Ant the incentive and opportunity to start
writing with Mike on a far more regular basis, freed as they were
from the need to play cover versions or to pander to anyone else's
tastes. Initially they used 'two electric guitars, fairly primitive and
unoriginal, which actually continued on into early Genesis.' They
spent as much time on their songs as was possible, although
difficulties arose from their being in different Houses at the school,
as their free times would not always coincide. At such times, Mike
continued to play alone, while Ant would sometimes sit in with
Tony and Peter, 'two older, more mysterious people'[4] who were
in the same House.

After a period of three months or so, Mike and Ant decided that they wanted to make a tape of five of their new songs using some basic recording facilities that were owned by a friend. In these early days, and with a strictly limited amount of money at their disposal, the songs had to be played directly on to tape without any recourse to overdubbing, as is the case now, so Ant and Mike needed a band to play their music. Ant suggested that they use the Garden Wall's musicians but Mike was initially very reluctant as he felt that they were 'a bit too jazzy, not really rock and roll, a little bit twee!'[4] Finally, though, the desire to record the songs overcame reservations and Phillips invited them to take part in the sessions. In the Easter holidays of 1967, Tony Banks, Mike Rutherford, Peter Gabriel and Anthony Phillips entered a recording studio together for the first time.

CHAPTER TWO

'All I hear is music'

The decision to enter Brian Roberts' primitive studio in Chiswick to demo some songs raised a number of problems, all of which centred around money and equipment – or rather the lack of it. Mike borrowed enough money to buy a Hofner Very Thin and managed to borrow a Futurama 30-watt amplifier – which he promptly blew up – while another friend lent Tony a Farfisa organ for the session. At first Gabriel wasn't invited to attend but Tony asked him along so that they could also demo the first song that they had written, 'She's Beautiful'. Ant was, initially, going to sing on the demos simply because he had written the lyrics and had always played the songs with his own vocal accompaniment, and indeed when Peter failed to turn up on the first day he did do the singing. Tony remembers it as 'really terrible'[4] and persuaded him to allow Gabriel to take over. 'In fact,' Phillips remembers, 'theirs turned out to be the only good song – the rest were absolutely desperate!'[4] At the end of two days' work they had a tape comprising 'Don't Want You Back', 'Try A Little Sadness', 'She's Beautiful', 'That's Me', 'Listen On Five' and the instrumental 'Patricia', a piece that Ant had written when he was thirteen and which finally became 'In Hiding'. Having recorded some songs the next question was what to do with them. Tony is clear on the point that they were all keen to get involved in the pop world and to take their songwriting further: 'We wanted a contact. Jonathan King was a Charterhouse old boy . . .'[4]

King had left the school in 1965 and had immediately embarked on a successful music career with a top five hit in July of that year, 'Everyone's Gone To The Moon'. Of more interest to the boys at Charterhouse was the knowledge that he had then moved into music production and publishing and was constantly on the alert for new artists and songwriters. King returned to the school on Old Boys' Day, so they decided to press a tape on to him. Being somewhat nervous and in awe of this youthful impresario they got a colleague, John Alexander, to leave the recording in his car. 'I returned after my first year at Cambridge University with a hit record and was given a tape which I just happened to play in the car on the way home. I thought it was fabulous – there was a great lead voice and some interesting songs.'[4] Tony says, 'The tape was very rough but he liked it. He asked us up to London to see him and he agreed to finance some demo tapes.'[4]

King was clear about what he wanted – very basic arrangements, featuring voice and guitar or voice and piano. King protests that this was in their best interests not a case of him foisting ideas on to the group. 'There's a totally erroneous story that I wanted them to be acoustic because it was the sound of the day – the reason was that it was much less expensive to buy acoustic instruments. Also, you can perfect what you are doing much better because you can hear your mistakes more easily. It made me unpopular because they were keen on organ and guitar solos which weren't very good and so I'd cut them back to the bare bones.'[4] Whether they agreed with King or not, they acted under his orders and put together another demo featuring 'The Image Blown Out' – later recorded and rejected for *From Genesis To Revelation*, a piece of prime psychedelia – 'Where The Sour Turns To Sweet' and new versions of 'She's Beautiful' and 'Try A Little Sadness'.

King was thrilled with these performances and decided to put this nameless group under contract. Tony remembers the situation: 'We signed a very long publishing deal – ten years – with Jonathan which we managed to get out of because we were still minors! It was just that we were so excited that anyone was interested in us – that's all we were looking for and we were prepared to sign our lives away!'[4] In fact, King's actions indicated his enthusiasm and belief in the young writers and were not as restrictive as perhaps it seemed on the surface. King signed them to a standard publishing contract for five years, with a five-year option, on what were considered to be fairly normal terms, Ant remembering that they each received an advance of £10! When the contracts were put before the boys' parents for ratification, they insisted that the term be changed to a one-year contract with a one-year option instead.

Contracts signed, King's first idea was for the group to release a single. The summer of 1967, the 'summer of love', was in full swing by August when the band went into Advision Studios to make their first record. *Sergeant Pepper* filled the air and Ant remembers the period vividly. 'It was an incredible time to be that age – I'd been on holiday with my parents in Tangiers, I'd been out there drinking mint tea, it was all so hip,' he laughs. 'I remember I saw Brian Jones there, he was my big hero in the Stones, he'd got a blonde on each arm, it was amazing! I'd managed to bring a kaftan back with me and wore it to the studio – Jonathan King called me a flower child!' Matching the naivety of the times, the single was to be 'Where The Sour Turns To Sweet'. Perhaps due to a combination of nerves and studio ignorance, the recording sessions didn't work out and the single was shelved.

Despite this early setback, King was still very drawn to the simplicity of their songs which were, to an extent, reminiscent of the innocence of his own hit record and those of one of his charges, Hedgehoppers Anonymous. They were grounded in the straight-forward melodies of the mid-sixties rather than the sounds of psychedelia which were starting to grip the country, a movement with which Genesis had little empathy. They appealed to King's musical sweet tooth, but there was more to it than that: 'I thought Peter Gabriel had a very distinctive voice and they were writing very original and intelligent songs.'[4] Peter agrees that their public school background led them to try to use intellect in rock music, although he has since expressed uncertainty as to just how good an idea this was.

Such intelligence and ambition gave rise to early conflict with King. He had asked them to record some more songs at Regent Sound in Denmark Street, London, studios where the Rolling Stones had begun their recording career. The group had been given fresh impetus by King's patronage and had been busily writing whenever the opportunity presented itself. Tony feels that the group progressed considerably over that period. 'As we went on, the music got more involved, what you might call more typical later Genesis stuff. The reason we were doing longer songs was that no one else was, so we thought that what we were coming up with was more fun.'[4] Ant concurs: 'In a very primitive way it was a precursor of the later longer and more rounded pieces, but not very convincingly played.' Unfortunately, King was less happy with the new direction and on receipt of a new batch of eight songs – none of which was ever released, but which included titles such as 'Barnaby's Adventure' and 'Fourteen Years Too Long' – his publisher wrote to Peter at Charterhouse to inform him that he didn't like the songs and felt that they should return to basics. 'As with so many young groups, they were trying to be better than they were,'[4] is Jonathan's view.

'Because he was in the business, we were a little in awe of him and we didn't want to let him go,' recalls Tony. 'We realized he wasn't into the new songs and so I sat down with Peter and wrote a song tailor-made to Jonathan's tastes. His favourite group was the Bee Gees so we did a Bee Gees pastiche, "The Silent Sun". He loved it and on the strength of that we were allowed to carry on.'[4] Ant wasn't so happy with the song: 'It seemed like a real compromise, though perhaps they were a little bit older and wiser and could see the need to keep hold of Jonathan – Peter was very ahead of the game in that respect, a wonderful combination of someone who is very shrewd and businesslike yet bizarrely creative in some of his ideas.'

Predictably perhaps, King remembers things slightly differently. 'That song was called a Bee Gees pastiche, but that's wrong because it was before the Bee Gees and Crosby, Stills and Nash were doing that type of thing.'[4] Whichever is the case, King did love 'The Silent Sun' and was sufficiently enthused to have it recorded for single release. They went into Regent Sound A in December 1967, with King producing and Arthur Greenslade brought in as musical director to augment the record with a string section, leaving everyone pleased with the outcome and looking forward to its release date, 22 February 1968, on the Decca label, home of King's own hit records.

In retrospect, 'The Silent Sun' is a fairly innocuous piece of mid-sixties semi-acoustic bubblegum and it's to the B-side that one must turn for any indication of the future Genesis. A Phillips/Rutherford composition, 'That's Me', showcased Peter Gabriel's voice more effectively, a voice far thicker and more emotional than one would have expected from one so young. The song boasted a quirkier arrangement than the A-side, with a fuzz guitar solo very redolent of the times, while the lyrics were interesting, echoing, at least in part, 'Nowhere Man' by the Beatles. The song lacked the requisite power as it built to its climax, but that was largely attributable to studio nerves plus the rather hesitant rhythm section featuring Chris Stewart on drums and Mike Rutherford on bass, an instrument he had been playing for just a few months. The single represented a step forward for the group, but before they could take an unsuspecting nation of record buyers by storm they needed a name.

Little attention had been given to finding a group moniker as they had had no need for one while they were simply writing songs and recording demos. Now, with a release date looming large, they had to come up with some ideas. Clearly Anon and the Garden Wall were out as the group now contained parts of both and, anyway, they needed a name that would reflect their new start. According to Peter, one of Jonathan King's ideas was 'to call us Gabriel's Angels! For some reason, I found the name very attractive, but the rest of the band didn't like it!'[3] Various other names came and went and Tony recalls that, 'Anthony Phillips came up with the Champagne Meadow, so I'm glad we didn't use that! We have to blame Jonathan for the name, he just suggested Genesis, it was purely arbitrary.'[4] Tony may feel it was arbitrary, but King thinks differently: 'The name seemed right at the time and I chose it because it was really the start of my production career. It had nothing to do with the group!'[4]

Whatever the case, Genesis had arrived and were expecting great things, as Tony explains: 'Jonathan King had a TV show at the time and so we thought we'd be on it. We went to Carnaby Street to get some clothes and we went for a black and white theme – I'm not a clothes man so Ant bought mine for me! We were young and naive, so we thought we'd cracked it.'[4] Ant remembers, 'We thought Top of the Pops was a formality so we went and bought some awful clothes!'[4]

'The Silent Sun' was first broadcast on BBC national radio by Kenny Everett, and the pirate station Radio Caroline played it regularly before it was forced to leave English waters. Melody Maker also liked the record, so the omens were good. But the great British public were thoroughly underwhelmed by the song and there was to be no Top of the Pops appearance this time. Looking back, the group are relieved that it wasn't a success. Banks claims: 'It was probably the best thing that ever happened to us because if we'd had a big hit then, I don't think we would have lasted. We'd have been compelled to stay in an area of music that we weren't particularly happy with.'[4] Ant adds, 'It would have been very difficult to regain any credibility if it had been a success.'

Even though Genesis had scarcely threatened the dominance of the Beatles and the Rolling Stones over the nation's pop charts, Jonathan King was still content to record a further single, which featured two more Banks/Gabriel compositions. Although the New Musical Express cited 'A Winter's Tale' as being a potential hit, Britain again reacted with indifference. The A-side was in a similar vein to 'The Silent Sun', a simple obsessive love song, but which showed Genesis in more confident mood. The central refrain concerned the hiding of emotions, both a call to a lover and a sly reference to the repression of their public school background. As with their début disc the B-side, 'One-Eyed Hound', showed a darker and rockier side to the group, opening with a nod in the direction of the Jimi Hendrix Experience and employing some of the vocal harmonies which were to crop up on *Trespass*. Tony's playing was very assured on both sides of the single and Ant and Mike were beginning to develop the acoustic guitar sound that was soon to become a Genesis trademark. But again when the band should have been moving up a gear, driving onwards and upwards, they were simply too mannered and deliberate.

It was shortly after the recording of 'A Winter's Tale' that Chris Stewart parted company with Genesis. He was still at Charter-house after the others had left and, as he had no input into their songwriting, there was no real part for him to play. Phillips feels that, at the time, he was probably as competent a musician as any of them, but that he lacked real dedication and was finally just phased out, being replaced by John Silver, a friend of the group.

Both before and after this first personnel change, the group continued to write new songs which were then passed on to Jonathan King, some of which were never to see the light of day, including one called 'Everywhere is Here'. Undaunted by the lack of success with their opening singles, King decided that their music was of such a standard that they should go ahead and make an LP. Even in its infancy, the Genesis sound and approach was probably better suited to the longer format than the single: they were already exploring more complex themes lyrically and musi-cally, so the single was too limiting for them. Given the oppor-tunity to record almost forty-five minutes of music, they decided to get some new material together, and spent time with John Silver's parents in Oxford and also at a manor house owned by the parents of another friend, David Thomas, who had played with Peter in the Spoken Word.

The sheer amount of time available to them on an album was a little overwhelming, so King felt that they needed a unifying theme. 'I came up with a very pretentious idea which really hadn't been done much at the time – a concept album. The album opened with the beginning of creation and would go through to the end of time!'[4] While the idea may sound pretentious now, at the time his concept didn't seem so outlandish. The LP had the working – and final – title of *From Genesis To Revelation*.

As King had intended, the images evoked by the story meant that Genesis had something to get their teeth into and they very quickly came up with the requisite number of songs. Ten days' worth of studio time had been booked at Regent Sound B in the summer of 1968 and so the band decamped to Thomas' basement flat in Earls Court, London. Once again recording was a fairly primitive affair, although for the first time they were allowed the luxury of two four-track recording machines. While this opened up new options for them in terms of types of sound available, the group as a whole were far too inexperienced in the ways of the studio to reap the benefits, something they found particularly frustrating. Mike now thinks of it as 'a starting point for us. It meant that we could see the possibilities.'[4] Ant adds that 'It did let us break out slightly from the verse/chorus approach.' Tony feels that it has very little connection with what came later, moulded as they were by Jonathan King: 'It's a bit out on its own.'[4]

As with the recording of the early singles, Jonathan King was at the helm, with Arthur Greenslade adding string arrangements. While everyone had been relatively happy with the colouring Greenslade had added to the singles, the band were less than pleased with the results of his labours on the album. Having envisaged a bank of strings complementing the twin acoustic guitars, they found that this time the section swamped the rest of the music, taking one of the stereo channels. (That separation does at least mean that by isolating one channel one can get some inkling of how it must have originally sounded in demo form.) There is little question that the strings are very intrusive and do the songs no favours at all, although one can also see that it was King's attempt to add some extra body to what were, at times, very slight songs. Listening to the album at this distance there is little indication that within two years they would be capable of putting together Trespass, though intriguingly 'Fireside Song' does boast a closing section leading into 'The Serpent' – itself a re-write of Tony's and Peter's first song, 'She's Beautiful' – that later found a home on 'Stagnation' on that album. As individuals, each member gives an indication of their potential, the twin acoustic guitar format pioneered by Ant and Mike being central to many of the songs and sounding at times very beautiful. Tony Banks contributes a number of pleasing moments, particularly on the introduction to 'Fireside Song' and Peter Gabriel's voice occasionally scaled the heights that he was later to achieve with ease. In general, however, it's an album of songs that while pleasant are fairly insubstantial and which certainly cannot withstand the beating they get from King's production. It promised much but this time delivered little, Tony admitting that 'I feel the album was a pretty terrible version of a lot of the songs we were doing.'[6]

When they heard the finished version of the album the reaction was one of universal anger, but their youthful reserve prevented them from making any attempt to change things, which simply allowed Jonathan King to press forward with his concept of what the group should be. Ant, whom Mike describes as 'the driving force, the keenest and most determined in the early days,'[4] was the only one to let his frustration show by stomping out of the studio on the final day.

'I think that some of Jonathan's disciplines were probably quite a good idea,' Ant is quick to point out. 'We were already writing fairly long, unwieldy pieces, some of which were interesting and some pretty awful. I think he wanted to turn us into a straight pop outfit, I don't think he saw where we were going.'[4] Accepting that King produced out of the best intentions, 'We were distraught about the production. There were some nice songs that we didn't really know how to play, but they suffered from the process. This thing was very naive and rough but at least it was very full sounding but when they mixed it on to one side of the stereo it sounded pathetic. We heard it and we couldn't believe what had happened. I felt they'd destroyed it, painted it a different colour. The strings were awful too. Around that time, Family had used acoustic guitar and full strings so I expected lovely big chords but instead we just disappeared down one side and these awful high things had the other – it was grotesque.'

In spite of the group's general lack of enthusiasm, the LP was released in March 1969 but not before King and Decca had encountered further problems. Decca discovered that there was an obscure American R. & B. band called Genesis and insisted that King make the group change its name. As the name tied in so closely with the music they had recorded, he refused. Instead, he sought a compromise by releasing the record without any group name, simply putting it out as *From Genesis To Revelation*. True to his word, on its release there was no name anywhere other than as a writing credit on the record's label. Some fifteen years before Spinal Tap's all-black cover for *Smell The Glove*, *From Genesis to Revelation* came out in a black sleeve, with only the title in gold Gothic script giving any indication of its contents. What Jonathan King saw as a clever way round the problem sadly backfired as the record unerringly found its way to the religious sections in many record stores and consequently was virtually impossible to find.

Dramatic, if somewhat pompous, advertisements for the LP were placed in the press, again in black and gold, proclaiming, 'Revelation is the giving of knowledge to man. Genesis is the source of new knowledge.' If such was the case, there were few seekers of this 'new knowledge' as the album racked up a pathetic six hundred sales and has consequently become a collector's item (although since that time it has been re-released numerous times around the world in different forms and under different titles making this archive material readily available to all).

Press reaction was almost non-existent, although Mark Williams in the influential underground paper *International Times* gave the record a very warm reception, describing it as 'a beautiful, entirely valid musical exercise', finding it difficult to come to terms with the group's youthfulness 'because the ideas they express . . . are already streets ahead of so many other groups',[5] and advising 'instant purchase'.[7] But this whole-hearted endorsement appeared in a week where distribution problems meant that the paper reached only a fraction of its usual readership. On the other hand, King remembers *Melody Maker*'s Chris Welch dismissing the album as 'terrible, pretentious and over-produced'.[4] King's view is that Decca had little idea of how to promote the record and 'it sank without trace. I think much of it was way ahead of its time – there were some gorgeous songs on it.'[4]

The recording of the album had taken place in the summer holidays of 1968 at the end of which the band went their separate ways to await the outcome of its release. Tony left Charterhouse to go to Sussex University to study maths, physics and philosophy, Mike went to Farnborough Technical College and Ant and Peter studied for further A levels. They still met during school holidays and Peter sometimes visited Tony at university. They all continued to write, Tony coming up with some songs – on guitar as there was no piano available to him – some of which didn't see the light of day until six years later on *A Trick Of The Tail*.

When *From Genesis To Revelation* was unleashed to general apathy, there was indecision among the group. Banks looks back on it as a time of general uncertainty. 'When it came out and failed, it was like "Was that it?" We just weren't sure what to do.'[4] A third single was put out on 27 June 1969 featuring two songs from the LP, 'Where The Sour Turns To Sweet' and 'In Hiding', in an attempt to stimulate interest in the LP, but to no avail.

With the band fragmented, Jonathan King started to lose interest and moved on to his next project. Genesis did some new demos for him but these were becoming more and more complex as the group began to evolve and construct the music that would form the basis of their style for the next few years. Songs were increasing in length to anything up to fifteen minutes, an idea totally opposed to Jonathan's philosophy. Finally, the relationship between band and producer came to a close, leaving Genesis to fend for themselves. King says: 'It was sad that it didn't happen, but they were coming under pressure from parents who wanted them to become lawyers and accountants, not musicians.'[4] (This is a claim refuted by Ant who states, 'They were a bit bewildered, but they were pretty sympathetic considering it was all so bizarre.'[4]) King: 'They knew I was losing interest and asked me if they should carry on, presumably as a result of that pressure. I'd usually tell people not to bother but I really felt they should carry on. I was delighted for them when they linked up with Tony Stratton-Smith because I knew he would look after them properly.'[4] For their part, while grateful for King's help in getting them a recording deal and for the experience it gave them, Genesis shed few tears at the end of their association with him and Decca. 'It was only after he had lost interest that we forged an original and dramatic strong style of our own. It was just because we had a real ambition to be special and different,'[4] claims Ant.

Decisions as to their future were fast approaching when they regrouped during the summer holidays of 1969. The makeshift methods of songwriting and infrequent meetings meant that the group was not making the progress that it should and was certainly not forging its own identity. Songwriting sessions were short affairs broken up by one member or another having to leave to return to school or university, thus preventing any sense of continuity. Another major problem was that school exams were being completed and career choices had to be made – the outside world was waiting for them. Tony was already ensconced at university but the others had offers of further education awaiting them, including for Peter an invitation to study at the London School of Film Technique. They were approaching a critical time.

Ant and Mike took the lead, deciding that they wanted to go professional and make music a full-time career. In spite of the failure of *From Genesis to Revelation* and their displeasure at the finished result, the experience had whetted their appetites and both felt that they could take things much further. Freed from the shackles imposed on them by Decca and Jonathan King's vision of the group, they felt renewed enthusiasm for the music, believing that the possibilities were so interesting that, even without Peter and Tony, they would continue. From April 1969 they had been writing together frequently and had developed their twelve-string approach more fully. This was the time at which Mike 'came into his element', as Ant recalls. 'Mike's role had been fairly shadowy previously, he didn't write too much for *From Genesis to Revelation* but he was a great guy to have around. Then from that April, we were really motoring, absolutely inspired. When the band got together, he and I would then go off for late-night writing sessions after rehearsals, though we'd get stick from the others about not getting enough sleep!'

'They decided that they would go professional at the start of that summer and so Peter and I said that we would help out but that we wouldn't stay with it because we wanted to carry on with other things,'[4] recalls Tony. Throughout that summer Peter and Tony had shared David Thomas' Earls Court flat, which they had previously used as a base from which to record *From Genesis to Revelation*. Tony remembers that 'the flat was very important for us both. There was the sudden introduction to women and the freedom – it was only a few months, but it seemed like years, that period lives on in my mind.'[8] It was also a very important period on a personal level, for it was through Thomas that Tony met his future wife, Margaret McBain. Not to be out-done, Peter also had the opportunity to deepen his relationship with a girl whom he had met at a Christmas party in 1965 and with whom he had since had a fairly on-off affair, Jill Moore. From the musical standpoint, the fact that Tony and Peter were under the same roof provided them with greater scope for writing together and gave a much needed boost to their collective morale. Over the summer Genesis continued to work on new music to such good effect that, by the end, Tony 'really felt that the music was very exciting and I thought it was an opportunity that might not come up again. I thought I'd regret it if I turned it down. Peter and I tended to swap roles daily, persuading one another to stay or leave.'[4] In order to test the water before finally committing themselves, Genesis made another tape of their new, more complex songs, which featured 'White Mountain', 'Family' (which finally became 'Dusk' on *Trespass*), 'Going Out To Get You' and 'Pacidy' which was later recorded for a BBC studio session. Again using Regent Studios, where old colleague Brian Roberts was now working as a sound engineer, they put down the tracks on 20 August 1969. 'We got no feedback or enthusiasm from anyone that we played it to, but we decided to carry on because we were so confident,'[4] laughs Tony.

The nucleus of the band now had to look for a new drummer, however, as John Silver left to go to school in America, provoking Ant and Mike to write 'Silver Song', a demo version of which has now finally been put on record with the recent compact disc release of Ant's *Private Parts And Pieces* album.

As a professional band, they needed some equipment. They each borrowed £150 from their parents and still had £300 from Jonathan King, with which Mike bought his first decent bass guitar, a Marshall lead amp, a Sims-Watt PA 100 amp and an organ. Again, critics regularly point to these privileges as though parental help and the middle classes have no place in rock and roll. As Tony points out, 'The finance from our parents was vital, but then lots of other people have received some help, being bought guitars or whatever.'[4] Steve Hackett, soon to join the band from a grammar school background, felt that 'there are no class barriers in music, thank God!'[4] and this petty sniping from the press over and over again can be put down either to ignorance of the real facts, to a selective moulding of rock history to suit a particular view or to simple critical ineptitude. Genesis were given no more financial help in getting started than were the Beatles, the Cure, the Smiths or countless others, none of whom have had to put up with the same adverse criticism.

Genesis had the equipment, they had the determination, they had some music and they had countless ideas. Now they had to become a professional group.

CHAPTER THREE

'Some of you are going to die'

As with any young band, rehearsal opportunities were scarce but absolutely crucial, particularly to one so uncertain of its future. Fresh from education, none of the members had homes of their own and throughout that decisive summer of 1969 Genesis regularly moved from house to house – as one band member's parents or friends went away on holiday, they moved their equipment in. It was the strength of the new material they were writing that finally convinced Tony and Peter that Genesis was a viable force and worth taking further – clearly the importance of that period and of the help they were given cannot be underestimated. At this early stage, the group was already inspiring great loyalty, respect, even devotion, from those around them and often people would go to extraordinary lengths to help the group. Brian Roberts, for instance, was very helpful, from providing them with the Chiswick studio where they made their first tape, right through to sneaking them into Regent Sound B, in August 1969 to record some of their newer, more complex material. He even arranged for them to spend part of that summer at his grandmother's home! Many people made similar attempts to help at this stage.

During this initial period as professionals, though, no one was as crucial to their development as Richard MacPhail. Originally a band-mate of Mike and Ant's at Charterhouse, he had left in 1966 and ultimately found himself in Israel working on a kibbutz. He returned to England to find Genesis set up at the home of Phillips' parents and was extremely impressed by the new music and the sense of purpose and self-belief that they now had. Having made the decision to go professional, the group had gone through a burst of creativity and put together a number of songs that would make up *Trespass*. It was also at this time that the abilities of the band as players went up exponentially, Rutherford finally having the time to get to grips with the bass, the others having the chance to concentrate on their instruments to a far greater degree. For the first time they were working as a fully fledged group, improvising together and coming up with more and more interesting ideas as a result of the group mind being in force – further strengthened by the recruitment of a new drummer, John Mayhew, via an advert in *Melody Maker*. Happy with the progress they were making, the main problems which beset them were logistical – having to uproot themselves physically week after week to new locations. Additionally the regular interruptions that were inevitable when using someone else's home meant that it was difficult to keep the thread of what they were doing. They all felt the need to find a retreat somewhere where they could cut themselves off from the outside world and be left to pursue their musical ideas and feel free to play whatever the hour.

MacPhail's parents owned a cottage in Dorking on National Trust land which they were planning to put on the market in the spring of the following year, as a result of which it was temporarily empty. MacPhail's father realized how involved his son was with Genesis and so allowed the group the use of the house, rent free, until it was ready to be sold. Not only that, he provided them with a bread van in which to carry their equipment, all paid for out of his own pocket, a piece of generosity that was the final piece of the jigsaw. Genesis now had the ideal location for writing and rehearsing and the means to tour the country.

In September 1969, just prior to submerging themselves in the countryside, the band played their first professional gig – at a dance at the home of Mrs Balme, where Peter Gabriel had attended Sunday School classes some years previously, for the princely sum of £25. The idea of Genesis playing at a local dance seems quite ridiculous in retrospect and their reception, while not hostile, was less than rapturous. Nevertheless, the cash was useful and they had got over the difficult psychological hurdle of playing their first gig as a band.

In November they retreated to the Dorking cottage where they were to remain until the following April, putting their heads over the trenches only to play whatever concerts they could arrange. Mike feels this was crucial to their development. 'We were completely removed from the business and any other outside music really. That was when we first learnt the way that we were going to be Genesis.'[4] While at the cottage, a wholehearted work ethic was their guiding principle with the group playing together for ten or eleven hours a day, improvising, piecing sections of music together, trying different arrangements of songs. Over those six months, *Trespass* was written, along with an enormous quantity of other material. The whole concept of the group changed from the one held when they had released *From Genesis To Revelation* just over a year earlier, as Tony Banks explains: 'We were committed to finding gigs and being a professional group and so the whole idea moved from a band trying to have a hit single to one that was trying to do something adventurous musically.'[4]

Even though the days in the cottage were very creative, tensions would sometimes boil over. 'We were very intense. We argued day and night,' is Mike's recollection of the time there, adding, 'I don't know how we stayed together!'[4] The proximity to each other was one source of the occasional flashpoints, exacerbated by the fact that they didn't really talk to one another about the personality differences that were becoming apparent, a by-product of the stiff-upper-lip attitude drilled into them at Charterhouse. The main cause of friction was in the committee set-up, when individuals tried to introduce new material to the rest of the group. Ant recalls it as 'a pretty savage forum, which was good – Tony Banks in particular was a real perfectionist. There were phases when we all struggled to assert ourselves in the group. During the Jonathan King era, I'd fallen away because I didn't like the fact that he was turning us into a pop outfit. Then later, a lot of the things that I wrote with Mike on two twelve-strings were being used while the other two weren't producing much, so the balance could shift, but once you were down, it was very difficult to get back up. There were communication problems.'[4] Ant found the intensity very intimidating at times: 'We were too young to realize that you need room to breathe. There was no life away from it at all – it seemed like such an ideal originally that the idea of turning away from it was a travesty. Gradually things started to fall apart because although the relentless hours of practice were very important, it wasn't great for our personal relationships.' The unremitting concentration on Genesis meant that they had to forsake their personal lives – girlfriends were forbidden, except on the very rare afternoons off! Naturally enough, each individual was particularly keen to have his material accepted and played by the group and would put ideas across as forcefully as possible, something not designed to assist group harmony. Tony's version of events is that 'Peter and myself were pretty stubborn and tended to get our way a bit, though Ant could be stubborn at times too.'[4] Peter did have particular problems to overcome though, as Ant remembers, 'His imagination was so bizarre, but he can be very inarticulate at times in trying to explain himself and because he wasn't completely on top of an instrument, he couldn't demonstrate things. He was interested in space and rhythm but we were powerful chord merchants, it was what we felt secure with.' Therefore Peter often found himself arguing alone, against the others.

Arguments or not, the importance of their period at the cottage cannot be overstated. The whole premise of the music which they would write and perform was evolved during this time – one has only to compare the pop tunes on *From Genesis to Revelation* to the far more ambitious music on *Trespass* to see that they underwent a major transformation between the recording of the two, a transformation that could be fully realized only once they had turned professional and could devote all their energies to the music. Not only were they given the time and space to work, but, thanks to their isolation from outside influences, had the opportunity to develop their ideas which gave them a far greater originality than other groups. Genesis heard little other music and so had only their own ideas to guide them, which explains why *Trespass* had such a unique sound.

Towards the end of their stay in Dorking, Genesis had also become a gigging band. Peter Gabriel in particular spent much of his time on the telephone to club owners and college and university social secretaries the length and breadth of the country in an attempt to get bookings for the band. Things were made easier for him by the broadcast, in March 1970, of a session that Genesis had recorded for BBC radio on 22 February, which featured 'Shepherd', 'Pacidy', 'Let Us Now (Make Love)', 'Stagnation' and 'Looking For Someone'. The first three were gentle pieces, dominated by the twelve-string sound and the use of two voices in unison (on this occasion Gabriel and Phillips, a forerunner of the successful style ultimately arrived at between Gabriel and Phil Collins). The other two songs were considerably different from the final recorded versions on *Trespass* and give a fascinating illustration of the steps taken between the first two albums.

A combination of Peter's persistence and the recognition they achieved from the session meant that they began to gain more and more success and started to become a regular live band throughout England, especially in the south-east. Some gigs were pivotal in their story, including their appearance at a showcase concert at Brunel University, which won them many new friends and a host of bookings. It was during this period that a lot of songs were further refined according to the reaction of the live audience, some changing, some being dropped altogether. 'It was tough, but a good way of getting the music into shape,'⁴ is Mike Rutherford's opinion, although over the initial period leading up to *Trespass* it did lead to further internal strife as Anthony Phillips found life difficult to cope with. 'There was a period on the road when I was going off the rails,' he admits. 'The fun went out of it a bit for me.'⁴ He elaborates: 'Because we had become very separate, we needed something to bring us back together. Being on the road meant that we didn't have time to rehearse new stuff and so we didn't get that new dynamic that you get with new material that causes you to communicate again.'

Nevertheless, over the next few months they played anywhere that would have them on any kind of bill – they supported Johnny Winter, Barclay James Harvest, Rare Bird, T. Rex, among a host of others – generally to enthusiastic audiences. Mike in particular expresses a fondness for their time as a support act because 'no one expected anything from us and we often got great reactions as a result.'⁴ Early on they were covering new venues all the time, but were usually successful as a result of their originality – few other groups were playing songs that had any edge to them. The times were dominated by simplistic pop tunes or endless dull musical workouts – Genesis were offering powerful, passionate, melodic songs which also contained interesting instrumental sections that were integral to their structure not simply tacked on for effect. Their set was unusual too, opening with soft acoustic numbers which featured Tony joining Ant and Mike on twelve-string guitar, building as they went along to a climax with 'The Knife', running at anything up to twenty minutes at that time. By the end of the show, they had normally captivated the audience, often because of their clear commitment to the music. They built up a very devoted cult following in a fairly short space of time, mutual respect between band and audience being the keynote.

Ronnie Scott's club in London was an important venue at the time for up-and-coming acts, situated as it is in the Soho district of London, the heart of the film, record and theatre business. A gig there meant that record company and management personnel would have good opportunities to see the band live and assess their potential, so the six-week residency in March and April 1970 was a godsend. One punter who found his way to their shows was John Anthony of Charisma Records who had worked with acts such as Rare Bird, whom Genesis had already supported. He was totally enthralled by their performance and the following week dragged his boss, Tony Stratton-Smith, along to the show.

Stratton-Smith had opened Charisma Records in the late sixties and was busily building a stable of interesting and innovative acts including Rare Bird, Van Der Graaf Generator and the Nice. Like Anthony, he could see the possibilities for Genesis and immediately asked them to join his label. Already aware of Stratton-Smith and Charisma, Genesis were instantly keen and, when promised the time to develop and grow, the signing was a formality. Without any desire to write short singles, the band knew that they would have to go on the road to find their audience and the willingness of Stratton-Smith to accept that view convinced them that they were dealing with a like-minded individual and record company. Tony Banks explains that it was critical that 'we were allowed to release albums without singles and just play live and build up a following – it was a slow process of playing a place as a support act and then go back a few weeks later as headliners.'⁴ The boost to their confidence was extremely important; someone as respected and influential as Stratton-Smith putting his faith in their long-term future gave them the necessary breathing space to let the music take its natural course without having to make any compromises. The financial backing that they now had meant that they could rely on a weekly wage – £10 – and could also buy some new equipment which in turn further helped to shape and transform their sound. Nevertheless, in spite of this success, Ant was continuing to feel the pressure: 'There was a period when people were coming to Ronnie Scott's and we had to prove ourselves to the bigwig managers – it was "Isn't this an important gig?" I found it very difficult to take.'

They continued to play live for the next few months, beginning what was to be a long and successful relationship with the Friar's Club, a venue that became their spiritual home and one which would guarantee them a warm welcome in the trying days on the road. Mike's verdict on the times was, 'We'd play Friar's and then try to find enough gigs for two or three weeks before we could go back!'⁴

In June and July 1970 they put a stop to concert work to go into Trident Studios to record their début Charisma album with John Anthony producing. The first question was very much one of material – which songs were going to find their way on to the record? Gigs had, to an extent, sorted this out for them – those songs which had worked with a live audience stayed in the set whereas those that hadn't were replaced as quickly as possible. In that way, they had whittled the material down to an album's worth of songs, although it wasn't to unanimous approval. Anthony Phillips was, and still is, uncertain about the final listing of tracks: 'I'm not sure that we recorded all the best songs. We recorded what had survived the road which were louder pieces and a lot of the acoustic things just didn't make it.'[4]

In many ways, *Trespass* was their first 'proper' album – the first since they'd turned professional, the first on Charisma, the first since they'd become a live band, the first where they had control over the material they were writing. It was essential that they came up with a record that reflected their new approach and one which would justify Charisma's faith in the group. They understood that they didn't have to produce an instant world-beater but they were very keen to capture the magic of their early concerts, thereby grabbing the attention of people who hadn't had the opportunity to see them live.

The opening track was idiosyncratic enough to set them apart from the herd within seconds. 'Looking For Someone' began with Peter's plaintive vocal over a restrained organ part before the rest of the band came in, the sort of start you either loved or loathed but couldn't ignore! From there, the album went from strength to strength. The six songs were all fairly long by the pop standards of the day, but their extended length gave the group space to stretch and experiment, an opportunity which they did not abuse, keeping the instrumental breaks concise and sympathetic to the context of the song. The over-riding feeling from the album was very much one of a pioneering spirit, an attempt to bring new sounds and new ideas to the music world. While Ant may have felt that some of the softer numbers had fallen unnecessarily by the wayside, there was still a good deal of acoustic music on the album – *Trespass* was perhaps most notable for the twelve-string guitar sound which Ant and Mike had been busily developing. Interestingly in a band with two guitarists, the lead instrument was often taken by Tony on piano, organ or mellotron. His lines were underpinned by the acoustic guitars and the effect of them together was quite stunning, sometimes offering two different melody lines running concurrently, this being the earliest hint at what was to become a Genesis trademark. So often in the future there was to be far more going on than appeared on the surface of a song, with every album repaying repeated listenings.

Lyrically, biblical ideas were to the fore again – 'Visions of Angels' had in fact been recorded for *From Genesis To Revelation* but wasn't used because, according to Tony, 'We didn't get the best out of the song'[1] – as was a fascination with the macabre that was to become central to much of their future output. Some of the album is rather twee and of its time, but Peter proved that he had some intelligent ideas for lyrics on 'The Knife', not a protest song as it was regularly described at the time, but a *parody* of a protest song. Taking a similar line to Woody Allen's Fielding Mellish character in *Bananas*, it propounded that revolutions against dictators tended not to provide solutions, just new dictators – those who want to govern are inherently unfit for the job. 'The Knife' was generally the most popular song on *Trespass* – indeed it was released as a single in May of the following year as Charisma sought to renew interest in the album, the nine-minute track split into two halves on the A- and B-sides and featuring a picture cover that depicted a Genesis line-up that included Phil Collins and Steve Hackett rather than Phillips and Mayhew who actually played on it! In spite of that, the cornerstone of the album was 'Stagnation' which contained elements of all that characterized Genesis in this embryonic state – sensitive acoustic guitar passages, a strong melody, a powerful bridge solo from Tony and an emotional closing vocal section from Peter. It's a track that has been under-rated over the years, but if there was a signpost for the future on the *Trespass* album that was it.

The feeling from *Trespass* is one of pastel shades, sensitivity, vulnerability, an impressionistic sound, melodic, emotional songs, a very visual form of music – oh, for the video age to have been in full swing in 1970. There was a range of different atmospheres on show too, from the power and bravado of 'The Knife' through to the delicacy of 'Dusk' where the acoustic guitars came into their own – probably the only emotion missing was humour, the band at this point taking things very (perhaps too) seriously. The dominant characters at this time seem to have been Tony Banks and Anthony Phillips, the whole combination of their differing visions of Genesis, working together to the best effect on ' Stagnation'. Peter's presence is relatively subdued with the exception of his performance on 'The Knife', while Mike still appears proficient only on guitar, the bass still not fully at his command. The weakness in the playing is unquestionably John Mayhew, who was a less confident musician in comparison with the others, maintaining the main Genesis problem at that time, a rhythm section with little drive. Admittedly, he's not helped by a drum sound that suggests he's hitting wet envelopes, but quite clearly he was unsure of taking the music into newer, more powerful areas – if proof be needed, one has only to listen to the version of 'The

Knife' on 1973's *Genesis Live* to see where it could have gone had Phil Collins been in the band for *Trespass*. Further problems came in the production itself – the guitars were muddy when they should have shone, the drum sound was uniformly awful, the essential clarity was absent from the record, although in fairness this was the case for the vast majority of records made at the time.

The album took a full month to record, a long period for a band so early in their career, but there was never any possibility of hurrying them along – the record would be ready when it was finished, not before. Studio inexperience on both sides of the desk – John Anthony was in his first year as a producer – did not help matters, but neither did some internal difficulties with Anthony Phillips feeling less and less happy with the music and his role in the group. 'I felt that the road had become too important – there was no time to rehearse new material and what we had was getting stale. To fashion something like "Stagnation" takes a long time and when we were playing almost every day, the time wasn't there.'[4] He had been having problems with their concert itinerary and was feeling increasingly isolated from the others: 'I just found the tension of the whole thing got to me. There were no specific disagreements, just the age-old band arguments about who was playing loudest on stage, that kind of thing. I was a bit younger than the others and I suddenly started to get paralytically nervous before the gigs. Then I got physically ill with bronchial pneumonia which didn't help. I just got very depressed as you tend to when you're ill and I had to ask myself, "Why am I doing this, it was supposed to be fun?" It suddenly became a job. It was very all-consuming – it was great to be committed and not dilettante about it, but I felt it was becoming threatening.' Finally, just after the completion of *Trespass*, having recorded it in a state of uncertainty, Ant decided that he couldn't work within the group situation any longer and had to leave. 'It was sad, but we were slipping apart. I think also, apart from the live problems, it was a case of too many cooks at that stage – the four of us were writing and it is extremely difficult when there are so many people trying to get their vision into one piece of work. There had to be a compromise and some-thing had to give, just as it did when Peter left later on.'[4]

The news came as a severe blow to the rest of the group. In many respects, Ant had been the most important member of the band to that stage – it had been mainly his energy that had driven them into turning professional and becoming a live group, factors that led directly to their future success. It was his ideas about the acoustic guitar and its place amongst electric instruments that gave their sound much of its unique appeal and he had a key role in defining many of the early song structures as a result. However, the difficulties that he found in working within a democratic set-up, allied to his problems on the road, meant that he had little choice but to leave the band. Mike, his closest friend in Genesis, remembers that, 'He had bronchial pneumonia towards the end of his time with us, and life on the road was tough then, it just got on top of him. He found it very strenuous and difficult.'⁴ Tony was 'very sad when he left – I don't think it was necessary. He felt he couldn't take the live performance, it made him too nervous. He'd been the most keen on playing live so it was odd that he found it the most difficult to take but he was very young and a lot was being asked. I also think he thought that we wouldn't carry on which made the decision easier – if he'd thought we'd continue, he might have thought twice about it.'⁴ This is something Ant denies: 'I went down quite a long way, the whole thing left me in a weakened state and then I was ill. I frankly wasn't capable of making a long chain of logical decisions, my life just seemed extremely grim and it was the only choice available to me. I was blitzed, I didn't feel I could talk to anyone about it and I just felt that my whole position with them was untenable.'

With a crucial member of the team gone, the question was very much could Genesis continue? Tony remembers, 'I thought it was the end of the group. He was vital to its formation and in many ways he was the strongest member. We felt that whatever was special about us was a combination of the four of us being together in the same room so I assumed that when he left, that was it.'⁴ Mike believes, 'That was the closest we came to busting up. For some reason we felt so close that if one left, we thought we couldn't carry on. Of all the changes we've been through, surviving Ant leaving was the hardest.'⁴

During the drive home from their final gig together at Haywards Heath, where they played to around twenty-five people, Peter and Mike decided that they wanted to carry on. Tony was still unsure but agreed, suggesting they use the opportunity to look for a new drummer: 'I thought it was important that we had one who was of equal stature with the rest of us.'⁴ The others agreed. Ant states that Mayhew was 'uncomfortable. He was unrelaxed about it. He was a bit older and there was this class problem – I wasn't conscious of it but I think he felt it. He never seemed very confident, he seemed intimidated and that was partly our fault.' Accordingly, John Mayhew was axed from the group who were now down to a nucleus of three.

In retrospect, Ant's departure was sad, but one which opened new horizons for the group and which pushed them onward, as he himself agrees: 'If I'd been in a healthy state, it might have ended like this anyway. Four writers were just too many.'

Phillips and Mayhew now out of the group, the rest started to look for new musicians. Their ultimate choices were to be vital to the future of Genesis.

CHAPTER FOUR

'I heard the old man tell his tale'

The recording of *Trespass* was completed in July 1970 with a release scheduled for that October. With colleges and universities closed for the summer, few gigs were available to an up-and-coming band in August and September and Genesis planned to take a short break, then write and rehearse new material which they would take on the road to coincide with the LP release. With the departure of Phillips and Mayhew, however, things took a totally different turn. The immediate priority was to line up some replacement musicians and integrate them into the band prior to playing live again. With a record to promote, some dates had already been pencilled in for the autumn and Charisma were obviously keen that they should be able to fulfill their obligations and help push sales of *Trespass*. With that in mind, Tony Stratton-Smith took out a box advert in *Melody Maker* looking for a 'drummer sensitive to acoustic music and an acoustic twelve-string guitarist'.

In the early seventies, the classified pages of *Melody Maker* assumed biblical significance for any musician looking for a band. One such was Phil Collins, a young drummer from Hounslow. He was born on 30 January 1951 and his background and personality couldn't have been more different from those of the Charterhouse boys. Phil was a natural performer from an early age, taking part in school plays and pantomimes, entering talent competitions on family holidays. This was nothing new to the Collins family, since they regularly performed at local charity events as a family unit, Phil's father singing, his brother – later to become a newspaper cartoonist – and sister doing various double and single acts. Phil was given a tin drum when he was three which immediately captured his imagination and by the time he was five he had been given a drum kit which could fit into a suitcase. His uncles had made it for him by putting together a toy drum, some tambourines and triangles, setting it up in the form of a real kit which Phil would then use to play along to music on TV and radio. Drumming was just a hobby at this point, and Phil spent more of his time acting and performing, including some infamous shots modelling for Emu knitting patterns! As with the members of Genesis, a major change in his life was just around the corner in the form of Beatlemania.

The pop music explosion headed by the Beatles, followed by the Stones, Motown, et al, captivated Collins and made his career decision for him – the future was drumming and his aim was to join a band as soon as he was able. At the age of twelve he sold a train set to buy a proper kit, although the train set actually belonged to his brother! None the less, with a full kit at his disposal, Phil was on his way.

In the meantime, school beckoned and he enjoyed a fairly happy spell at Chiswick County Grammar School, becoming involved in school plays as well as the sports teams. He worked his way through occasional BBC TV appearances, voice-overs and assorted other bits of work, including the terrible chore of being paid to watch the Beatles as one of the crowd during the TV show section of their *A Hard Days Night* film. At the age of fourteen he got the part of the Artful Dodger in the West End production of *Oliver*. The school were unwilling to give him leave for the necessary period and so he moved to the Barbara Speake Stage School which allowed him to take up the role, a position he occupied for some nine months until his voice finally broke, leaving him embarrassingly scrambling for notes he could no longer attain. At the end of his run with the show, he turned his attention more fully to a group that he had put together almost as soon as he'd reached stage school, the Real Thing. In 1967 he decided that acting was no longer for him, a result of a miserable experience in the Children's Film Foundation epic, *Calamity the Cow*, where ongoing rows with the director led to him being written out of the film.

Around that time he linked up with Ronnie Caryl, a guitarist who had achieved a good reputation in the locale. Together they started a new band, recruiting the requisite members and regularly playing together at Phil's house. Phil was in and out of other groups for a short period before Ronnie alerted him to a new opportunity as the backing band for the Gladiators, a poor man's Four Tops. They already had a guitarist and keyboard player, but

Caryl and Collins were able to fill the remaining slots. Unfortunately, the backing band were far too good for the Gladiators and soon left, forming Hickory who went on to work all over the country, sometimes working with the Walker Brothers' John Walker. This band teamed up with a couple of writers, Ken Howard and Art Blaikley, who had just been involved with the Herd and needed a new outlet. They provided Hickory with a concept record, a sci-fi epic, *Ark II*. The name of the group was changed to Flaming Youth and the promotional hype machine went into overdrive – the record, a very naive, poppy affair got rave reviews in the press, they secured their own TV special for NBC TV in America and seemed set for the big time. Unfortunately, the excitement came only from the management and record company – the album was studiously ignored by the public and the band were unable to secure any gigs. In fact, a guest review in *Melody Maker* by Pink Floyd's Roger Waters summed up the public's view most accurately, slating *Guide Me Orion* as 'very contrived'.⁹ It was with this background that Phil, who had contributed some lead vocals on the album, decided it was time to start looking for a new band.

At the time, one of Phil's favourite groups was Yes who regularly appeared at the Marquee. During one of the shows, he was told that their drummer, Bill Bruford, was leaving the band to go to university. After the show he went backstage to talk to their singer, Jon Anderson, who invited him to arrange an audition. At the same show he ran into Tony Stratton-Smith, an old friend, and, remembering the advert he'd just seen in *Melody Maker* for a Charisma group, he asked who the band were, thinking Strat would give him the job. On hearing it was Genesis, Phil was impressed, since he'd seen their names appearing with monotonous regularity in the press gig guides. Strat informed him that if he wanted the job, he'd have to audition as the band were very fussy. Deciding to give it a go, Phil did not call Jon Anderson – 'I've always wondered about that, because I knew the song backwards. I'm sure I would have got the job and would have ended up in Yes.'¹⁰ Nevertheless, he decided to fix his sights on an audition with Genesis, having already tried out for the likes of Manfred Mann and Vinegar Joe. One of the big attractions of the Genesis gig was that they were looking for both guitarist and drummer, so Phil was hopeful that he and Ronnie Caryl could stay together. He telephoned Peter Gabriel who invited both of them to audition at his parents' house. 'We turned up at this wonderful farmhouse – there was a grand piano on the patio, a sunshade over the drums, swimming pool! I was early so they told me to go for a swim. So while I was in the pool, I was listening to all the other guys audition, so by the time I did my bit, I tried to make it look a bit hard but I knew all of the pieces and waltzed through it.'⁴ On the way home, however, Caryl told him that he thought that he'd got the guitarist's job but that Collins had blown it!

Genesis meanwhile were busily deliberating over the relative merits of the musicians they'd auditioned. Having spent their career to date as virtually a four-piece with a drummer tacked on as an afterthought, it was vital that whoever was recruited was of equal standing with the others in musical terms. If any part of their music had been a particular weakness it was the rhythm section, revolving around drummers who followed rather than gave time to the rest of the group, and consequently the requisite power and drive was seldom there. This time they were determined to get it right and held extensive auditions. Tony says, 'We saw about fifteen drummers. We worked out all the bits they should play and there were two or three who would have been good enough but Peter and I were very keen on Phil – he seemed very inventive and we got on well with him which was important. He told lots of jokes and he was enthusiastic about the group – we wanted people who wanted to be in the band, not those who'd treat it just as a job.'⁴

A couple of weeks went by before Peter telephoned Phil to tell him that he'd got the job. Phil was naturally delighted, not just because he was back in work again, with the incredible wage of £10 a week, but because he could see a very definite role for himself in Genesis, both musically and in terms of helping break the internal tensions by acting as 'class clown'⁴ as he puts it. 'A drummer is the goalkeeper of the group – you can have a bad band with a good drummer and it sounds fine, but if you have a good band with a lousy drummer it sounds terrible.'⁴ Having given Collins the place at the drum stool, 'they went off on holiday for two weeks, which was when I had my first proper job, working as an exterior decorator with my girlfriend's dad.'⁴

Genesis now had their first fully integrated drummer, but were still short of a guitarist to step into Anthony Phillips' shoes. They had spent a long time auditioning as many guitarists as drummers, but none of them had come up to scratch. While recruiting a drummer was, in some respects, an easy task, a replacement for Ant had to be rather special. Every prospective guitarist had to match not only Ant's ability as a player and writer, but also live up to his stature as a crucial group member. Mike had particularly stringent demands, having had such a close personal as well as musical relationship with Phillips – obviously he was keen to find someone with whom he could continue to develop Genesis' unique twelve-string sound and with whom he was musically sympathetic. These requirements went unfulfilled and the band were unable to find a guitarist in time for the start of their dates in support of *Trespass*, so they began to rehearse as a four-piece. By Phil Collins' testament, things were fraught: 'There was a lot of friction, which I guess came from their background. Tony and Peter, the best of friends, were at each other's throats. There was still some doubt as to whether the group would work without Ant. Apparently he was a very integral part of the writing team and there were anxious moments as a result. We rehearsed at the Maltings in Farnham and people would just walk out and you wouldn't see them for hours!'[4]

While these early dates as a four-piece did restrict the sound somewhat, it was a very valuable period for the group and Tony in particular. 'We worked as a four-piece for a couple of months. That was important for me as I had to play all the guitar parts to all the songs that we'd done to that point on keyboards. I simulated the guitar parts and taught myself how to play two parts at once, which became important later on . . . Some of the songs sounded good and some didn't.'[4] While things had begun to come together, Genesis needed the additional sounds and options that another guitarist would provide and this realization brought the mood within the group down.

Better news was around the corner with the reviews of *Trespass*. Jerry Gilbert in *Sounds* called the band 'extremely good', singling out 'Visions Of Angels' and 'White Mountain' as 'exciting'.[11] *Melody Maker* was more expansive – 'tasteful, subtle and refined' – pointing out the album's flowing continuity.'[12] Buoyed by this encouraging reception, accompanied by generally favourable live reviews at regular intervals, the band's spirits were revived sufficiently to take on a new guitarist.

Mick Barnard was a guitarist from an Aylesbury band, Farm, who was recommended to Genesis by David Stopps from the Friar's Club. Keen to broaden their sound again, they took his advice and drafted Barnard into the group. Over the two months to Christmas, he started to fit in and the music began to open up once more, so much so that they included two new songs in their set, 'The Musical Box' and 'Twilight Alehouse'. However, improving though he was, it was clear that Barnard did not have the same level of experience and musical expertise as his new colleagues, an expertise that had grown out of their intensive working schedule over the previous year. Though Barnard was an able musician and might have fitted into the Genesis of twelve months earlier, they had now reached a higher rung on the ladder and so the rest of the group felt he was very much a temporary member. While in their embryonic form they could cope with a drummer who wasn't really contributing to their sound, the guitar and guitarist were crucial to them. There was no way they could countenance the idea of having a guitarist who was still feeling his way into the group and didn't contribute to the writing and arranging of their songs. Having finally plugged the hole in the rhythm section with the recruitment of Phil Collins and being able now to take the music forward into new areas, there was no way they would create a different weak link, sacrificing the melodic inventiveness that Ant had brought to the group. It was essential that they became a true five-piece group with each musician having the same vision.

That being the case, they kept a very close eye on the classified section of *Melody Maker*, looking for any guitarists who might be like-minded and available. One such musician was Steve Hackett, a Londoner born on 12 February 1950, the day before Peter Gabriel. Steve took to music almost as soon as he could walk, picking up on the harmonica at the age of three. 'I was playing tunes on that before I could read and write,'[4] he remembers with a smile. Steve's father played harmonica, had been a bugler in the army and also played guitar, Steve recalling that he often used to hear him strumming along. Music was very much part of his household as he grew up, though none of his family were actively involved in that world, his mother working in advertising, his father a painter. In the same way that the comedian avoids bullying by making people laugh, Steve won the approbation of his classmates by playing tunes for them in the playground, ensuring his survival despite the handicap of having to wear glasses at a very early age!

Like all his future colleagues in Genesis, the great leap forward came with the invention of rock and roll. 'You just hear songs around you as a kid, but then there was something different happening in music with bands that were using electric guitars – Cliff and the Shadows!' In the middle sixties, Steve was beginning to play the guitar – until then he'd been too small to play his dad's guitar – and inevitably became a follower of the Beatles and the Stones. 'I felt a bit closer to the Stones – the instrumental work with the electric guitar and the harmonica was more prevalent with them.' The next turning point for Steve came from a less obvious source, Segovia, playing a piece by Bach. 'It changed my idea of what the acoustic guitar was capable of – I'd thought that the acoustic had really been superceded by the electric guitar, but that showed me that I was wrong. My perception of the use of acoustic guitar changed further when I joined Genesis.'

Music became his true passion and he left Sloane Grammar School at the age of sixteen, working during the day and playing guitar at every opportunity. He was already placing line adverts in the music press to attract the attention of other musicians and was in and out of a few groups, including Sarabande, Canterbury Glass and Quiet World – with whom he recorded an album in 1970, *The Road*, though he confessed that he'd only joined them because they already had a record deal! He absorbed lessons from the sixties guitar heroes, as well as the original blues records which 'Clapton and Mayall turned into the souped-up streamlined white man's blues.' As he points out, by that time, 'I'd gone off technique – there were a lot of prototype heavy metal bands, and it all seemed to be just faster and faster. That's all right, but really I wanted to push guitar into areas where it hadn't been before.' Hackett's pioneering spirit was very much in keeping with the Genesis ethic, as was his concentration on melodic playing, but he was unable to find kindred spirits with whom to work. As his disenchantment with work and with other musicians increased, his classified adverts became more and more elaborate. Finally, by December 1970, they read: 'Imaginative guitarist/writer seeks involvement with receptive musicians, determined to drive beyond existing stagnant music forms.' As Hackett put it, 'I thought, at least I'll get someone who's idealistic, even if they're completely bonkers!'[4]

Still on the lookout for a guitarist, Peter Gabriel saw the advert and called Steve. He advised him to listen to *Trespass* and invited him to a free show that Genesis were playing at London's Lyceum on 28 December, informing him that Mick Barnard was unlikely to be with them for much longer.

Steve was suitably impressed with the album: 'The delicate pastel shading was very good but then when they were ready to rise into an area of power, there was something lacking.'[4] This particularly excited him because he felt that here was a part of the music where he could have an immediate impact – 'There was an aggression in my playing that I felt I could stamp on to them.'[4] At that time, in an issue of *Sounds*, Jerry Gilbert had given Genesis a rave review for their gig at Godalming Gin Mill, (the group 'scaling great heights'[13] in his opinion) which only increased Steve's interest in the group. At the Lyceum, a thousand Genesis devotees turned out to give them a rapturous reception as they played another in a string of remarkable shows and Steve was sure that this was the band for him. He spoke to Peter after the show – 'He was painfully shy'[4] – and invited the band to his parents' council flat in Victoria so that he could put on a show for them as opposed to doing a conventional, and more nerve-wracking, audition. Tony and Peter were the representatives for the group, Mike being ill at the time, and they were immediately excited at the possibilities they could see in Steve's playing and the new ideas that he could bring to Genesis. Steve was invited to join them and went to see Mike who further auditioned him from his sick bed. 'I went to see him and he asked me what I played, we went on to talk about twelve-string guitars, swapped guitar shapes and ideas, so we had an immediate rapport.'[4]

Back to the fully complete five-piece, Genesis were ready to resume their all-out assault on the Great British public. Steve naturally felt very nervous in the early stages, but the band were remorseless in their progress across the country. They would play any gigs they could get with no regard for location, and in the first half of 1971 were playing six or seven nights a week.

Life was given some order, however, when Tony Stratton-Smith decided to set up a nine-city package tour using three of his up-and-coming acts – Lindisfarne, Van Der Graaf Generator and Genesis. Van Der Graaf were led by an individualistic frontman, Peter Hammill, a writer and performer who had much in common with Peter Gabriel. The group were mining the same live circuit as Genesis but had already dented the album charts in April 1970 with *The Least We Can Do Is Wave To Each Other*, so the two bands complemented each other well. Lindisfarne were a band from the north-east who had a poppier element to their music – they were light years away from the novelty act they became in the late eighties when they released a party album and then aided England footballer Paul Gascoigne in clubbing to death their anthem 'Fog On The Tyne'. In 1971 Lindisfarne were the best known of the three and on the brink of hit status with their *Fog On The Tyne* album which went to number one, followed by two top-five singles the following year.

This sell-out tour was very helpful to Genesis, an act whose following was very much restricted to the south-east of England. Lindisfarne and Van Der Graaf both had a wider acceptance and so were able to draw in to the shows people who had never seen or heard Genesis before. Having little to prove and nothing to lose, Genesis regularly stole the show, forcing *Melody Maker*'s

Michael Watts to concede that they 'emerged with the greatest honours and audience acclaim'[14] on the opening night of the tour at the Lyceum on 24 January. The tour made its way across England taking in various points across the north of the country before ending on 13 February at the Winter Gardens in Bournemouth. By its conclusion, Genesis had conquered a whole new group of people and were starting to make their presence felt on a national scale. They followed the tour with their own concerts throughout England and by supporting a group called Bell and Arc. Quite simply, they'd play for anyone that would have them and they zig-zagged their way across the country, playing around one hundred gigs in the first six months of the year. In one of the few gaps available, Peter and Jill were married on 17 March 1971. Jill's father, Sir Philip Moore, was the Queen's assistant private secretary and so his daughter was allowed to marry in a royal chapel, St James's, the reception being held at St James's Palace. Following a brief honeymoon in Tunisia, paid for by Jill's parents, memorable for the fact that Peter contracted violent food poisoning, the two returned to set up home in a small basement flat in Wandsworth.

The live side of the band was assuming ever more importance to them and their record company. For a group that had no regard for success in the singles market – and no material suitable for it even if they had been interested – live work was the only means of building up a fan base. As has remained the case in Britain, radio is largely interested only in top-forty pop hits with anything outside that rigid format condemned to just a few hours a week on 'specialist' shows. This means, quite simply, that the only way for a band that does not reflect the charts to grab a following is by playing to people. Genesis were fortunate in that in the early seventies, venues were available for bands to play, a far cry from today where so few good club gigs exist. Genesis were one of the last bands able to make its way through the club and university circuit, playing for peanuts but building up their stage craft, honing their musical abilities and attracting new fans all the time. It can still be done, as bands like U2, Marillion and Ned's Atomic Dustbin would testify, but it's now the exception rather than the rule. The punishing live circuit that Genesis embraced so wholeheartedly is one of the major reasons that they were ultimately able to step up into the big league and yet still retain their musical integrity and the ability to put on a powerful live show.

The first six months of 1971 were formative for the new line-up. Hackett, as good as his word, succeeded in injecting a new harder

edge to the existing music, while Collins was an astounding drummer. Songs which had plodded now strode confidently forward,
driven on by his tasteful playing, creating, along with the ever-
improving Mike on bass, a capable and consistent rhythm section
which underpinned the music and provided Tony and Steve with
the opportunity to stretch out and experiment. Their music was
still a mix of acoustic and electric instruments but over this period
it became more dynamic, more purposeful, more confident. The
nightly opportunity to play their songs both old and new before
audiences who were still largely unaware of Genesis was demanding, but it very quickly enabled them to discover where they had
struck gold, conversely holding any musical deficiencies up to the
light.

Trespass, while giving hints of the music that was to come and of
the band's potential, had been a slightly fey affair, the harmonies
perhaps being a little too angelic, the lyrics too airy-fairy at times
to capture the casual listener's attention. Those songs had been
the result of their writing period locked away from the real world,
and that showed up a little too clearly on the finished record. By
the middle of 1971 Genesis were an altogether different, tougher
proposition: the result of constant work on the road, the music
had slimmed down and was able to flex its muscles more convincingly. By that time too, Phil and Steve had carved out their own
niches within the group and become integral members of the unit,
as musicians and as personalities.

Phil was very much the joker in the pack, and the infusion of
enthusiasm and vitality that he brought to the rest of the group
fundamentally changed the outlooks of Gabriel, Banks and
Rutherford as songwriters and as individuals. Suddenly things
weren't quite so intense, Genesis were no longer a force isolated
from the outside world but a group of friends enjoying making
music and the possibilities that doing that afforded them. Humour
became a far more important ingredient in the concept of the band
and in their songs. 'Harold The Barrel', for example, would never
have made its way on to *Trespass*, which for all its good points
– and there were many – was a rather po-faced offering. The
involvement of Phil and his battery of jokes lightened the mood
immeasurably. Musically, he truly was a revelation, transforming
old songs and giving powerful direction to new ones although in
these early days his major role was as an arranger for the music
written by others, changing the feel of songs and suggesting new
approaches to them.

Steve's influence on the group was perhaps subtler than

Phil's, but no less important for that. Like the Charterhouse contingent, he was a rather reserved, introverted character which in a strange way made it both easy and difficult for him to fit into Genesis – easy in that they were like-minded personalities, but difficult because he often felt a little shy around his new colleagues. 'I think both Phil and myself found it hard at first. The band had been together so many years and it seemed like they had their own language and were on a different wavelength sometimes. Three of them had grown up together and I didn't always know what they were talking about!' The ideas that Hackett brought to the group were quite different to what they'd done in the past: 'I think my influence was quite radical – I found a kindred spirit in Peter because he was equally radical, always on the fringes.' As Steve freely admits he was far more of a player than a writer at that time and his main interest was to find new sounds from the guitar. His experimental views tied in well with their adventurous songwriting, giving a new, more coherent musical voice to some of their wilder flights of fancy. He also began to remove some of the more fey aspects from the music and helped the group stand up as a rock band, albeit a very different one.

Life on the road for a struggling band was far from easy in the early seventies and Genesis, now at full strength in all departments, were no different to any other group in that respect. They 'paid their dues' just like everyone else, battling around the country in the back of a battered bread van, carrying all their equipment and setting it up themselves with the help of Richard MacPhail, getting little sleep as they went from gig to gig. Mike remembers, 'We never stayed anywhere – we'd drive to Newcastle, do a gig, drive back to London, get a couple of hours' sleep and then go and do a gig in Southampton that night!'[4] By his estimation, in the period up until *Selling England By The Pound* which came out in the autumn of 1973, Genesis were playing around 250 gigs a year. Money was inevitably tight – Collins recalls that they used to fight over Green Shield stamps – but the constant touring was very much a part of their education and their drive towards achieving a greater musical maturity. Inevitably, there are horror stories of life on the road, but one which Mike recounts sums up their eccentric way of dealing with things. 'We had to go to Aberystwyth and we broke down again and again on the way. We finally got there at midnight for a six o'clock gig, didn't get paid and started straight back! I remember waking up in the van at four in the morning, parked by an AA box, hearing this strange Indian sound – it was Pete playing his oboe in the box, wrapped up in towels to keep warm!'[4]

Stories of a different kind were becoming more central to the Genesis live experience. At the time, most of their songs were fairly complex affairs, and between songs guitars would have to be tuned, causing long breaks. Initially, Peter would simply stand at the microphone looking embarrassed and waiting for the ground to swallow him up, but as he became more and more assured in front of a live audience, he began to develop stories that he would tell during these lulls in the proceedings. Some of them would be descriptive of the song that they were about to play while others were surrealistic vignettes exposing the soft underbelly of repressive English culture, the first indications of where many of Peter's lyrics would take the group over the next few years. In some respects it was Gabriel's stories as much as the music that captured the imagination of many of their earliest followers, people who would trail the group with an almost evangelical zeal, setting Genesis even further apart from the mainstream 'Hello Cleveland! Let's party!' presentation of a lot of groups. These idiosyncratic tales had a further value to the band – in their earliest days playing tiny clubs the PA systems were very primitive and so the vocals were often indistinct from the rest of the music. On songs like 'The Musical Box', a long, fairly complex lyric, a first-time audience would have difficulty deciphering what it was about simply from the performance, so Peter took the opportunity between songs to give them some indication of what they were about to receive. Audiences were truly thankful.

The approach that both he and the rest of the group had towards their stage work certainly endeared them to many – a group of studious, shy musicians, all seated, hunched over their instruments, all clearly committed to giving the best possible performance of their songs. While at the front Peter would draw the crowd into Genesis' own world, a world that owed little to the reality that the fans were forced to inhabit in their daily lives. Sometimes a desperately quiet and reserved figure, Peter would suddenly come alive, leaping around the stage, arms flailing, perhaps pausing to kick out at the bass drum (the only piece of his precious drum kit Phil would allow him to use) more in anger than for musical effect. A charismatic performer, shamanistic almost, Gabriel was blessed with the gift of being able to hold an audience in the palm of his hand, coupled with the sensibility never to abuse that power. Strong interplay between performer and audience was essential to Peter and he successfully overcame his own reservations and naturally shy demeanour to bridge the gap that existed between the two.

Gabriel's stories and burgeoning talents as a frontman were to be decisive in their progress towards success, but first, as 1971 went on, a new album was required.

CHAPTER FIVE

'Play me my song'

As had been the case with *Trespass* a year earlier, Genesis looked towards the summer, a time when gigs were thin on the ground, as the point to take a break from the touring treadmill and settle down to finish writing and recording their second Charisma album. Up until then, though, it was full steam ahead on the live front. Inevitably for a new and largely unknown group, they found that some gigs, however hard they tried and however well they played, were disastrous, audiences calling out for them to play songs they could dance to. Genesis can't dance now, and they certainly couldn't in 1971, so the calls fell on stony ground. Such gigs chipped away at the group's morale and brought the hardships endured on tour into sharper focus, leaving them looking forward to returning to strongholds of support they had already succeeded in building up in various parts of the country.

One such was Friar's in Aylesbury, a venue where they regularly went down a storm and where they returned in June 1971 just prior to retreating to the country for work on the next record. Ready for their break from live work, Genesis took flight from the word go, with Peter particularly wrapped up in the gig, and the packed crowd reciprocated in full, reacting ecstatically to both old and new material. As usual, following their set they returned to the stage to perform 'The Knife' as an encore. Midway through the song, in a piece of prototype stage-diving, Peter ran across the stage and launched himself into the audience. What had started out as a spectacular piece of theatre ended in disaster, as Gabriel landed awkwardly and broke his ankle. Promoter David Stopps and Richard MacPhail went into the crowd after him and carried him back to the stage, where he finished the song before an ambulance arrived to take him away. Fortunately, the Genesis gig schedule had come to an end so Peter had time to let his ankle mend, but the few gigs they did play through the summer featured the strange sight – even for Genesis and 1971 – of the lead singer sitting in a wheelchair!

Again, location was crucial for their rehearsals – a setting similar to the MacPhail cottage was required. Help this time came from Tony Stratton-Smith who allowed them to use his old Tudor home, Luxford House, near Tunbridge Wells, where they worked on existing songs and pieced together a range of new material. Though Steve and Phil had both been in the band for more than six months their impact had been primarily on Genesis as a live unit, fleshing out the songs from *Trespass* and helping the stage presentation evolve. Writing together was still largely uncharted territory.

Nineteen seventy-one had been relatively kind to Genesis and the introduction of the new musicians had added a musical strength on stage that had hitherto been noticeable mainly by its absence. Consequently their gigs were more and more impressive and they achieved far better responses from their audiences, being accorded cult status particularly in the south. There was undoubtedly a buzz surrounding this up-and-coming band and anticipation was running high for their new record – the first time they were to record under the weight of external expectations, a source of anxiety in itself, the individuals all having worries of their own to deal with. The Charterhouse triumvirate generally felt more secure, buoyed by a year of reasonable reviews and considerable live success, which left them content in the knowledge that they had been right to persevere with the band. Positive as to their long-term future they were all nevertheless worried as to how the writing process would work without Anthony Phillips. They were sure that the group would ultimately emerge stronger than before but robbed as they were of such a key part of the writing team there was some apprehension, a concern that was further increased by Tony's decision to move from piano as his major instrument to a combination of organ and mellotron. Accordingly, their approach to the album was very much more workmanlike than that towards *Trespass*, the three being preoccupied with potential difficulties rather than simply focusing on writing new songs.

Phil and Steve came to the rehearsals with some trepidation. As this was their first real chance to contribute to the writing, they were particularly keen to make an impact on the music. Working as a writing team is completely removed from working together as a live act and so the initial weeks were very much a time of getting to know one another in a different context, examining the possibilities of the new line-up and evolving a way in which they could work together harmoniously. Tempers were occasionally frayed as everyone battled to keep their emotions in check, but things were rarely as fraught as they had been at the cottage the previous year. One reason was a decision that the group had taken some time before, and employed on each release to that date, whereby all the song credits would be shared under the umbrella 'All Titles Done By All'. The first benefit from this was that royalties would be divided equally, so there was no financial necessity for anyone to push their songs ahead of those by other members. This in turn meant that, theoretically at least, the strongest material would get through irrespective of writer, an idea which appealed to the committee-style organization of the band, Peter remarking to the NME that 'We want to avoid bitching and fighting for composer royalties and glory.'[15] It was also widely felt that no one member of the group was more important than any other and so by communal credit they hoped to deflect press attention away from individuals – an unwanted and often unwarranted spotlight which had torn apart many groups in the past – and towards Genesis as a working entity. Finally, as Steve explains, there were very good artistic reasons behind the idea. 'We considered the arrangement was as important as the song itself. Just because someone comes up with the framework, it doesn't mean the spaces in between aren't important. We all had a crack at filling in the spaces, racking our brains to come up with original bits of detail, usually within each other's songs. We tried all the possible combinations, sometimes collective, sometimes individual, but at its best the group mind was in force.'

Despite this idealistic co-operative approach, Genesis comprised some very competitive individuals who could be ruthless in their determination to get their songs through the committee and would, according to Peter, devise endless manipulative strategies to bring the others round to their way of thinking. As Genesis was the only outlet that each had for their songs, record space was at a premium and so it was essential to each member that they got as much material as possible on to the current album. This tension was at the very centre of the group's dynamic, every good idea brought in by one person spurring the others to produce something equally, or more, exciting to ensure that they did not lose out on the democratic vote and surrender valuable album time. The clamour created by five writers vying for attention meant that they were able to maintain a high quality of material.

As to the rehearsals themselves, Steve can still vividly call to mind his thoughts: 'We got away from gigs and spent an idyllic three months writing and then recording. It was great for me – my first band, first time as a professional earning money! We'd just got a mellotron and everything was opening up, it was a very nice growing period. I was really learning how to write – I'd been a player, but writing hadn't really occurred to me, so this was the big time, even though for Pete, Tony and Mike, it was less of a milestone. They'd done it before, so it was a little less exciting for them.'[4]

There were already some new songs available that had been played live, including 'The Musical Box' and 'Twilight Alehouse', which had been put together during their time as a four-piece – some parts having been around when John Mayhew was still with them – and guitar parts were gradually written for them as Steve got to grips with the material almost on a concert-by-concert basis. The rest of the album gradually came together over two months, a combination of reworking old ideas and material written from scratch, Phil being a particular catalyst, eager as he was to jam with any of the others at any time of the day or night. There was no shortage of experimentation either, with Banks and Hackett beginning a musical relationship that was to define a large portion of their sound for the next few years. The two had a number of similar musical ideas and both were very keen to explore new avenues with their music. Songs were still of paramount importance, Steve agreeing that 'the band's work ethic was really that of a songwriting collective', but he encouraged the others in the use of interesting sounds to augment songs and take them into areas that had yet to be explored while still making them accessible to a pop sensibility. Tony responded to this stimulus well and the two created some startling effects on the new album, something to which Steve is keen to call attention. 'In early Genesis, we didn't have synths and a lot of the weird and wonderful sounds we got were from a combination of very basic guitars and keyboards. People used to ask if a certain sound was a synth and it used to please us that we'd managed to confuse them!'

The new rehearsals progressed fairly slowly but Genesis were developing a wide range of material for such a new team, which hampered things accordingly. Finally, in August, they were ready to go back to London's Trident Studios to put their new songs on tape, with John Anthony again producing, this time using David Hentschel – the tape operator on *Trespass* – as his engineer. What is striking about *Nursery Cryme* is the difference in sound quality from its predecessor – Anthony this time putting the group into a more sharply defined picture, giving the instruments a clarity that had been sadly lacking before. Ideas regarding the sound of the record were far more to the fore, reflecting their greater experience as a group and the new confidence they'd built up after a year on the road. The input of the new musicians was pivotal, removing some of the excesses of the past which gave each member the space to make their point more clearly and concisely. Always a band keen to learn, they realized too that Peter Gabriel's voice, while distinctive, did create problems for the rest of the music. His vocals had a very thick, throaty quality and as such used up a lot of the available sound frequencies so that the rest of the music had to be arranged to complement him, rather than become involved in a battle for supremacy as had previously been the case. These were lessons that were digested by the group and, though things were still far from perfect, led to a vast improvement in the quality and warmth of the sound, adding new colours and textures to the music.

In some respects, *Nursery Cryme* was a transitional record for Genesis, bridging the gap between the more acoustic feel of *Trespass* and the harder edge that was to characterize future offerings, much of the credit for which can be laid at the feet of Collins and Hackett. The stand-out track at the time was 'The Musical Box', a long piece in the tradition of 'The Knife', a story that very definitely grew from Gabriel's increased confidence and the first lyric that really set Genesis apart from the crowd. It centred around a particularly vicious game of croquet in which young Henry has his head gracefully removed by his companion, Cynthia. Returning to the house, she discovers his musical box and, on opening it, unleashes the spirit of the dead boy, now an old man who has never fulfilled any of his physical desires, an omission he attempts to correct with the young girl. Evoking thoughts of nursery rhymes and of *Alice In Wonderland*, the song was quintessentially English, placed in the Victorian age and bringing forth comparisons with Edward Lear, though Gabriel's world was far more barbarous and disturbing. Henry's sexual frustration has clear parallels with Gabriel's perceptions of the widespread repression of English society and its accompanying sexual hypocrisy. The lyric was accompanied by the strongest music that Genesis had yet put on record. Opening with their *Trespass* trademark twelve-string sound, this time chiming brightly where it had formerly been stifled, the track built up to a powerful instrumental climax, mirroring Henry's desires, Steve and Tony combining superbly above an invigorated rhythm section featuring a vastly improved bass part from Mike. At the heart of it all was Peter, living and breathing the part of Henry; desperation, lust, frustration all communicated in a vocal *tour de force*. Songs of ten-minute duration were soon to be mocked as indulgent and irrelevant, but 'The Musical Box' stands today as a potent, emotional piece of music. If the *raison d'être* for soul music is that it offers the opportunity to perform music with passion, intensity and integrity whatever the subject matter, then 'The Musical Box' is soul music at its best, the only quibble being Mike's assertion some years later in the *NME* that 'The studio version doesn't have the bite that the song did live.'[16]

Having opened so robustly, it was perhaps inevitable that the rest of the album be a little disappointing in places. Certainly 'For Absent Friends' – which gave Phil Collins his first shot at lead vocals – 'Harlequin' and 'Seven Stones' were fairly lightweight, but they were all enjoyable, showing that the group was capable of two- or three-minute pop songs. Though they were little more than fillers, stylistically they were consistent with the rest of the record and did a great deal to give *Nursery Cryme* a feeling of completeness, almost thematic continuity.

The major revelation from *Nursery Cryme* was that, contrary to prevailing opinion, Genesis had a great sense of humour and weren't the serious technicians people had taken them for. There was the blackest of humour in 'The Musical Box', but their wit manifested itself most openly in 'Harold The Barrel', a comic opera of sorts with the same brand of off-beat imagery that John Lennon had used in *In His Own Write*:

> Harold the Barrel cut off his toes and served them all for tea
> He can't go far, he hasn't got a leg to stand on.

Any pundit who censures Genesis for being strait-laced puritans after hearing that is far more narrow-minded than his accused!

The rest of the album gave the new five-piece room to flex their increased musical muscle. 'Fountain Of Salmacis', a mythical tale built around the legend of Hermaphroditus, featured Steve's most impressive contribution, a shimmering, liquid guitar solo leading into a mellotron choir that was to become his signature, and 'Return Of The Giant Hogweed' was an eight-minute rocker, propelled by Tony – the lyric again eliciting a wry smile with its tale of a rampaging plant attacking the human race. (It's odd that it wasn't until later that Genesis were unfairly branded as partners in crime with Pink Floyd, where in fact the only valid comparison between them came by way of Genesis' very English whimsicality, a trait not too far removed from that of Syd Barrett's Floyd.)

On the whole, *Nursery Cryme* was an artistically successful
album though ironically the spectre of Charterhouse seemed to be
skulking in the shadows far more than had been the case with
From Genesis To Revelation. The subject matter, coupled with Paul
Whitehead's sleeve design, gave the whole package a Victorian
resonance which for those aware of the group's origins conjured
up visions of that bygone world the public schools endeavoured
to perpetuate. The cover of *Nursery Cryme* was particularly striking:
a depiction of 'The Musical Box' featuring a young girl with old,
evil eyes wielding a croquet mallet, surrounded by severed heads,
while in the background there was Harold The Barrel about to
plummet to his death and a hogwood growing in blissful isolation.
The painting was dated 1871! Inside the gatefold this effect was
maintained, the lyrics printed in a beautiful recreation of an old
family photo album, each song having an accompanying picture
in full colour, instantly giving an impression of the spirit of the
music contained within. Sadly, though the compact disc reissue
of *Nursery Cryme* gives improved sound quality, its attendant booklet has butchered the sleeve, destroying its concept and giving no
indication of its original attraction.

The album complete, the band were less than ecstatic with the
final product. Tony in particular felt that they had not progressed
as they should, reasoning that they had not yet fully come to terms
with the loss of Phillips. While it is true that there was a shortage
of truly outstanding songs on the album, 'The Musical Box',
'Salmacis' and 'Hogweed' proved that the band were far from
burnt out but were instead a cauldron of ideas fighting for
expression. Musically there were great strides made on *Nursery
Cryme* – Banks and Hackett dovetailed inventively, Rutherford and
Collins in partnership were already forming an exceptional rhythm
section and Gabriel was developing a persona all his own, a narrative figure guiding the listener around the strange twists and
turns of the music. Similarly they had ditched some of the cloying
harmonies of yore and were instead cultivating a fascinating vocal
interplay between Gabriel and Collins where it was often difficult
to tell just who was singing and which allowed the record to throw
up new surprises on subsequent listenings. Good strong songs
were again at the core of the work, but instrumentally they had
moved them on to a new plane as each musician became more
confident of his abilities. Lyrical ideas were more experimental,
but concise story-telling was still their medium.

Happy or not, Genesis plunged headlong back into the live
circuit in September, awaiting the album's late November release,

their set enlivened by the inclusion of some of the new songs. The album was greeted with reasonably encouraging reviews. Jerry Gilbert, writing for *Sounds*, was particularly enthusiastic: 'The line-up's changed since the last album . . . giving the group a far more positive sound. An extremely fine and absorbing album.'[17]

Charisma did not promote *Nursery Cryme* with the enthusiasm that they had put into *Trespass*, Tony Stratton-Smith actually telling the group that he wasn't happy with the album, and as a consequence Genesis again failed to reach the LP charts. This was particularly unfortunate as the record was a very real improvement, if only in terms of sound quality and musical execution. But Charisma were concentrating their efforts towards Lindisfarne, then just beginning a fifty-six-week run on the album charts with *Fog On The Tyne*, leaving *Nursery Cryme* to come out to an uninterested and uninformed public, one besotted with Led Zeppelin's fourth album released in the same month, a record festooned with hippy-drippery. While Zeppelin's anthem 'Stairway To Heaven' filled press column inches and rock radio, Genesis aficionados had just cause to believe that, had they been exposed to a wider audience, songs like 'Musical Box' and 'Salmacis' could have been equally successful.

In spite of the indifference from the record company – the only real boost from them being the organization of another package tour for October – Genesis continued to slog their way around the country, playing such delightful venues as Windrush Twilight Club in Gloucester or the Hobbit's Garden – a real sign of the times! While never arguing with their arduous schedule, the wind had been knocked from their sails and the overwhelming feeling was that they were standing still, a hammer blow when one recalls the buoyant spirit just prior to rehearsals for *Nursery Cryme*. They continued to play astonishing concerts and pick up new fans along the way, but there was the feeling of preaching to the converted at gigs, without any real sign of achieving a significant break-through to a wider audience. The future of the group was never in any question, but things had undoubtedly gone flat and there was a growing impatience within the ranks which sometimes blew up. Tony remembers an incident at one gig which had been 'terrible. Mike was so pissed off he didn't want to do an encore but I said we had to do one, just to be professional! He threw a chair at me, but we went on. All the way back to the stage, he kept trying to kick me over!'[4]

Salvation was at hand, however, for mainland Europe was beginning to take Genesis to their hearts.

CHAPTER SIX

'Today's a day to celebrate'

By the end of 1971, Genesis had played somewhere in the region of four hundred gigs in their homeland, constantly chipping away at their potential audience, building up a ferociously loyal cult following, but were still some way from any kind of public acceptance. Meanwhile their press profile was subdued, consisting of album reviews when appropriate and the occasional gig review which, though welcome, by no means reflected the hard work they were putting in, nor the interest the fans had in them. Questions were inevitably being asked as to just what they had to do to get on to the next rung of the ladder in Britain, their stock response being simply to work harder. Their strategy was very much one of breaking through in Britain before giving any real thought to other territories and so it was with some considerable surprise that they received the news that *Trespass* had reached the number-one slot in Belgium, learning at the same time that Italy was also beginning to fall under the Genesis spell.

The news from Belgium could not have been more welcome for the band, though it was slightly perplexing that they should have such success abroad without having put in any groundwork whereas in their native country they were considered little more than a mild diversion from the likes of Led Zeppelin and Deep Purple. The news turned 1971 on its head, transforming it from a year of stagnation into one where important new ground had been broken. Closing the year with a Christmas gig at the Kingham Hall in Watford, Genesis were prepared for their first overseas jaunt, to Brussels, in January 1972.

Looking forward to playing to new audiences – audiences that were already familiar with the songs and who were anticipating a celebration of the music – the band drove to Dover where they caught the cross-channel ferry, sat up overnight on the boat because they couldn't afford cabins, drove to the gig, played and drove straight back to the ferry and home, arriving exhausted after a couple of days without sleep – 'We were so determined that we'd put up with anything!' explains Steve.

However exhausted they were, the show in Brussels was a complete success and on the strength of that a Belgian TV company asked Genesis to play a number of their songs in a TV studio as part of their *Rock of the Seventies* programme, a series that was to feature other English bands such as Yes and Van Der Graaf Generator. The group were clearly ill at ease in front of the cameras but played for thirty minutes, performing 'Fountain Of Salmacis', 'Twilight Alehouse' (at that time still unreleased), 'The Musical Box' and 'Return Of The Giant Hogweed'. The earliest film of the group, this show – which still gets occasional airings on late-night television – is a fascinating historical documentation of their early approach to live performances. Peter is clearly the focal point and he is keen to project himself as forcefully as possible, both to give the songs a clear narrative figure and to draw attention away from the rest of the band – there are times when Peter is patently embarrassed by the reticence of the others, their refusal to do anything other than play their instruments: Tony hunched over the keyboards, Mike and Steve actually sitting down, not exactly a spectacle to rate with the Jimi Hendrix Experience! While in many respects Peter was later to create a monster with his use of costumes and stories it is obvious that he felt very keenly his responsibility to provide audiences with a visual focus to comp-lement the music. Indeed, the TV appearance suffers from the loss of his stories between songs and to casual viewers Genesis must have appeared an aloof, even arrogant, group of very serious young men, so uninterested did they seem in communicating with any audience. While this was far from the case, their shyness did often conspire to create this false impression, one that Gabriel was keen to eradicate.

Following their return to England they heard that *Nursery Cryme*, an album totally ignored at home, and one filled with incompar-able lyrical as well as musical imagery, had reached number four in Italy. Again they were mystified as to the reasons, but in retro-spect it comes as little surprise that the Italians took to them so strongly. With their grounding in classical music and opera the Italians were looking for groups that were offering a little more complexity, a more ambitious style of composition, allied to an

emotionally strong performance. Genesis provided that in spades
and the Italians took them to their hearts in the same way they
had Charisma label mates Van Der Graaf Generator. With gigs
already organized throughout Britain, the band were unable to
travel immediately to Italy to exploit the situation fully, but at least
they could return to their routine with renewed confidence, secure
in the knowledge that their songs were beginning to reach people.
If part of mainland Europe was sufficiently impressed to buy their
records in quantity without ever having seen them, surely it was
just a matter of time before Britain would follow.

Anticipation was high in the Genesis camp for the visit to Italy
and that air of expectation was further increased by Charisma who
invited *NME* journalist Tony Tyler to spend a few days there with
Genesis, a smart promotional move which guaranteed them their
first major press feature. Although the band came a very definite
second to Tyler's Whickeresque observations on the Italian life-
style in an article entitled 'The Spaghetti Scene', he did bring
Genesis into his monologue on occasion, pointing to the 'Fountain
Of Salmacis' as having 'the kind of drama that is international'[18]
and leaving the firm impression that Genesis had become superstars in Italy. Such exalted status was not quite theirs yet but
the tour was very successful in many ways. Mike has very fond
memories of Italy. 'It was great because at least we felt that we
were getting somewhere – they took to *Nursery Cryme* and were
the only people that really liked us. They were very enthusiastic
and it was just a nice country to be in. We toured funny little clubs,
playing in the afternoons and evenings, as well as larger places.'[4]
The first Italian tour was an eye-opener in the same way that
recording *From Genesis to Revelation* had been – it gave them a
glimpse of what the future could hold, an idea of the possibilities.
In England they were struggling around the club circuit but in
Italy they found themselves playing a mixture of venues, both
clubs and sports stadiums! Steve, like the others, was bewildered
by the Italian passion for Genesis but feels, 'Maybe our passion
for the music struck a chord with them, our spirit and theirs just
seemed to coincide. Italians are a law unto themselves, they'd
applaud in the strangest places, it's just like nowhere else!'[4]

Fuelled by the euphoria of success, at least in some parts of
mainland Europe, Genesis had written some new material,
'Happy The Man' and 'Can-Utility And The Coastliners', short
acoustic-flavoured pieces, similar in style to the short songs on
Nursery Cryme, though both were much sharper. Italy itself was
inspirational too, for it was there that they put together what went

on to become 'Watcher Of The Skies', the music being formulated during the soundcheck for the gig at the Palasport in Reggio on 12 April and the lyrics written in Naples seven days later. 'Watcher' is a lyric which immediately conjures up a vision of the song in the mind's eye and one which was a cornerstone of Peter's later experiments with costumes. The music throws up its own visuals too, the huge introductory mellotron passage making it an obvious concert opener, Steve remembering that on occasion it made venues shake, giving the impression of 'a spaceship coming in to land!'[19]

After a series of positively triumphant shows throughout the country, Genesis returned home, their confidence and morale having been transformed by the experience, even allowing for the odd outburst, usually a result of exhaustion. Phil recalls stopping late at night outside a café. 'Tony and Margaret went for a cup of tea – it was a real rough place, so I said, "You go in, I'll stay here, I'm not going in there!" There were bikers everywhere, but they went in. He was winning all these tokens on a one-arm-bandit waiting for the queue to go down and eventually he went to pay with all these tokens but the woman at the counter told him he could only buy cigarettes with them. He told her he didn't smoke, so she laughed and said, "Well they're no use then!" He threw all these tokens at this woman – they went everywhere while all these bikers were sitting there watching. He never did get his cup of tea!'[4]

The inevitable treadmill of gigs continued throughout the UK but invigorated by their success they put their all into the shows, sure in the knowledge that what they were doing was beginning to strike a chord and also happy with the collection of new songs that they were amassing ready for that summer's recording sessions. They recorded 'Happy The Man' for a single release, again using John Anthony as producer, but the sessions progressed very slowly and the escalating cost caused disagreements between Charisma and Anthony which culminated in a parting of the ways, leaving Genesis hunting for new producers for the forthcoming album.

Writing and recording aside, Peter continued to develop a more and more commanding presence on stage and was always looking for new ideas that would shock or surprise the audience. He had been encouraged by his success with the Italians, where he had even, at least partially, introduced the songs to them in their own language, something which endeared himself and the band to them even further. His next tactic, in time for their appearance on the bill with the Beach Boys, Slade and Lindisfarne at the Lincoln Festival during the Bank Holiday weekend in May, was to wear a heavy jewelled Egyptian collar, thick black eye make-up and, most striking of all, to shave the front of his head. Unfortunately, in a tradition that follows Genesis to this day whenever they play an outdoor concert, it poured with rain and the 50,000 crowd, up to their knees in mud, had little interest in a relatively unknown group playing in broad daylight, performing songs that they didn't know – they opened with the yet to be recorded 'Watcher Of The Skies'. Despite a reaction akin to that which ancient Rome reserved for the Christians, Genesis, and more particularly Gabriel, had begun a whole new era in terms of presentation and projection, an era that was to catapult Genesis on to another plane. Just the simple act of shaving his head had sent the press into a fever, Peter later giving *Zig Zag* a list of possible reasons why he had done it, which included, 'It's a cheap gimmick', 'The lice cross from the left side to the right every evening at exactly 7 p.m. and I can swat them more easily', 'I've got a subconscious desire to join the Hare Krishna movement' or 'It's the result of a very nasty shaving accident!'[19]

As they had done the previous year, just prior to taking their break for writing and recording Genesis played a triumphant Home Counties gig, promoted by David Stopps who had taken out various national press adverts heralding the 'Genesis Convention' at Watford Town Hall on 28 June 1972. It was attended by one thousand devotees, each of whom received a Genesis rosette specially made for the show. The crowd afforded them a rapturous welcome; the band responded with a show that had all the power, majesty and delicacy of their extensive and impressive repertoire. From the opening strains of 'Watcher' through to the closing notes of 'The Knife', they poured themselves into a passionate perform-ance later reported ecstatically in *Melody Maker*, Chris Welch giving them probably the most approving review that they had received. The celebration was completed by the fact that, this time, Peter Gabriel did not seriously injure himself!

Recording and writing sessions were waiting, most of the rehearsals being conducted beneath a dancing school in Shepherd's Bush, although this year they were to be broken up by Tony and Margaret's wedding on 27 July and later by a further brief concert tour of Italy. A number of songs were already com-plete, including 'Can-Utility And The Coastliners', 'Watcher Of The Skies' and 'Get 'Em Out By Friday', the first two having already been road-tested. These three were all arranged and re-arranged prior to recording, 'Watcher' having its vocal line changed considerably, all the time putting together the pieces of a jigsaw to form another track for the album. As was so often the case on going into rehearsals, various members already had sections of music that they'd written separately, but which were far from complete songs. Tony had a piece that he'd initially written at university and which he'd continued to work with, turning it into 'The Guaranteed Eternal Sanctuary Man', Peter had a short song called 'Willow Farm', and there were a number of other bits and pieces. Slowly, over a month or so, these bits were linked together until they eventually had a piece of music some twenty-three minutes in length, a work that was to take up almost a side of the new record.

In the words of their Charisma boss Tony Stratton-Smith, speaking at the time to Richard MacPhail after having heard the album for the first time, 'This is the one that makes their career.'[5] The record was to be called *Foxtrot*, its spine was to be a song called 'Supper's Ready'.

CHAPTER SEVEN

'All change!'

As with virtually every other aspect of their career, record production was a subject on which Genesis had very firm ideas. Deprived of the services of John Anthony and David Hentschel with whom they'd recorded *Nursery Cryme*, there was some disappointment that the advances made by the whole team could not be continued. That being so, they were very keen to produce themselves, using only an engineer for the technical side of the operation. Phil Collins is still clear in his view on using outside people to produce records: 'If you haven't got any ideas of your own, that's when you need a producer. A producer is just an interpreter – it's like a painter getting someone to do a painting for him by telling him what colours to use and where to put them. In the end, it changes the thing, you just get his interpretation of what you wanted, not your own.'[4]

Charisma didn't see it that way at all. Tony Stratton-Smith felt that they needed another voice to help direct the songs – he hadn't been happy with the previous record and so he certainly wasn't going to leave them to their own devices. With Stratton-Smith calling the tune, a couple of producers were tried out: Bob Potter, who frankly admitted that he didn't like the music, and Tony Platt, with whom there were personality clashes. The band finally settled on David Hitchcock, with John Burns, a big fan of the group, as engineer, although Genesis did prevail sufficiently to become co-producers.

As far as the sound of the record goes, *Foxtrot* is a slightly odd animal. There are sections which don't have the punch of *Nursery Cryme*, as if the new team was feeling its way in the recording process without too much success and yet there are sections that

sound as strong and powerful on a technical level as almost anything recorded in the early seventies. The lasting impression is
that the band themselves took more control as things went on,
working more in tandem with Burns than with Hitchcock.

As to the songs – pure Genesis! With *Foxtrot*, they succeeded
in drawing together all the most impressive elements of their
repertoire to date, along with an abundance of new ideas in one
spellbinding statement of intent – once released, no one could
again accuse Genesis of being dilettantes, rich kids dabbling in
pop music. *Foxtrot* was a musical declaration of assurance and
variety, a manifesto that delivered emphatically and yet promised
even more, a clarion call to those disenchanted with both top-
twenty chart fodder and muso indulgence – this was a band that
believed passionately in what it was doing, was melodic, light of
touch, with an eye for the absurd and blessed with the ability to
laugh at itself and at the rest of the world.

The centrepiece of the album was 'Supper's Ready', a song
which took up almost all of the second side. Its length immediately
raised the hackles of some critics – how could a song of twenty-
three minutes' duration be relevant to the pop kids of the day?
The fact that it was so long was sufficient proof for some that
Genesis were dull, pretentious prog-rockers, so why bother to
listen? Where should one begin in answering such all-encompass-
ing criticisms? Those that did actually listen to the song found that
it was in fact a collection of short songs, connected by musical
bridge passages and a strong lyrical theme. Certainly it was an
ambitious idea, but it was superbly executed with no excess bag-
gage, no needless musical or lyrical decoration, a triumph of the
application of intelligence to rock music. Why is it so intrinsically
harmful to be ambitious and intelligent? If the Beatles hadn't had
the same exploratory, inquisitive nature that fuelled Genesis, the
world would never have had *Sergeant Pepper*. Why should rock
songs be restricted to three minutes? If a theme merits a longer
time-span – and this did – why shouldn't it be given that space?
How many classical suites are made up of shorter sections which
together create one flowing movement? Lengthy classical pieces
are rarely accused of being passionless simply because of their
length. Just as classical music embraces good and bad ideas, the
successes and the failures, so too can rock music – and 'Supper's
Ready' was an emphatic success. It may have been an epic work
on the grand scale, but Genesis did not over-reach themselves
– they brought home the (human) bacon without any trace of
pomposity. Dogmatic dissension dismissed, what of the song
itself?

It was gradually put together during the rehearsal period prior to recording, ideas tossed into the melting pot to the point where they had a ten-minute piece in the mould of 'The Musical Box' or 'Stagnation'. Unwilling to repeat themselves, the song needed to go in another direction, a direction that opened up when Tony suggested that after a very romantic acoustic passage they should just stop the song and launch into a new one, Peter's 'Willow Farm', a real oddity, filled with clever wordplay and imagery in the same style as 'Harold The Barrel'. The change from romance to absurdity gave the song the injection of pace it needed and paved the way for its completion, probably the finest piece of music that Genesis have ever written and performed, 'Apocalypse In 9/8' and the closing 'Aching Men's Feet'. Musically those latter stages were awesome, born out of improvisation by Mike, Tony and Phil – a pointer to the future – and inspiring a potent vocal performance from Peter, one which heroes like Otis Redding would have been proud to call their own. By his own testament Peter 'felt as if I was singing from my soul – almost like singing for my life.'[20] Once more, Genesis proved themselves to be light years apart from the progressive rockers with whom they were clumsily classified, Mike explaining that even on a song of this length, 'we were simple and melodic.'[4] The song displayed their customary grasp of dynamics, and its length was required not to massage musical egos but to get the themes across.

For something so strong, 'Supper's Ready' came together almost by chance. As it was being written the band had little idea just what the final product would be. They certainly never considered that it would become a musical milestone, Mike telling the *NME* in 1976: 'We didn't realize quite what we'd got. We were worrying more about other tracks,'[16] noting later that 'we stumbled into it really!'[4] Tony, in the same *NME* piece, describes it as 'The loud against the soft and the very romantic against the incredibly stupid . . . by doing that you make the romantic more romantic and the stupid more stupid.'[16] Phil responded particularly well to the improvised nature of 'Apocalypse In 9/8', still calling it a 'very moving piece of music',[4] while Steve describes it as a culmination of two year's work, a combination of 'lyrical ideas and lyrical playing'.[4] Musically then everyone was delighted, but the final piece of the puzzle fell into place with Peter's lyrics, a tale of the battle between good and evil that could have been the basis for a film script, the visual imagery giving a good indication of the avenues his writing and live performances would take. The initial stimulus came from an experience that he and Jill had had in the company of John Anthony at Jill's parents' flat at the Old Barracks in Kensington Palace. Anthony was very interested in spiritualism and had been talking to Jill at length about the subject and the idea of power and strength of will when the atmosphere in the room changed dramatically, Jill going into a trance as the windows blew open. Peter described it as 'like a Hammer Horror film except that it was for real'[5] adding, 'We saw other faces in each other. It was almost as if something else had come into us and was using us as a meeting point.'[8] Naturally, Jill and Peter were terrified by their ordeal; Peter exorcized some of his fears by writing of the age-old battle between the forces of light and darkness, ending in the final revelation. Bluntly stated in this way, it's evidently a subject that could have become a collection of horrifically pretentious, self-indulgent witterings, however in this case it came straight from the heart. It is to Genesis' credit that it was treated with great subtlety allied to a nice line in cynicism – any creeping pomposity deflated by the inclusion of 'Willow Farm' and its theatre of the absurd – and that, by the end, the many different emotional strands had been satisfactorily gathered together with incomparable power to produce a song perhaps unequalled in the canon of rock music.

Some twenty years later, 'Supper's Ready' is still recognized as a masterpiece so it is tribute indeed to the quality of the other songs that they were not dwarfed by its presence. It's easy to think of them as being appetizers for the main meal but that would be a grave injustice. 'Watcher Of The Skies' used an imaginative sci-fi lyric by Mike and Tony, inspired by the view from the roof of their hotel in Naples that April, when they had looked out on to a totally deserted landscape. The towering adagio mellotron introduction gave the record an atmosphere all its own, a flavour that was to be repeated countless times to even greater effect in concert, the melodramatic chords welcoming the audience into a completely new world with the promise of an escape from day-to-day mundanities. 'Time Table' and 'Can-Utility And The Coastliners' were both shorter songs, but of greater substance than those on the previous album. Romantic in theme, 'Time Table' yearned for a return to old values of honour and decency, 'Can-Utility' a tale of the folly of blind faith and of King Canute, unable to hold back the waves.

The remaining song was a further offering from the Peter Gabriel school of comic opera, 'Get 'Em Out By Friday', another story of good and evil – the evil coming this time in the form of voracious property developers buying up houses and turfing out the occupants into blocks of flats 'in the interest of humanity'. The developers get their own way by the liberal use of bribery, and we're transported forty years into a future where people are restricted to a height of four feet, so that 'they can fit twice as many in the same building site'. The news of this is transmitted via a newsflash on TV dial-a-programme services, a nod to Peter's father who invented a cable TV system called, of all things, 'Dial-a-Program'! It was odd snippets of lyrical detail such as this – inconsequential to the casual listener if noticed at all – that charmed a host of fans and won him a congregation of followers, most of whom appeared to take it in the tongue-in-cheek way that it was meant. Peter told the press in early 1973: 'I do like to have the detail there so that if anyone did want to spend their life rooting around the lyrics, it would be like a little paper chase for them – very unnecessary, but great fun!'[21]

That attention had already wormed its way into the sleeve design for their Charisma albums and Paul Whitehead obliged again for *Foxtrot* with a painting that had fans scouring it for clues, although in retrospect it was perhaps too busy, lacking the striking simplicity of his *Trespass* cover or the strong central image of *Nursery Cryme*. The focal point this time was a fox in a red dress – of which more later! – floating on ice, using its cunning to escape the clutches of the fox hunters, four horsemen of the apocalypse (in '9/8'). The cover also features the *'saintly shrouded men'* from 'Lover's Leap', with echoes of former glories coming in the form of Cynthia's mallet and a giant hogweed both afloat in the sea. Less successful than previous covers – it was Whitehead's last for the band – it still stood out from the crowd and gave some suggestions as to the surreal nature of the contents. As with its predecessors, the only way to fully appreciate Whitehead's work is as an LP sleeve – the CD booklet has again been destroyed by some butchery tool.

The powerful narratives and descriptive imagery that ran throughout the album tended to give the impression that Genesis were a one-man band, a problem that was to become worse later. The truth was, of course, very different, with all the members able to feel justifiably proud of their input on *Foxtrot*. To a degree, Tony Banks was the guiding musical light, the rich variety of sound that he was able to coax from his very primitive battery of keyboards was a revelation and gave Genesis a very individual, dramatic identity. His contribution to the writing was immense and he feels now that 'Particularly through the seventies, my tastes controlled the group more than the others, perhaps because I got the most unpleasant if people didn't agree with me!'[4] In tandem with Tony, Mike had moved to the forefront, contributing both lyrics and music, his understanding with Phil improving all the time – the three of them were always keen to play together to come up with new material, 'Apocalypse In 9/8' being the major fruit from those sessions on *Foxtrot*. Phil merely reinforced what everyone already knew – here was a rock drummer with few peers, whose energy was a wonderful source of inspiration to those around him, his gifts as an arranger saving numerous songs from the scrapheap, 'Get 'Em Out By Friday' being a classic example.

The only member of the band not on an absolute high was Steve who, despite the inclusion of a beautiful unaccompanied acoustic guitar piece, 'Horizons', still felt slightly apart from the others. He was less keen to get involved in the jams that Phil, Mike and Tony were developing, working in greater isolation, in the same way that Peter often did. Steve did in fact ask the others if they thought he should leave simply because he felt that he wasn't writing enough material. They quite rightly reassured him, recognizing the contribution that he made with his guitar sounds, the unique textures and odd noises that were a valuable part of their sound-scape, often transforming the feel of a song. Tony was very keen to further refine their partnership, pointing out to *Electronics and Music Maker* in 1983 that together they would experiment to come up with different sounds. 'Steve and I would play games, one inventing a new sound and the other trying to imitate it. By combining the two, we got another sound and went on from there.'[22]

The LP came out in October 1972, accompanied by the single 'Happy The Man', a curious promotional move since it was not on *Foxtrot*, was coupled with 'Seven Stones' from *Nursery Cryme* and had employed a different production team! Despite a nice picture sleeve featuring an action shot of the band in Italy, the single flopped, but the album crashed into the UK charts on the 14 October, reaching number twelve during its seven-week residency. In the press it met with generally positive reviews, a timely boost as Genesis were set to embark on another tour of the country, again in support of Lindisfarne.

Prior to the UK tour, the band visited Dublin at the end of September to play a concert at the National Stadium, a venue normally reserved for boxing matches. The gig proceeded in a fairly regular way, the audience impressed by the selection of old and new songs. Towards the end of the show, Peter told one of his stories and they began to play the final song of their set, 'The

Musical Box'. As was his wont, when the band moved into the musical section partway through, Gabriel went off stage, waiting to return for the denouement. This time, however, he returned wearing a long red dress that he had borrowed from his wife and a fox head, mimicking the character on the cover of the new album. The crowd were stunned, staring at the singer in a mixture of shock and awe, while the band were equally surprised since Peter hadn't told them what he was going to do. There was something of an inquest later, Peter defending his actions as the logical extension of his storytelling persona, expressing emphatically that since everyone else took such a sedentary role on stage it was up to him to do something dramatic to make their concerts a visual as well as a musical event. Some of the others were less sure; Mike went on to become very enthusiastic about Peter's costumes, but was less comfortable in this case. 'Musically, it didn't have much to do with anything, so I didn't think that it worked,'[4] although he concedes that the band let Peter have his (fox) head on the subject. Steve was rather more keen because 'My attitude was very much that we should put on a show and bit by bit he added little bits of theatre – the haircut, the necklace and then the costumes.'[4] Defending Gabriel's lack of consultation, he says, 'If he'd asked, maybe it wouldn't have been accepted!'

The idea for the costume which finally took Genesis into uncharted theatrical territory, was originally Paul Conroy's, then working for Charisma. He felt that dressing someone as the fox from the sleeve would be a good way of promoting the record, but Peter immediately seized upon the suggestion, deciding that it would make him the undoubted centre of attention. Even if the group were uncertain about this new departure they were forced to agree that it gave them an extra dimension on stage and provided journalists with a lot more to write about than just another group of musicians and photographers with something more interesting at which to aim their cameras. Genesis were very soon to appear on the front cover of *Melody Maker*, something which dramatically raised their profile as well as their appearance fees.

Finally on the road to success at home and with Italy and Belgium treating them as superstars, the next step was to conquer America. Their records were being distributed through the States by Buddah, an organization that found itself confused by *Nursery Cryme* – indeed it wasn't reviewed by *Rolling Stone* magazine until October 1972, when Richard Cromelin pointed out their 'refusal to indulge in gratuitous eclecticism at the expense of rock and roll', and described Genesis as 'the new contender for the coveted

British weirdo-rock championship.'[23] However, Buddah felt it had a better chance of selling *Foxtrot* to America. Aware that the band hadn't played there and also accepting that Genesis would have to grow on their audience gradually, they contacted Tony Stratton-Smith in London for advice. Between them, Buddah and Charisma decided to launch Genesis in America by playing a one-off show as a headline act at a prestigious venue, flying in influential press and radio people from all over the States to witness the occasion. It was hoped this would create both a buzz for the new record and a ready-made and expectant audience for their return visit, tentatively scheduled for the following spring. The date was set for 13 December, the venue New York Philharmonic Hall for a Christmas charity show, an annual event organized by New York radio station WNEW and which was consequently guaranteed saturation advertising and media coverage. Playing their first show in the vital American market under such close scrutiny before a press that didn't care if they were a success or failure represented a huge gamble for all concerned. (In terms of cash outlay alone, it cost Buddah and Charisma $16,000 to stage.) But, as Stratton-Smith told *Sounds'* Jerry Gilbert in his article on the gig, such a gamble could only be done 'with a group that (a) had a really fine show and (b) that was coming to the top of the curve in terms of confidence. It was a tremendous challenge for the band.'[24]

Military-style plans were laid for the show, with Richard MacPhail and the rest of the crew travelling out a week earlier to check the hall, organize the lighting and effects and arrange a warm-up show, which they played two nights before the New York gig in a university in Boston before an audience of thirty. The audience, or lack of it, was the least of their worries as they were beset by monstrous technical difficulties, largely caused by electrical voltage differences between America and England, causing the organ to run sharp and giving problems with the rest of their equipment. The only consolation was that they'd organized a three-hour soundcheck for the Philharmonic Hall, a suitable amount of time to sort things out satisfactorily.

The day dawned inauspiciously, both Steve and Peter waking to find themselves struggling with flu brought on by the inadequate ventilation in their hotel rooms, and things went downhill from there on. On arriving at the venue, they weren't allowed in because the New York Philharmonic Orchestra had decided to rehearse for their concert the following evening – it wasn't until six-thirty that they left the hall, with the doors scheduled to open at seven o'clock. For perhaps their most important concert to date,

Genesis didn't even get a soundcheck! Already nervous, their collective mood was scarcely improved when their support act, fellow Charisma act String Driven Thing, went on to face a slow hand-clap and were subjected to constant equipment problems. Nevertheless, on they went, opening as usual with 'Watcher Of The Skies', which Jerry Gilbert described as 'one of the best versions of [it] that I have heard.'[24] Already struggling with his voice, Peter brought out the red dress and fox head and it was this typically English eccentricity which Gilbert thought 'won the evening for Genesis'[24] as they fought through breakdown after breakdown. By the middle of the set, Mike in particular was beset by a terrible humming noise from his bass to add to a general buzz on all their equipment, worsened by having to use a hired amp after one of theirs had blown up just before the show. When they played 'Supper's Ready', still in its infancy as a live song, Peter's voice gave out, 'disappearing at worst into a hoarse and inaudible whisper.'[24] Finally reaching the end of their nightmare, they went straight to their dressing room where Mike in particular was inconsolable, throwing his guitar to the floor, the group refusing to admit any intruders. They all felt that it was probably the worst gig that they had ever played and that they had blown their chances, Tony describing it as 'a complete disaster'.[4]

Meanwhile the crowd was ecstatic: the ordinary punter, the record company executive and radio DJ alike – America had never seen anything like Genesis and they wanted more. While the group couldn't understand why everybody was so delighted, they quickly gathered that they'd been a hit and had won over a whole new collection of fans. The following day at their record company's New York office there was real excitement in the air, staff busily taking calls from press and radio throughout the city, anxious to know more about this strange group from England. Spirits revived, Mike recalls leaving New York thinking that 'we'd conquered America!'[4]

Most of America had yet to hear of the band and there was a lot of hard work still to be done, but as 1972 came to a close Genesis could look towards the new year with confidence.

CHAPTER EIGHT

'Stepping one beyond your show'

A rock group aiming to carve a long and successful career in the music industry must at some time look towards America – the potential audience is huge, the financial rewards commensurately high and the challenge irresistible. The first glimpse of the 'new world' has affected different acts in different ways. Some have become transfixed, like a rabbit in the headlights of an oncoming lorry, blotting out all else, until America runs them down and leaves them with nothing. The wiser few ensure that they don't betray their roots and endeavour to cultivate the new market while simultaneously attending to their bedrock support – this means working twice as hard, but the final crop is richer as a result.

Having had their eyes opened by their brief Stateside experience, Genesis set to the task of promoting *Foxtrot* in Europe, including a triumphant return to Italy where, almost inevitably, they had the number-one album. In what was a very satisfying turnaround of billing, proving how far they had come in so short a time, Genesis headlined a Charisma festival that took in a combined audience of 28,000 at the Palasports in Reggio and Rome, and featured Peter Hammill and Lindisfarne as support acts! The shows were fanatically received and the Italians were given their first sight of Peter's increasingly theatrical performance. Italy was, however, a prelude to the headline British tour that was awaiting them that February during which they would grace Town and City Halls around the country.

Most prestigious of all was the concert they were due to play on 9 February at the Rainbow Theatre in Finsbury Park, London's premier venue for rock bands, the final confirmation that the UK had at last recognized Genesis for the force they were. With such a big show in prospect, it was expected that the group would do something rather special to mark the occasion, but nobody could have foreseen just what they had in store. The music was already in place – the new material from *Foxtrot* having been thoroughly played in by now – so the band could afford to turn its attentions more towards the presentation. In spite of the increased confidence generated by their continued success, they were still very reserved as a live act and there was a desire to make the stage set look interesting, rather than cluttered with equipment in front of which sat a collection of fairly anonymous musicians. Obviously, if they hid their equipment behind a curtain, it would absorb some of the sound and detract from the music. Their stage manager had come across a gauze curtain which was fine enough to be transparent to sound, but unfortunately it was also fine enough for people to see through. The problem seemed insoluble until they hit on the idea of shining ultra-violet light on to the curtain, which made it appear solid, thus disguising their equipment! Tony's thoughts were that by 'making the set look interesting . . . we could be trendsetters. It first came together at the Rainbow and it was stunning. It was very simple, but the point was that it had never been combined with rock – we turned the stage into the personality!'[4] He and the rest of the band realized that they'd found something special when they opened with 'Watcher Of The Skies', as Tony recalls: 'We lit the curtain with the UV lights and Peter had UV-sensitive eye make-up on. It was incredibly exciting and it just gave everything a power.'[4]

It wasn't only the new lighting set-up that was exciting. Peter had taken to the stage wearing a long flowing black cape and a pair of 'batwings' around his shoulders, fixed by a headband. Unlike his previous dalliance with costume – the fox head in Dublin – this time Peter gave notice to the others that he would be wearing a range of masks and clothes – he told them on the day of the concert. Steve believes Peter's decision not to tell anyone in advance was simply because 'he was against the idea of committee',[4] feeling that it diluted the impact of the individual, a portent of what was to come. He needn't have worried – this time, having been introduced to the idea and having seen its benefits, there was a greater degree of agreement from the band because the costumes tied in with the music. Mike says, 'We enjoyed it, they worked well'[4] – the batwings in 'Watcher' conjured up the alien visitor, giving Peter a new presence before the audience, who were intent on playing their part in this celebration.

Peter was so absorbed in his role that he broke precedent after the opening song and welcomed everyone to 'the world of

Genesis', introducing the rest of the group rather than leading into a monologue. These introductions were characteristically off-beat, as if they were players in a film – 'Michael Mellotron playing the part of Tony Banks, David Drums and Sally Cymbals as Philip Collins, myself, Peter Gabriel, played by Patrick Moore, Michael Rutherford by Richard Rickenbacker and Steve Hackett by Gary Gibson himself' – clearly this wasn't going to be an ordinary show! Gabriel adopted and then shed costumes and personas as naturally as a snake sheds its skin. For the closing section of 'The Musical Box' he wore a disturbing, malevolent old-man mask, miming Henry's sexual climax and thus making further sense of the musical accompaniment in a tremendously strong piece of theatre. There was a range of costumes for 'Supper's Ready' – a flower head for 'Willow Farm', a strange box mask for the '666' section and a black cloak that at the end of the song was torn off in a flash of light to reveal Peter in a shining white suit, the final triumph of good over evil.

As a frontman, Peter was transformed by his props. Far from being something to hide behind, his masks were used, as they are in African and Indian cultures, as means by which his personality, and the people that populated the songs, could come through more clearly. Peter was now on his way to becoming a 'rock star', though as Steve says, 'He never really saw himself that way.'[4] The press were unanimous in their praise for the Rainbow show and on the cover of the following week's *Melody Maker* there was Peter staring out from his flower mask. 'Has Peter Gabriel created a monster?'[25] asked Chris Welch in his review, a question more prophetic than he might have imagined at the time.

Welch was unstinting in his praise of Genesis, noting that the whole band was on top form: 'From a shout to a whisper, Genesis seem completely in control.'[25] He gave all the members of the group equal credit, elaborating on how inventive and talented they were, what a powerful grasp they now had on the art of songwriting, their instinctive feel for musical and theatrical dynamics and finally describing the semi-hysterical response from the crowd. The review closed with yet another reminder of the band's roots and of how far apart they were from the 'progressive rock' movement, a reminder which went unheeded: 'Peter gave a remarkable performance . . . savouring a delightful variety of voices, sometimes resembling Anthony Newley or Fagin, or a soul singer. After all, were not the masses affected? Did not youths and maidens dance as if possessed? And you can't blame it on rock and roll, because Genesis don't play any.'[25]

Welch was a lone voice in the dark, however, as Genesis were soon lazily grouped with the likes of ELP, Jethro Tull and Pink Floyd, something which still rankles with the group to this day and a completely erroneous categorization. Comparisons on a musical level were aggravating for the group but soon equally fallacious visual comparisons were found, ranging from the obvious – David Bowie (just about to announce his retirement as Ziggy Stardust) and Alice Cooper – to the more bizarre – Gary Glitter! Yet again, the press seemed determined to miss the point completely – Gabriel's costumes weren't pure ostentation, designed just to give audiences something to look at, neither were they garish decoration or fashion statements, they were an extension of the songs, complementary to the music and intended to convey the fantasy of their lyrics to people who might not know all the words, especially at a time of poor PA systems. Press criticism aside, Genesis' ever-growing army of fans loved this new development, and as pictures of Gabriel made front covers of the papers and as their reputation grew as a live band of the highest class, they could by-pass the critics and achieve success on their own terms.

Following the reports of the Rainbow gig, everybody wanted to see Genesis and they toured the country in triumph. The shows at Manchester Free Trade Hall and Leicester De Montfort Hall were recorded for later broadcast by an American radio station in its King Biscuit series, a programme which was set to go out in early March, just as the band were returning there for a tour of the east coast.

After their great success the previous December, and Mike's parting comment that they felt that they'd cracked America, the group were devastated to discover that New York had forgotten all about them, and that the rest of America had no idea who they were. Refusing to compromise, Genesis played only headline shows in America, with a couple of exceptions included a 'battle of the bands' show with Lou Reed in Canada, where they met with hostility from Reed's fans. According to Peter, a brawl ensued, much to his delight since he felt that it made the band work all the harder to capture the attention of an aggressively disinterested crowd. They had no intention of restricting their stage show in any way, or of leaving any of it behind – they insisted on using their full rig night after night, which meant that it was a virtual impossibility for them to play as a support act, even if they wanted to and if there had been suitable bands to work with. Allied to that, having been spoilt by their success in Europe and the UK, they enjoyed playing to people who specifically came along to see Genesis. This meant that conquering

America was to be a long, hard struggle, more difficult than it might have been, but they approached it philosophically and were pleased with the pockets of support they had at some gigs, such as at their return to the Philharmonic Hall that April. It also meant slogging their way across the country in cars and vans – far from the glamorous image of touring the States possibly envisaged by the folks back home.

Tensions inevitably built and Phil has vivid memories of a visit to New Orleans where they soiled their previously spotless image: 'The hotel was holding our rooms until four o'clock. We'd been driving for hours and got there at ten past four to check in and they said, "Sorry, we've given the rooms away." We were shattered, so Mike picked up this vase and threw it across reception, but being America it was plastic with plastic flowers, so it just bounced off the wall and fell on the floor. We couldn't even do that right, but we did get the rooms!'[4]

The group's only qualms about America revolved around their record company, Buddah. Following the success of their first American visit, they had hoped that Buddah would be able to promote *Foxtrot* to a wider audience, but returned to find that little had improved and that they were still almost total unknowns, an indifference which sometimes made it difficult to motivate themselves despite audience responses that were generally very strong. This lack of motivation proved infectious, and soon their faithful assistant Richard MacPhail decided to leave the band because he felt disenchanted by the harsh reality of big business.

Coming off the road, their natural habitat since the release of *Foxtrot* six months earlier, Genesis faced the prospect of putting together a new album for release later the same year. They had not had a break since the recording sessions for the previous album, so hadn't had the opportunity to write any material, being left with a few ideas that hadn't come to fruition during their last sessions. For the first time since their days in the Dorking cottage, they set aside time purely to write new music, from scratch, as a group, using the same rehearsal facilities they'd employed a year before – the dancing school in Shepherd's Bush and a doctor's house in Chessington. Charisma gave them a three-month period to come up with the material and initially all went very well with much new music being written in the first few weeks, but then the open-ended time span bit back, Mike terming it 'the kiss of death'.[20] The very fact that they were given such a large amount of time to write meant that once they had a piece of music they tended to keep returning to it, re-arranging it, changing bits, to a point where it looked as though they could have problems completing the record in time. That July, Tony told Chris Welch in *Melody Maker*: 'When we started rehearsing, we worked too slowly because there seemed plenty of time, but then we found ourselves pushed.'[26]

Charisma were beginning to fret over the future of this new record and once it became clear that Genesis would fail to meet their deadline, Tony Stratton-Smith proposed that they release a live album to fill the gap rather than rush its completion. The group weren't keen on the idea – Peter felt that by cutting out the visuals the power of the show would be lost and the others were unsure as to just how good it would sound, Phil arguing that they had never felt their live sound was as good as the recordings. To obtain their final approval, Stratton-Smith agreed to release it at a budget price, which meant that it could go into ordinary chain stores such as Woolworth and W. H. Smith to a far greater extent than ever before, immediately making it more accessible to the casual buyer. The choice of what to release was restricted – the only tapes available were those used for King Biscuit from the UK tour in February, so Charisma obtained the original unmixed versions and put Genesis into London's Island Studios with John Burns, engineer on *Foxtrot*, to mix it, for release in July 1973.

Genesis Live is a fairly impressive document of how the group sounded at that time, though Peter was right to predict that it would lack the unique power that the combination of music and visual elements gave them as a live act. Chris Welch, perennial Genesis supporter, gave it a good review, writing, 'While other groups babble of passion plays and rock operas, Genesis quietly extend the boundaries of rock music, keeping its spirit of excitement and humour.'[27] The album served as a nice potted history of the group to date, the songs generally more powerful than their studio counterparts, with the main points of interest being 'The Knife', where Gabriel had changed some of his original lyrics, and the inclusion of one of Peter's between-song monologues on the back cover. The album did its job, filling the gap and maintaining Genesis' profile nicely, reaching number nine in the charts. But the group were not happy with it and it was briefly deleted following the release of 'Seconds Out' in 1977. It has since been reinstated as part of their catalogue.

Rehearsals for the new album continued throughout the summer months, but progress remained slow and there was a general sense of disillusionment over the project – Phil, in particular, felt very unhappy about the state of affairs. One of the things that he'd brought to Genesis over the three years he'd been with them was a greater sense of spontaneity, the idea that there can be magic in the particular moment of creation, a magic that can be lost with the constant picking through of songs with a fine toothcomb. As a result, the performance and songs on *Nursery Cryme* and particularly *Foxtrot* had been a lot fresher, livelier and less laboured than on *Trespass*, and Collins was keen to see this continue, especially as his passion grew for bands like Weather Report, whose more improvisational mode of working appealed very strongly to him. Certainly Phil was kicking his heels and Mike revealed in *Sounds* in 1976 that there had been worries that Phil might want to leave the group. As the sessions dragged on, Phil relieved some of his frustration by playing with a pick-up band called Zox and the Radar Boys which featured Peter Banks, Yes' original guitarist, and a couple of school friends, a line-up that played a few gigs, including one at Aylesbury Friar's.

Among the rest of the group there was agreement with many of Phil's feelings towards the rehearsals. Mike remembers that half of what finally came through was actually written in the first couple of weeks, some by means of improvisation, some from songs that were brought in largely complete. Tony had written an early draft of 'Firth of Fifth' around the time of *Foxtrot* but it had met with a cool reception, so he'd continued to work at it over the intervening period, bringing it back to the group who were now much happier with it. Peter had some short piano pieces which became the basis for the first part of 'Dancing With The Moonlit Knight' featuring a guitar figure of Steve's. Another riff of Steve's saw the whole band jamming around it for hours until it became a fully fledged song – 'I Know What I Like (In Your Wardrobe)'. 'My guitar riff had been around since *Foxtrot*, but everyone thought it sounded too much like the Beatles. I kept playing it and finally everyone else joined in and it became our first hit single – no one else has ever said that it sounds like the Beatles!' Another long improvisational session between Mike, Tony and Phil bore fruit with the very strong instrumental section at the end of 'The Cinema Show'.

Several other pieces in tow, the band returned to Island Studios in August to record their fourth album for Charisma – prior to a headlining performance at that year's August Bank Holiday Reading Festival – with expectations higher than they'd ever been. Could they come up with another album to match *Foxtrot*? Would there be a song as good as 'Supper's Ready'?

Charisma kept faith with John Burns for this record, recognizing the partnership he was building with the band who had been suitably impressed with his efforts on the previous records. The move unquestionably paid off because *Selling England By The Pound* gave them their best sound to date. Genesis responded well to this improvement by playing better than ever, and this was perhaps the only time where technique threatened on occasion to take precedence over the songs. The record opened strangely with 'Dancing With The Moonlit Knight', beginning like a traditional folk song, Peter singing unaccompanied, and this eccentric, highly original approach kept coming thick and fast right through to the closing 'Aisle of Plenty' which reprised the guitar figure from 'Moonlit Knight' and had Peter disclosing the prices at his local supermarket amid a welter of truly excruciating puns – who but Genesis would try to get away with a line like – 'Thankful for her Fine Fare discount, Tess co-operates'?

The vinyl grooves were crammed to overflowing with a bewildering array of themes and ideas. Interestingly, and perversely, now that success in America was very much on the agenda, they could hardly have come up with a more English-sounding record! Gabriel was very conscious that the British press would be looking for the smallest signs of the band slanting things towards American ears and was keen to avoid the trap by filling the lyrics with English references such as Green Shield stamps (a tortuous pun around the legend of Sir Gawain and the Green Knight) and by insisting that the album carried the moniker 'Selling England By The Pound', the title of the Labour Party manifesto at the time.

If the album had a theme, it was the decay of English folk culture and the country's rapid Americanization, represented by the Wimpy hamburger, an allusion to the correlation between junk food and junk culture, though Hackett sums up the mood of the record best; 'It's just kind of mad, surreal, the references are so scattered – the whole package always makes me smile. It's very strange music, you just can't pin it down!'[4] Tony and Mike in particular have mixed views on *Selling England By The Pound*, feeling there are some very high points but also some very low points, but Steve is quick to argue that it is his favourite Genesis record. 'I was very happy that the band's playing was good, my guitar sound was good, there was some weird and wacky stuff on it, it was pretty broad. There were some genuinely funny moments on it, we certainly had a good straight love song, the playing was hot, lots of what I wanted to do was on it.' He adds, 'Everyone was being natural, working to the same ends.'[4] One key decision he recalls was not to join 'The Cinema Show' and 'Moonlit Knight' into one long song as had been intended – there was a conscious desire to avoid repetition from one record to the next, so the idea of a long song beginning with twelve-string passages and ending in a strong instrumental section was abandoned, the passion to do something new being a characteristic of the group to this day.

'I Know What I Like' went on to become their first hit single when released the following year, ideal in that it reflected the band's music rather than being an unrepresentative bid for a place on top-twenty radio. Peter opened the song, sounding like the White Rabbit in *Alice In Wonderland*, backed by the mechanical whirr of the 'cosmic lawnmower', before heading into an everyday tale of repressed folk. It gave a good indication as to his areas of inspiration – the seething wildness held beneath the formal restraint of Englishness, neatly described by Michael Wale in *The Times* in January 1974 as the 'reflection of a world where nothing is quite what it seems'.[28] In an ironic turnaround, this time the album featured a song that had been inspired by what was to become the cover, Peter having seen Betty Swanwick's painting 'The Dream' at a London exhibition, whereupon he was immediately inspired to write the lyrics for 'I Know What I Like'. The band approached her to do a new painting for the sleeve, but because of time restrictions she modified the existing one, adding the lawnmower and garden fork. The result was one of their best-loved covers and one which rooted the album more firmly still into an image of the English way of life.

Steve freely admits that following *Foxtrot* he wanted to approach *Selling England* purely as a player, with no great interest in writing, 'Yet I ended up writing a couple of key things for the band.' An important writer on the two opening tracks, on Tony's 'Firth Of Fifth', he contributed an emotionally charged solo, which many still regard as the crowning moment of his time with the band. He also provided the basis for an impressive instrumental workout on the second side, 'After The Ordeal' – a track that caused something of a stir as both Peter and Tony were very keen to keep it off the album. All this meant that Steve had become a far greater force in the band, another writer to be reckoned with. Not surprisingly, he says, 'I have fond memories of *Selling England* as a time when, although my personal life was in turmoil, the group was breaking new ground. We were going where no band had gone before!' In a situation similar to that in which Phil Collins found himself some six years later, Steve's first, short-lived marriage – the wedding had taken place at the beginning of the year – was in the early stages of collapse and he sought refuge in his work with Genesis, pouring all his time and energy into it as a means of escape from his domestic problems.

Peter had freer rein as a lyricist than ever before too, 'The Battle Of Epping Forest' being an impressive contribution, despite not working in total harmony with the music. The idea was based on a gangland battle over East End protection rights which Peter had read about in a newspaper some years before. In spite of his attempts to obtain more information, including placing an advert for help in *The Times*, sources had disappeared without trace, leaving him to populate the story with his own characters – Liquid Len, Harold Demure, Sweetmeal Sam and the Bethnal Green Butcher. Reading the lyrics on the album insert, it's one of the most appealing, perhaps the funniest, idea that Gabriel has ever used, but unfortunately the feud between the music and words saw more bloodshed than the battle itself! Perhaps the one time where Genesis employed a too-clever-by-half approach and actively invited comparisons with prog-rock. Fans were especially grateful for 'The Cinema Show' which closed the record on a high, its improvised instrumental ending being a live favourite right through to the 1984 'Mama' tour, a piece of music which embodied high emotion.

Not an unequivocal success by any means, *Selling England* did still have much to commend it – the best production and playing to date, a potential, yet fully representative, hit single, a keen sense of fun, and, in 'More Fool Me', a tender, romantic song that exposed a completely new side of the band. Written very quickly by Phil and Mike, it featured Phil on lead vocals and a one-to-one conversational slant to the lyrics, proof positive that Genesis truly were a group of songwriters, one far more inventive than the majority of their competition.

Selling England By The Pound was released in October 1973 to reviews inevitably, and probably quite fairly, less ecstatic than those which greeted *Foxtrot*. For example, Robin Denselow in the *Guardian* wrote: 'Much of the material is indistinctive and tedious in the extreme . . . they are just good in parts.'[29] But the response from the public was everything that they could have hoped for, the album reaching number three as Genesis began a sell-out tour of the UK which continued throughout October, taking in venues the length and breadth of the country. They were now a very big proposition, at least in Britain, and one would have expected touring to go like clockwork, but this was not the case. Opening their first tour since the departure of Richard MacPhail at Green's Playhouse in Glasgow, the show had to be cancelled with the theatre full and the support act already finished. For various reasons the crew hadn't been able to satisfactorily set up the lighting rig, leaving their road manager, Adrian Selby, to tell the promoter that he couldn't allow the band to go on stage as there was the very real possibility of electrocution. Green's had something of a reputation as a 'difficult' place to play at the time, so it was hardly with a song in his heart that the promoter sent everybody home, promising to reschedule the gig for the following week.

The promoter was Tony Smith, one of the most respected figures on the rock scene. Back at their hotel after the show, Smith pointed out to Genesis in no uncertain terms that they had to get themselves a manager of some quality as soon as possible, because unreliability such as they'd just experienced would cost them dear. The band had already been giving the idea some thought, particularly with their increasingly high profile in the States, and felt very keenly that they needed someone to handle their business affairs. They had already gone through one unsuccessful relationship with lawyer Robert Hirshman, having previously been turned down by David Stopps from the Friar's Club. On tour, they continued to discuss the problem, deciding that Smith was the man for the job, though he was less than sure about the idea at first. Mounting boredom with his role of promoter finally won him over and he took on the job believing that 'it was just a question of getting them organized. It was only later that I discovered that they were £150,000 in debt. That's at 1972 values too. It'd be about a million now.'[30] Tony Banks remembers the chaos things were in: 'We were protected from our debt by Charisma, but 1972/73 was a bad period, in the USA especially, as touring was very expensive without the receipts – on one tour, no receipts were kept for anything and the Inland Revenue decided we'd made a huge profit when we'd made a big loss. We needed a manager and when Tony agreed, he was very dismayed with our affairs. He's filled all the gaps without affecting our music, so it's been a very successful partnership.'[4]

Back on the road, Genesis were playing better than ever, the mixture of old songs with the new material and an improved stage show cementing their place firmly at the top. Even returning to Green's, where Steve admits they were very unsure of their reception, 'They gave us a standing ovation when we went on and they couldn't have been kinder!'[4] The 'Selling England' tour of the UK was filmed for possible cinema release, Stratton-Smith feeling strongly that the band should be captured on film during what

was a very exciting period both in terms of audience acceptance
and of their live performance. But the band felt that the film was
not of a high enough standard and so refused to sanction its
release. It's a great shame that the film isn't commercially available
because it really does illustrate how out on a limb and how far
ahead of the crowd Genesis were. While Pink Floyd wanted to
impress you with technology, ELP just wanted you to be
impressed and King Crimson were a little irritated that you actually
dared to be in the same building as them, Genesis radiated the
feeling that everyone was in this together. Peter may have been a
strange, alien figure during the songs and the band may have
seemed very distant when playing, but there was a very real
warmth between stage and audience. This and their very obvious
commitment to providing value for money – sets were already
running at almost two hours – persuaded people to take Genesis
to their hearts and the astonishing degree of loyalty that they still
receive from their fans is a testament to that.

Genesis were now a major concert draw, but press reactions
were beginning to give some cause for concern. Although Phil had
the chance to move to the front of the stage to sing 'More Fool
Me', Steve played 'Horizons' and Mike and Tony were colouring
the sound with great taste and skill, the press only had eyes
for Peter and his new assortment of costumes (which this time
included an East End thug with a stocking over his head during
'The Battle Of Epping Forest' and Britannia for 'Dancing With The
Moonlit Knight'). The band were united in their desire to provide
a memorable live show in both visual and musical terms, but there
was an inevitable annoyance that Peter was being singled out in
the press reviews and was the one asked to do all their interviews
– Genesis had always tried to present itself as a democratic unit
and a true five-piece group where everyone was equal, but the
press were giving the impression that Genesis were 'The Peter
Gabriel Band', an impression strengthened with every front cover
that Peter received. Even though it was played down publicly,
and there was no resentment directed towards Gabriel himself,
Peter was feeling less and less at ease with his position within the
band, often using interviews to ram home just how great the
other's contributions were, rarely expressing his increasing disenchantment with the business and the never-ending workload of
gigs. In March 1974 he broke that self-imposed silence and told
Crawdaddy's John Swenson: 'The pace we have to keep is frustrating – I can't really see myself doing this for more than another
year or two.'[31] As if to emphasize his growing disillusionment

with the music industry and perhaps with Genesis, Peter and Jill moved to a cottage in Bath in the same month. While the rest of the group lived in and around London and the music business, Peter found it necessary to distance himself from that, at least geographically.

However, when Peter was on the road, he and the band pulled out all the stops. Returning again to America in November for a tour to take them through to Christmas, they were at last making some headway and were able to headline two shows at the Felt Forum in New York, closing the tour by playing two shows a day on the 17, 18 and 19 December at the Roxy, a renowned rock venue in Los Angeles. All the band have very fond memories of that particular residency, the sound being excellent and the audiences, in the main, composed of wildly enthusiastic people who attended most if not all of Genesis' six concerts there. Peter got into the spirit of things on the final evening by dressing up as Father Christmas, telling *Melody Maker* on their return, 'It was one of the best welcomes we've ever had. We found that we had a sort of underground mystique.'[32] The band, thoroughly enjoying themselves, played at peak form and were in particularly good spirits having learned that tickets for their five January shows at the Theatre Royal, Drury Lane, had sold out within hours of going on sale. It wasn't all plain sailing, though, for one of Peter's on-stage ideas did not quite work as he had anticipated. 'I had hiccups for two days solid in LA – I had tried using helium on stage to get a Mickey Mouse voice. It was really quite worrying, although I thought it was funny at first.'[32]

With things moving ahead on all fronts, the Drury Lane engagements were everything they could have wanted, although Peter again fell foul of his theatrical antics. At the conclusion of 'Supper's Ready', normally there was a bright flash during which Peter threw off his black cape to reveal a white suit. This time, he took advantage of one of the theatre props that was in situ, as Phil explains: 'He decided to go up on these "Peter Pan" wires. They took him up, but the wires got twisted so Peter was stuck up in the air, slowly revolving, and he was trying to sing and right himself with his leg!'[4] Accidents aside, the mood of celebration was heightened further a few weeks later when 'I Know What I Like' was released as a single, backed by old live favourite 'Twilight Alehouse', finally released after three years. It went into the charts and peaked at number twenty-one. It probably could have got far higher, but the band were unable to promote it with a *Top of the Pops* appearance because of their touring schedule, similarly rejecting a promotional film that had been made to accompany it. Without any real push, the single stalled after promising initial sales and dropped out of the charts.

The early part of 1974 was consumed by tours of Europe, where they played to more than 50,000 people at four Italian shows, and then a longer stint in North America and Canada which continued into April. After eight months on the road, Genesis had consolidated their first-division status in Europe and were getting better and better reactions throughout America. Still massively in debt, financial success was some way off, but the signs were that within a couple of years, given a continued concerted effort, the group would finally break even, particularly as they had laid the foundations in the crucial American market. It seemed that all they had to do was to keep their line-up and their output stable. The workload was, however, beginning to take its toll on the band and some of the relationships within it. Peter, in particular, felt more and more frustrated by life on the road and further alienated by his ever-increasing media profile, so a short break was required before Genesis could get back together and make their next, vital album, the one that both they and Charisma hoped would herald their final breakthrough in the States.

CHAPTER NINE

'In the cushioned strait-jacket'

They had spent the better part of four years together working on one aspect of Genesis or another, so there was some relief when the 'Selling England' tour came to a close and the band could take a break from one another. There were various tensions simmering as a result of this enforced closeness on both a personal and a musical level. Phil was still frustrated by the structured music that had come to the fore on *Selling England* and began to play with a variety of other musicians, something which was to lead ultimately to the formation of Brand X, a very loose jazz-rock outfit – 'It was like a band completely free, without any inhibitions at all, it was open.'[33] Brand X took the lid off the pressure cooker for Phil throughout the late seventies, acting as a safety valve, along with the phenomenal amount of session work that he also undertook.

This time, though, Phil wasn't the only member who wanted to get involved in extra-curricular activities, Mike teaming up with Anthony Phillips to make an album. Since leaving Genesis, Ant had studied music further in order to increase his all-round understanding of form and composition, until finally he felt the time was right to return to recording. There was a great deal of material that he and Mike had written together in the early seventies which had never made it on to record and so they intended to rectify this, hoping to write some more music to complete the album. Phil was also called in to help with the project, the three of them exhuming 'Silver Song' with the intention of releasing it as a Phil Collins solo single, although that never saw the light of day. Recording began that summer, but Mike's commitments with Genesis meant that they were unable to complete it before he went on tour with the new album, the results of their labours ultimately being released in 1977 as Ant's first solo album, *The Geese And The Ghost*.

Genesis had decided to get together towards the end of May to begin work on the next record, which they had decided would be that much-maligned – often with reason – 1970s beast, the concept album. During the final leg of the 'Selling England' tour, the group had been throwing ideas around as to their next move and felt that using an underlying theme throughout the course of an album would give them the necessary space to develop some of their lyrics more fully, and the challenge of capturing specific moods and atmospheres in the music to help the story along also appealed. They needed a storyline – Peter's vision of what became the story of Rael finally won the vote, though the democratic process was, according to Peter, 'bullshit on my part, as there was only one story which I was going to develop.'[34] There had been other suggestions, but to Peter in particular it was vitally important that this album took Genesis into entirely new territory. Their pre-occupation with fantasy, science fiction and with myths and legends was something that had to go. Perhaps more than the others, Peter had his ear to the ground as far as the nation's musical climate was concerned and could feel that the winds of change were getting ready to blow up a storm. Two years before the Sex Pistols arrived on the scene, Gabriel devised Rael, a proto-type punk, an aggressive, ballsy character, light years away from tales of Romeo and Juliet or Hermaphroditus, though Mike recalls: 'Rael wasn't the beginning at all. It was getting so obscure we needed a central character.'[16] As Peter has said, 'We were beginning to get into the era of big fat supergroups of the seventies and I thought "I don't want to go down with this Titanic." '[20] Gabriel wanted to pare down the lyrics, to take them away from the fey flights of fancy that had typified a lot of their earlier work, to give Genesis a new credibility in the face of the new-wave onslaught. Having got the go-ahead for the storyline he wanted, he then insisted that he should be solely responsible for the lyrics. The idea was his baby and he didn't want anyone else's views clouding his reading of it.

Although there were misgivings, the band acquiesced to Peter's demands, Mike and Tony, the other principal lyricists, in particu-lar backing off. Both felt they could have made important contri-butions to the lyrics and the band as a whole were rather dubious as to whether Peter would be able to come up with the required amount of material in the time available, given that he was a very deliberate writer who took as much time as possible before coming up with a finished version of a song. Nevertheless, the band went into rehearsals, renting a house which gave them the opportunity to work whatever the time of day, a situation reminiscent of their period in the Dorking cottage prior to *Trespass*.

Headley Grange in Surrey was a house owned by Led Zeppelin which they sub-let to other groups. The very fact that it was owned by them meant that it was inevitably in a state, but it had been further abused by visiting guests. Genesis arrived to find the grand old country house in terrible disrepair, as Phil recalls: 'It had been raped – by that time, rats had become the main occupants. You'd walk down the hall and these rats would slowly scurry across the floor and then scurry back, it was horrible – but we spent three months there driving each other crazy.'[4]

Personal problems were very much a part of the Genesis land-scape over this period. Peter was unsure of his future and Jill, his wife, was reaching the end of a difficult first pregnancy, causing him to commute regularly between his home in Bath and Headley Grange, so he was therefore unable to give his full attention to the group. Added to that, their marriage had been rocked late the previous year when, just after conceiving the child, Jill had had an affair with Genesis' road manager, Regis Boff, a close friend of Peter's. She later described this as 'my pathetic little bid for atten-tion'[8] as a result of Peter's concentration on Genesis, and it was to have a profound effect on his relationship with the group and his plans for the future. Though the group had always allowed wives and girlfriends to accompany them on the road, it was very difficult or uncomfortable for them to do so and so they often remained at home. Inevitably this put a very heavy strain on a number of relationships, something from which Steve was also suffering as he endured the final breakdown of his marriage, a misery exacer-bated by the situation in which Genesis found themselves. 'We got into this idea of rehearsing in the country and that was difficult. We used this derelict house in the country and I like to be comfort-able! Maybe it was a "back to the dorm" philosophy, mattresses on floors – it was pretty spartan, which got me down.' Despite all the difficulties, Phil recalls that it was 'a very productive period and maybe the subliminal tensions made for some good music.'[4] The band quickly realized that the album was going to have to become a double to accommodate the wealth of quality music that they were producing, intensifying Peter's composing headaches – he now had to come up with a double album's worth of lyrics.

After rehearsing for a short time, Peter received a telegram from William Friedkin, director of *The Exorcist*, who intimated that he would be interested in working with him. Friedkin had read the story on the back of *Genesis Live* and had also seen the group at the Roxy in Los Angeles where he had been fascinated by Gabriel's stories. Friedkin was hoping to get a science fiction film off the ground and wanted to involve a new writer, a 'Hollywood virgin', in the project and thought that Gabriel's work illustrated a keen visual mind. With the problems of his wife's pregnancy obviously at the forefront of his mind, Peter was particularly excited by Friedkin's vague proposals – it would give him a break from working at Headley Grange and working on the screenplay at home would allow him time with Jill. It could also lead him into an avenue of work that had always intrigued him – in 1969 he had turned down a place at film school so that he could continue with Genesis – his later promotional videos illustrating just how important visual elements are to his work.

All this in mind, Peter went to the group and asked them to stop work while he went away and collaborated with Friedkin, even though Friedkin hadn't at this point given a definite yes to the project. Understandably, the rest of the group reacted in horror to Peter's suggestion – one member didn't have the right to leave the others in mid-air just to satisfy some personal pet project. Phil concedes: 'It was a good time for him to stop and think, but the band couldn't stop at that time.'[4] If Peter went off to do something by himself, what were the others going to do? Would he even come back to the group afterwards? Tony was particularly adamant that Peter couldn't do both. 'At the time, it just would have been wrong for us to allow people to do that. We were totally committed to the group.'[4] The band was finally beginning to reap the rewards of its long years of hard work and, as America was starting to open up for them, it was crucial that they maintained the pressure and continued to work as a group. While audience size was increasing at a consistent and encouraging rate, the band were still very heavily in debt thanks to their elaborate stage shows, a debt that could only be eradicated by continuing to work under the Genesis banner. Allied to that the music was still breaking new ground, the material they had so far for the new album was exciting, there were plenty of new ideas around and the band was still artistically rewarding – Genesis certainly had plenty of steam left in it, so why should there be any need to stop? Faced with this reaction, Peter felt himself backed into a corner and decided to leave the group in order to explore the project with Friedkin, returning home to Bath.

Phil remembers the group sitting in the garden at Headley

Grange trying to decide what they should do. He thought they should continue as an instrumental group, 'because we had a lot of music written'.[4] The rest of the group were in agreement that they should go on, but in a similar form to that which existed, Tony pointing out that 'The song was the reason for Genesis' existence. Everything was based on the song, everything was complementary to that,' and Phil later agreed that 'Mike and Tony wrote songs that needed singing.'[4]

With Peter gone, the others continued to write together, intending to work later on a storyline to fit in with the music. In the meantime, however, Gabriel's collaboration with Friedkin became more and more vague. Phil believes that it finally floundered as a result of Friedkin's reluctance to be the cause of splitting up Genesis, only really wanting some ideas, not a serious full-time commitment. At this point Charisma, clearly worried about its investment in Genesis, became involved and it was Tony Stratton-Smith who instigated a compromise package so that Peter could return to the group without anyone seeming to back down and lose face. The rest of the group agreed that Peter could look into other projects at a later date, providing he committed himself to recording and touring this new record. This uneasy truce in place, Peter returned to Headley Grange to complete work on the album, although he was still troubled by his wife's state of health. Their daughter Anna was born in July, partway through the rehearsals, and during the first two weeks of her life medical staff held out little hope for her survival. By comparison, the recording of a rock record was a trivial matter, one in which Peter had little interest – it was perfectly obvious to him where his priorities lay. The rock-and-roll treadmill was becoming less and less rewarding and it was through gritted teeth that he turned his thoughts to the task in hand.

All this time the others were piecing together more and more material for the album, working very much as a group, sometimes with, sometimes without Peter. A lot of very strong music was written, much of it in the same kind of extended improvisational sessions that had yielded 'Apocalypse In 9/8' and the closing section of 'The Cinema Show', a conscious effort by the band to move away from the kind of over-rehearsed and over-elaboration of ideas that had marred some of the music on *Selling England By The Pound*. One piece which Phil vividly remembers was the writing of 'The Waiting Room', which went under the working title 'Evil Jam'. 'We started to play and the only guidelines were that we should start off with "nasty" and finish off "nice" and where we

went in between was up to us, so we started with these really
nasty sounds and suddenly the weather changed – thunder and
lightning, it poured with rain, it was extraordinary. As the music
got nicer, so the sun came out!'[4] He still regards 'The Waiting
Room' and its companion piece, 'Silent Sorrow In Empty Boats',
as being among their finest moments, 'pieces of ad lib music,
things that don't date',[4] they were similar to the 'sound pictures'
that Brian Eno was recording at that time. (In fact, Eno did work
briefly on the album, the result of a chance meeting in the studios
and Gabriel admits that Eno was very able with the synth treatments that would have taken the band twice as long.) Similar ideas
were used to come up with the music for, among others, 'Fly On
A Windshield', 'Ravine' and 'Hairless Heart'.

With Peter back in the group, the writing continued. Much of
the ill feeling had subsided and, though there were frustrations,
everyone was in a far happier state of mind. Steve, however, still
had some reservations: 'There was a lot of strain so I didn't really
relax into the feel of the album, which having come from one I
was really happy with was hard. It was becoming a monster –
double album, concept, which I was rather anti at that point.'

Finally, rehearsals were complete and in August the band
moved to Glosspant in Wales, where they recorded the album in
another old house, using the Island Mobile Studio, John Burns
again producing. The music written, the band were able to put
down the backing tracks within a fortnight, but a month later they
were still waiting for Peter's lyrics and a lot of the melodies. Always
a slow worker, the personal problems that had been heaped upon
him had meant that he was still a good way from finishing, but
was unwilling to accept any offers of help from the others. The
words and music had been written in isolation from one another
and Peter found himself in need of more music to link the songs
together, or music to fit lyrical ideas – 'The Grand Parade of Lifeless
Packaging' being an example. He asked the rest of the group to fill
in the gaps while he continued to work on the words, which didn't
exactly endear him to them at the time although they did write
the necessary material.

Genesis were scheduled to open their world tour in England,
playing in Newcastle in late October, but it was obvious that it
would be a struggle to complete the recording and mixing of the
album before they went on the road, let alone actually have it in the
shops in time. With that uppermost in their minds, they worked
feverishly at Island Studios in London on the mixing of the tracks
until the album was finally ready, the first fruits of their labours

being 'Counting Out Time', released as a single on 1 November 1974, backed with 'Riding the Scree'. Both songs were a very real step away from what the group had done in the past, particularly on *Selling England By The Pound*, which had a very lush, polished sound, its songs having clearly been crafted over many hours. In contrast, these new tunes had a fresher, more spontaneous feel to them.

Having opened their new account by presenting a different facet of the band, Genesis were still very concerned that they were being misrepresented in the press and, with two bones of contention uppermost in their minds, they set about correcting these misconceptions. Peter's frustration at his role within the band largely stemmed from the fact that he was seen as the star of the show, the others mere acolytes. Everyone was unhappy with this distortion of the facts but Peter felt that it gave rise to a deep-seated resentment of him, which, though never expressed, resulted in the others being less inclined to give him any opportunity for expression outside the band, also causing them to restrict his role within Genesis and forcing him into a greater degree of working isolation. He believed that they thought he was already getting a disproportionate amount of praise and so were unwilling to give him any additional leeway, feeling that he already had more space than he deserved. Peter wanted to redress the balance, in part for his benefit and in part to show that the others were very capable songwriters in their own right. The rest of the band were equally keen to prove that Genesis was a *group* as having left the band once there was every possibility that Peter might do so again. It was very important, therefore, that they establish themselves in the public eye so that if Gabriel did leave things wouldn't fall apart.

One of the earliest interviews they gave to promote the new record was in the *NME*, where Peter stressed: 'We've always thought of ourselves as a songwriter's co-operative first and foremost. For us, the songs are the most important things about Genesis.'[35] His words often fell on stony ground, however, and in the following April he was still preaching this gospel, telling Piccadilly Radio in Manchester, 'It's nice to approach people on more than one front but we'd really like the songs to get through more.'[36]

The second item on their agenda was to dismiss the comparisons with the 'progressive rock' supergroups, not the easiest of tasks when presenting a concept album to critics. They could see that the good ship progressive rock was sinking and while they'd never been part of that movement, it was time to make the contrasts

even more obvious. Tony was the first to discuss it in *Sounds*:
'People think we're more airy fairy than Yes or ELP but I've never
thought we've been at all like those bands and I think this new
album will end those comparisons for ever. The most important
thing to us is the songs – we're not as concerned with flaunting
musicianship. It's our most direct album – although the songs are
related, they stand up separately,'[37] – not a comment that the
discerning listener would have applied to 'Tales From Topographic
Oceans' for instance. After these early pronouncements, the public
got their opportunity to judge *The Lamb Lies Down On Broadway* for
themselves when it was released at the end of November 1974.

Peter had anticipated some of the backlash, telling the *NME*,
'We expect a good slagging this time, particularly since this is a
concept album which is ideal for the critic to get his teeth into.'[35]
Those critics ate a hearty breakfast and the commercial reaction
was commensurately disappointing, the album peaking at number
ten, never threatening to rival the success of *Selling England By The
Pound*. A public that had welcomed concept albums in the past
had become cynical in the face of the cosmic dross that was regularly being foisted upon them, so any concept, no matter how
different, was not likely to get a fair hearing and this was unfortunately the case with *The Lamb*. Critics roasted the *idea* of the album,
ignoring the content, and the public merely treated it with indifference. The passing of time has given *The Lamb* an almost mythical
status, but the feeling in 1974 was that it was a stiff. Chris Welch
wrote, 'I wish that rock musicians would learn the importance of
self-editing. A few golden miraculous notes and some choice pithy
words are worth all the clutter and verbiage in the world . . . I have
the feeling it is a white elephant.'[38] Barbara Charone, however, was
enthusiastic, noting that '[it] sticks out of the present vinyl rubble
like a polished diamond'.[39]

Looked at rationally, the album contains some of the best work
that Genesis has ever produced and can certainly be listened to as
a collection of songs as Banks described, ignoring their thematic
continuity if you choose. Songs such as 'In The Cage', 'The Carpet
Crawl', 'Back in NYC', 'Lilywhite Lilith' – a reworking of 'The
Light', a very early Genesis song – and the title track still stand up
as strong, concise rock songs. The more experimental instrumentation on tracks like 'Fly On A Windshield', 'The Waiting Room'
and 'The Colony of Slippermen' are impressively ambitious and
totally successful, taking Genesis into completely different areas
of music, aided by a sympathetic production. Gabriel agreed that
'We've lost some of the polish we had on *Selling England* but it's

been worth it to get the right feel.'[36] Unquestionably their most straight ahead collection of songs since the naiveté of *From Genesis To Revelation*, they used the extra time available on the double album wisely, producing music which encompassed myriad moods and conjured up strong atmospheres but which still dealt in the currency of the best popular music, liberally laced as it was with irresistible melodies.

As always, the songs triumphed over any desire to flaunt their by now impressive musicianship and the album warranted a far kinder reception than it received. This was no flatulent ego trip, but a valid musical excursion. The music contained sufficient depth and variety to sustain the interest over the four sides – a major achievement in the field of the rock double album, where variety was very rarely the spice of life after its high-water mark, 1968's *The Beatles* which contained a similarly staggering diversity of material. *The Lamb* was at turns emotional, compulsive, witty, diverting, savage, soothing, frightening, enchanting but always highly entertaining and listenable. It appeared that musically they had trimmed down almost to a trio of Banks, Collins and Rutherford, lead guitar taking a back seat to the keyboards, Steve admitting that some of his ideas 'weren't getting through' partly because of his lack of enthusiasm for certain aspects of the project.

The real sticking point for critics of *The Lamb Lies Down On Broadway* was simply that it was a concept piece – many immediately closed their ears to the music on principle. On their behalf, though, it has to be said that any weakness that the album showed was in its storyline. Peter's tale of Rael had to fail simply because of the immense wealth of detail that he tried to get across. On discussing the idea of turning the album into a film, Tony pointed out that there was enough going on in the story to make ten films: 'There was too much information – some of the lyrics were too cumbersome.'[4] It was this verbosity that was its downfall. In part, some of the difficulties might have been overcome had Peter allowed Mike and Tony the opportunity to contribute lyrics, his only concession to them being 'The Light Dies Down on Broadway'. In comparison with Peter's idiosyncratic, absorbing style their lyrics were more linear, giving them a more approachable, understandable slant which could have greatly benefited the album. While individual songs successfully made their points – 'In The Cage' and 'The Lamia' in particular – as a whole the story doesn't really flow and is often wilfully obscure, Peter admitting as much to *Sounds*: 'The story is printed on the sleeve because it was too encompassing for all the songs to contain the action – its a

clothesline on which you can hang up the songs.'[37] Even the story
is sometimes difficult to follow, cloaked in darker, denser imagery
than Gabriel had ever used before: at times moral fable – the only
cure for hideous disfigurement brought on by a casual sexual
encounter is castration – and at times semi-autobiographical – 'I'm
putting [a character] down to watch him break up, decompose
and feed another sort of life'.[40] Here is a clear portent of Peter's
future, a sign that his time with Genesis was limited.

Peter was to draw further parallels in an interview with the *NME*
in Paris during their world tour: 'It's the idea of him being an
outcast in a totally alien situation. I identify with him to a certain
extent.'[41] It's very tempting to project a work on to the writer and
look for an autobiography that isn't there. With a writer as sharp,
intelligent and mischievous as Gabriel, this is asking for trouble,
but just like the apple on the Tree of Knowledge, the temptation
to take a bite is too strong to resist.

Rael's story is that of a split-personality, a characteristic often
attributed to Peter – the shy, retiring, inarticulate figure off-stage
and the charismatic attention-seeker onstage. Similarly Peter pro-
fessed to disliking the star machinery that was being created
around him and yet there were many times when he courted
that machine shamelessly, and his enthusiasm for the wonders of
collaboration contrasted with his disdain for the committee. Rael
is a character that, according to Peter, felt 'as if he was a waste of
material, part of the machinery. He doesn't even think about his
position in society – all he can do is escape or give up.'[37] Again,
the similarity between Rael and Peter is striking, particularly if
one looks at the lyrics to 'Solsbury Hill', Gabriel's anthemic song
about his departure from Genesis:

I walked right out of the machinery.

The idea that Peter used Rael as a form of self-analysis once
removed gained additional weight over the years as he talked
about the album, describing it as a form of therapy and an effective
expression of his erotic/neurotic fantasies. But if Peter was projecting himself on to Rael – something which he tacitly admitted to
Armando Gallo: 'I am sure that my own doubts and searches
were built into the story, although I didn't really understand the
connection until I was performing *The Lamb* live'[34] – then there was
a complex mix of emotions running riot within: Kafkaesque self-
loathing – in part because of his position as a rock star, in part
because of his wife's infidelity and his role in that – battling with

an incurable optimism. In hindsight, it seems fairly evident from the story and the lyrics that Peter was rapidly heading towards a major turning point in his life, a point where he would have to make some difficult personal choices. He could no longer sustain the vision of himself as a rock star, concerned that it could ultimately destroy his music. The performance side of his role had begun to detract too much from the songs and Peter was as sensitive as the others to the fact that their part in Genesis had been sadly underplayed. 'Cuckoo Cocoon' seemed to intimate that he was becoming too comfortable inside the trappings of rock stardom – 'I feel so secure, that I know this can't be real' – and did the 'cushioned strait-jacket' of 'In The Cage' refer to his internal battle between financial security and his need for artistic freedom, a freedom he felt denied within a group structure? Was the production line indicating individual profit potential in 'The Grand Parade Of Lifeless Packaging' a symbol of his disgust for the music industry? 'The Chamber Of 32 Doors' his cynical view of all the business suits who claimed to have his best interests at heart while clearly protecting their own? The lyrics point to a man unhappy with the way events had gone. Gabriel was torn between the desire to take Genesis further and the need to have complete control of his destiny, the yearning for success and recognition against the requisite compromising of ideals, the appreciation of the power of his position and yet the revulsion he felt for the 'star trip' he was being forced into. Should he give up or should he try to escape?

The story aside, the other major criticism of *The Lamb* was that the band were looking towards, and only interested in, America. Banks retorted in *Sounds*, 'The album is American in the sense that it has had an effect on us over the last few years.'[37] Other than its New York setting and some scattered cultural references, the music was as quintessentially Genesis as anything they had done previously – the context had changed, but the basics were similar: songs of emotion and melody if more aggressive and taken in new directions. Talking to *Beat Instrumental* in April 1977, Peter explained the germination of the idea and the reasons why it was placed in America – reasons artistic rather than economic. 'One of the first things you notice when you go to New York is the steam rising from out of the manhole covers in the streets. It's a very strange sight and it gave me the idea of a vast underground world going on which we are not aware of as we walk on the surface. It all ties in with the conscious and the subconscious mind.'[42] Everyman's split personality is at the heart of *The Lamb*, Rael's adventures in this underworld becoming an exploration of his and, by extension, Gabriel's subconscious. Indeed if his statement to Gallo is to be believed, Peter was consciously writing about the sub-conscious but sub-consciously writing about himself! The role of the sub-conscious mind is clearly of universal significance and so it was important that Genesis moved away from what people saw as their fundamental Englishness to a more global stance, involving characters that had nothing to do with their own experience so that the listener could more readily comprehend that they were addressing questions of personality, not nationality. The idea of a group of white boys from England writing about the problems of a greasy Puerto Rican punk in New York is faintly risible until you make the mental leap necessary to grasp that they were in truth writing about Everyman. Rael could be anyone, anywhere – even the name was chosen with great care so that it would be essentially rootless, not founded in any particular race, creed or country.

The album complete, the next step was to go on the road and take *The Lamb* to market.

CHAPTER TEN

'Leaving your cocoon'

If the recording of *The Lamb Lies Down On Broadway* had been a difficult, sometimes traumatic, period, then the world tour which followed it was scarcely a picnic either.

As with any band playing a tour of Britain, dates had been booked well in advance of the album's completion to ensure that the bigger venues were available. The show was to open in the UK on 29 October, despite the fact that the album wouldn't be completed until partway through that month, a consequence of the delay on Peter's lyrics. As a result, the band found themselves mixing and re-mixing the double album in shifts, while at the same time putting together the stage show, perhaps the most far-reaching and complex rock show ever designed at that point in time. There was a sense of unreality about the final stages of mixing, Phil admitting that what he would be mixing in one shift would then be re-done by Mike and Tony in a later shift as every-one began to lose sight of what they were doing – indeed at one point there was even talk of releasing the album as two LPs at a six-month interval to give the band extra time to work on it. Tony remembers that making the album turned into a form of torture by the end. 'It took about five months and we were all really fed up with it.'[4] Tempers frayed, and at times individuals lost interest in the music, particularly Steve Hackett: '*The Lamb* happened despite me, not with me. I really felt it was very indulgent and I couldn't quite get to grips with it or contribute something great in a guitar sense.'[20]

If the internal dissent and his personal dissatisfaction with the music and his contribution to it weren't enough, Steve's marriage had by now irretrievably broken down and he was beginning to find the mounting pressures too much to cope with. 'It was a sort of depressing time – my first marriage was on the rocks, we were mixing the album which had been fraught, we'd been away recording in derelict houses with mobiles . . . One night, I went to see a Sensational Alex Harvey Band gig – they did an incredible show and I went to a reception and had a bit to drink. Someone said, "Oh, they'd be nothing without Alex," and in my drunken stupor I drew the parallel with us and Pete. I tensed and I broke the wine glass I was holding – I severed a tendon and a nerve.'[4] Steve was rushed to hospital where the doctors patched him up but the UK tour had to be postponed while the wound healed – the injury had been serious enough for there to be worries as to whether he would lose his thumb. In retrospect, the postponement was a blessing in disguise for the band, releasing them from the onerous task of playing the entire *The Lamb Lies Down On Broadway* opus to their home audience who hadn't even heard the 'Counting Out Time' single, let alone the album. Even then, with Steve fully fit, they were exposed to that dubious honour when they opened the tour in North America, a country still to fall completely for their charms. As Mike puts it, 'It was a big mistake!'[4] Phil remembers it as 'suicide',[4] adding that 'It was very hard work. We played the whole double album, an hour and a half of new music, until we got to the encores, but by then it was a bit late!'[4]

The recorded version of *The Lamb Lies Down On Broadway* remains their most controversial piece of work, but the accompanying live show generated almost universal acclaim, a theatrical *tour de force*, an innovative forerunner of later mixed-media presentations. Playing a brand new album from start to finish without any old material was a major triumph in itself in the aftermath of Yes' 'Tales From Topographic Oceans' tour fiasco, where they had initially set off on the road to play their double album in its entirety but were forced to bring back the old favourites within weeks as bored ticket holders walked out of the show – Genesis at least had the songs to maintain interest, even though they were barely known by the audience. Allied to the music, as the band played on, the story would unfold behind them using 1450 slides in eighteen different cassettes projected on to three screens by seven projectors. The lighting was powerful, designed to show the slides to best effect but was impressive on its own and there was appropriate use of strobes and flash powder, those essential ingredients for a mid-seventies rock show.

Within this elaborate setting, Peter adopted the guise of Rael. His skin coloured to represent the Puerto Rican punk, he wore a leather jacket and jeans, using nothing more exotic than that until the latter part of the show when, during 'The Lamia', he would become engulfed by a cone which revolved around him and from which he would ultimately emerge in probably the most extraordinary costume of his entire tenure as lead singer. Portraying the Slipperman, he wore a 'huge bulbous outfit'[4] as Phil was to describe it, a grotesque yellow body stocking, covered, in Peter's words, with 'lumps and bumps and slimy humps' coupled with one vital extra for all aspiring rock stars, inflatable genitalia.

Towards the end of live performances of The Lamb a life-size dummy of Peter was required to illustrate the split personality. To make the dummy as lifelike and accurate as possible, Peter 'had a life mask made – I had pipes up my nostrils to breath and was totally encased in plaster – very claustrophobic.'[43] As Peter suffered for his art, the dummy brought extra problems for the road crew – security backstage had to be tightened to ensure that no particularly zealous fans walked off with their hero's likeness!

The tour broke new ground in terms of its theatricality, but its complexity meant numerous running problems – this was 1974/75 and their collective imagination ran far beyond what the relatively primitive technology of the day could successfully and consistently provide. Problems abounded in every area – on discussing the slide show, Tony points out, 'It never all worked, though on the four or five times it came close, it was great!'[4] Slides sometimes stuck, were changed at the wrong times or, on those occasions when Peter didn't talk to the audience for long enough in the breaks between songs, the projectionist might be left with too little time to change the cassettes. The lights were generally fine, but some of the special effects gave problems. Phil remembers with a smile: 'In "The Lamia", this cone came down from the rig and started to revolve – the microphone cable kept getting caught and so Pete would be desperately trying to free it and sing at the same time – a bit Spinal Tap!'[4] In France, Peter's dummy was replaced by a naked roadie, but another memorable disaster came in Oslo, the first date in Europe. 'At the end of The Lamb there was a flash and Pete would be one side of the stage and the dummy would be the other, then the strobe would start and you weren't quite sure which was Peter. The first time Peter Hart did it, he got too much bang and not enough flash – there was a deafening bang, we just stopped playing, the audience were stunned and this guy poked his head round the curtain and said, "Sorry!" '[4]

Crowds were enthusiastic, Peter remarking, 'We've been getting a switch round in audience – some people who did like us don't like this tour and some who didn't think it's the best thing we've done.' He went on to note, 'The leather jacket and jeans I wear as Rael has given us a more raunchy appearance and we can sense a change in the audiences,'[43] their reactions being far more boisterous than in days of yore. Critics too were generally dazzled, certainly by Peter, though sadly few described their reactions to the music, Barbara Charone being a rare exception, opining, 'The stench of rock and roll boredom reeks, but Genesis don't smell!'[37] The only carping note that was regularly sounded was that Peter had left his assortment of previous disguises behind and hadn't taken any of them for the ride down Broadway. 'If you're going to get up on stage and occupy a role, you have to discard previous roles you've adopted and not simply adopt the standard rock role'[37] was his riposte, adding elsewhere that Rael had to be divorced from his previous creations. 'The idea was to present someone earthy who people could relate to and who would be a point of reference in each situation.'[37] He was also dismissive of those who said that visual imagery had no place at a rock concert. 'If the visual images are conceived at the time of writing and you don't use those visuals then you're not allowing the audience to listen to the song in the full strength of which it was created. That's what you're after, to give the audience as much in a song as you get from it. Visuals are only rubbish if they're not integrated with the continuity of the music.'[37]

The Slipperman represented the furthest extreme to which Peter had taken his version of 'rock theatre' and though it was visually powerful, it was starting to alienate some of the band. Phil, in particular, was becoming increasingly annoyed with the direction that their live shows were taking: 'With some of the costumes, the staging had got to a point where it was difficult for Pete to get a microphone near his mouth and I felt the music suffered.'[4] He states, 'The props had reached a point where they were taking over and the fact that they all centred around Pete made it like a one-man show to sections of the audience.'[20] He emphasized the point further in a *Melody Maker* article in April 1975: 'It's a good thing that the show can get across by the visuals, but a lot of people don't listen to the music. I find it incredibly frustrating to play say very well one night, not very well the next and for people not to know the difference. I'd like to get booed on an off-night!'[44]

Musically, the tour was unrewarding too, as Tony recalls: 'It was a very rigid show, we had to play the songs in the order of the album without any changes – the first half of the album was better too, which meant finishing with the weaker half.'[20] Mike was upset by the fact that 'we were stuck with some sections that weren't great live, just because they were part of the story.'[20] Some areas had been left open for improvisation, particularly 'The Waiting Room', which quickly became a forum for them to work out their frustrations – as the tour progressed so did that piece, the group going so far as to record it live in Los Angeles for inclusion on a future single. Not all the tensions and frustrations were rooted in the live show, however.

As the personal and technical problems mounted, Peter Gabriel's departure, first mooted and dealt with some six months earlier, became irreversible fact. Just a few short weeks into the tour, Gabriel confronted manager Tony Smith with the news that he wanted out. Smith asked him to reconsider, but two days later the rest of the band were informed. 'I had no idea what I wanted to do, but I knew I was sick of rock, the business, and everything about it. I was beginning to dislike myself for doing what I was doing'[20] – sentiments already expressed in the very album that they were touring! If not exactly shocked by the news, having gone through a similar situation during the recording of *The Lamb*, the band were upset and angry. Their immediate concern was for the future of the tour – venues had been booked as far ahead as May 1975 and cancellations would have been astronomical in terms of cost, while the damage to their reputation might be irreparable – cancelling a tour, losing their frontman and having no new songs or a replacement singer would make great press. Peter had some feelings of guilt about leaving the band and was persuaded to continue to the tour's conclusion, also agreeing not to reveal his decision to anyone despite the fact that he continued to give interviews up until the end of the tour. This made life very difficult for him, tip-toeing through a minefield every time he was asked about the group's next project, also giving him no release for the emotions that his imminent departure had stirred within. 'I found some very gigs very depressing,' he was to tell Chris Welch later. 'I'd come away wet-eyed. On the last tour, it did feel that an important chapter of my life was about to change. It was quite highly charged with emotion.'[45]

With his departure postponed, the others were caught between the desire to make Peter change his mind and their righteous indignation that he should want to leave the group. There was an over-riding feeling that they had worked hard to reach a position where they were on the verge of international success, a point where they could reap the rewards of their groundwork and that the loss of such a distinctive and powerful frontman would mean the end of the band, at least in the eyes of many fans and journalists. Still heavily in debt, the others felt that Gabriel was deserting the ship and could destroy the band's future, something with which he felt unable to agree, being more confident in their ability to succeed than they were.

'Peter had been getting distant when we made *The Lamb*'[4] points out Tony, and Steve reinforces this view, 'Pete was working in increasing isolation and it was an uneasy balance so the parting was being illustrated throughout.'[4] They were scarcely taken by surprise, therefore, by his announcement and following the initial reaction to his decision the tour continued fairly harmoniously, the tension relieved now that everyone knew exactly what they had to deal with. Mike remarked, 'None of us wanted Pete to leave, but when it happened it was easier than the build-up, we could get on with things.'[4] 'The Lamb' made its stately progress around the world, heading towards its final shows in France where Peter would make his last appearance with Genesis, something they were working up to as Phil recounts: 'His last gig was supposed to be in Toulouse, and the night before we were in the dressing room in Besançon and someone came in and said, "We're not playing tomorrow night, this is the last show," because they hadn't sold enough tickets. It was terribly anti-climactic because we'd all built up to this last gig with Peter and suddenly this was the last gig and we weren't prepared. Peter played "The Last Post" on his oboe and we went out and played *The Lamb*. Extraordinary really.'[4]

On that fairly downbeat note, Peter Gabriel ended his days with Genesis. Why did he feel he had to leave? His reasons were broadly similar to those which had caused the false start when they were making *The Lamb* at Headley Grange. He was unhappy with his role in the band and the superstar machinery that was being created around him – he didn't want that position and he was painfully aware of the injustice that it heaped upon Tony, Phil, Steve and Mike. He admitted that he found it all unreal and that he had been hollowed out by the experience. He was also very unhappy with the way many of his contemporaries had been packaged and with the excesses, both musical and personal, to which they were falling prey and he was particularly keen not to fall into that trap.

Genuinely repulsed by the music industry, he felt very strongly that having achieved success, Genesis would find themselves inside the belly of the beast, entrenched as part of the establishment that they had worked outside of for so long. Not only did he dislike the idea of becoming an establishment figure, there was a very real possibility that by doing so he and the band would be obliged to churn out formularized product to maintain their position. His artistic integrity and idealism were taking a savage bruising at the hands of the music business and he needed to get out, making the point to the *NME* midway through the tour, 'We're not going to be a band to sit still. We'll self-destruct before we stop running.'[41] Peter's fear that they might be shackled by success caused him to 'self-destruct' as far as his place in Genesis was concerned.

In a similar vein, the very success which he once craved had robbed him of much of his freedom, artistic and personal, and tainted the initial idealism with which they had all approached the band. As he later told *Melody Maker*, 'For me, some of the fire had gone. In a musical sense I was proud of my involvement in Genesis and in terms of taking it on the road. But when things get to such a scale, it does tend to drain the humanity out of it.'[45] This was a topic he returned to in the lyrics of his 1978 single 'DIY':

> *When things get so big, I don't trust them at all.*

As Genesis became a larger concern, tours were being booked well in advance, in bigger and bigger venues, playing to more and more people. To Peter this seemed soulless, and, more importantly, he found the idea of his future being planned way ahead abhorrent, leaving him with insufficient time to explore other creative ideas or be with his family. One of the most important factors in his final decision was Anna's birth, something which, coupled with his marital difficulties, sharply redefined his priorities. While the rest of the group were less sympathetic to this at the time, Tony now recognizes the impact that this had on him. 'He was the first of us to have a child – perhaps he grew up quicker than the rest of us at that time . . . Peter was the first to get the idea that there was more to life than being in a rock group, he wanted to balance it out differently and so he had to leave.'[4] The discipline of the group at the time was fierce. Peter pointed out to *Melody Maker* that 'certain areas of Genesis weren't flexible,'[15] the band all pushing not just for a wider audience, but more importantly to maintain the musical momentum of the group. Having been pleased with the way *The Lamb* was written and with the finished product, the others felt there was a lot more exciting and inventive music to be made and were unwilling to take a break, thereby risking the loss of that impetus. Tony agrees that Peter 'wanted more time than the rest of us felt we could give so he felt he had to leave.'[4] Peter's work as a solo artist, particularly through the 1980s and into the 1990s, illustrates that it would have been difficult for him to function within a group format – the time he chooses to take to make records and the diversity of his other activities would have made scheduling of group work impossible – though working as a musician was far from his mind at this point. The album-tour-album-tour treadmill had worn him down and the time was right for him to change his way of life and to sever his ties with the money-mad industry.

Having taken on full responsibility for the lyrics on *The Lamb*, Peter must have recognized that the band wouldn't let him do that again, something which clearly aided his decision. Mike agrees that 'He would not have found it easy to go back to our previous method of songwriting. Perhaps he felt that *The Lamb* was a good final statement on which to leave.'[20] Steve remembers that when he first joined the group, Peter had said to him, 'I don't think composition by committee works, do you?'[4] Having made the compromise for several years, Peter no longer wanted other people working on his ideas and so a group environment wasn't a healthy one for him any more. Also, as Phil and Steve progressed as writers, there was less and less space available on the records for each individual – Rutherford says, 'When there were five of us, it became hard because there were so many ideas around.'[4] Something had to give and that something was Peter Gabriel. In many ways it was an obvious departure point, the lyrics signposting the way, supported by interviews in which he had stated that *The Lamb* 'has given me the most satisfaction'.[36] Part of that satisfaction came from the show, but Peter recognized that they had taken the theatricals as far as they could by that time and their next show would have to be scaled down for many reasons – the press response, the alienation of Gabriel within the band, the desire to present the music as the main item on their agenda and the need simply to break out of their existing roles and do something different. Peter was well aware that it was time to re-invent himself and Genesis before they became too anchored in their positions and became a caricature – he chose to do that by leaving, they chose to do it later by changing their approach to the music. This had the additional benefit of providing Peter with new credibility as far as the press was concerned – after all, he had left the bloated capitalist dinosaur that they thought was Genesis, something which stood him in good stead in the face of punk's onslaught.

Gabriel's departure was finally underlined with the odd

combination of practicality and theatricality that had marked his contribution to the band. Eschewing the opportunity of talking to the Fourth Estate, he decided that he would be better able to express himself in written form and personally delivered a letter explaining his resignation to all the music newspapers. Inevitably, the letter was idiosyncratic in tone and at times concealed more than it illuminated but it was clear that Peter had become disenchanted with the music industry and was upset that the idealism that had fuelled the group in its earliest days was being replaced by a solid professionalism, often finding himself thinking in purely business terms. Accepting that the group was still a strong musical force, he hinted at his desire to explore 'my creative bits and pieces',[46] adding that 'even the hidden delights of vegetable growing and community living are beginning to reveal their secrets'![46]

In many respects he sounded like a jaded company executive aching to get away from the rat-race and there was little in the missive to suggest that he would be pursuing an active career in music as a solo artist. Acknowledging the strain that Genesis had placed on domestic life, he noted that it was 'important to me to give space to my family, which I wanted to hold together, and to liberate the daddy in me'.[46] Emphasizing that there was no animosity between himself and the rest of the band, he insisted that he had not left in search of a solo career as defined by the likes of Bowie or Ferry, giving no real indication as to what his future plans were outside his family life. As the passing of Gabriel as an artistic force was mourned, many were equally pessimistic about there being any further output from Genesis, but as the death knell was being sounded for 'Gabriel's group', Banks, Collins, Hackett and Rutherford were deep in rehearsals for a new album.

CHAPTER ELEVEN

'Into the fire and into the fight'

Although they had lost what many would have considered to be their prime asset, fortune smiled on Genesis in as much as they were together on the road when Peter made his final irrevocable decision to leave. Having coped with their initial doubts, the remaining four were given valuable breathing space to work out their future, especially once Peter agreed to keep his decision under wraps. Steve Hackett, in particular, was at first very unsure as to whether Genesis *sans* Gabriel was a viable proposition. 'We were worried that we were going to decline because everything had been slanted so much towards Peter.'⁴ He went on to say, 'I thought that the future was uncertain with Pete leaving after the tour, so I really built up my first album there with material that didn't fit in with Genesis – basically it became *Voyage Of The Acolyte*.' While taking care of his own future by laying the foundation for some solo recording, Steve continued to discuss with Phil, Mike and Tony what identity Genesis might now have, and as the tour progressed, 'We all felt that we wanted to go on and prove that we hadn't just been Pete's backing musicians.'⁴

This determination was very much the order of the day within the camp – after all, they'd been increasingly unhappy with the unflattering and inaccurate manner in which the press had portrayed them as back-up musicians. To give up would only have made it appear that the press had been right all along. They were now offered the unwanted but nevertheless perfect opportunity to prove that they were the real power behind the Gabriel throne, that they were a talented group of songwriters and musicians, that 80 per cent of Genesis would continue under that banner. 'The band was more and more identified with Peter so we wanted to show that we could carry on without him,' explains Tony. 'We knew we could withstand it as long as the audience was prepared to follow us,'[4] a concern echoed by Phil: 'I never thought we'd stop, I was just frightened about what other people might say.'[4] Steve's view was 'We knew we could produce something, but were people going to buy it?', while Mike informed one journalist later, 'We were confident that we could do a good album because Peter was really only one-fifth of the writing team.'[47] The writing and recording period for *The Lamb* had given the four an insight into working without input from Peter, and the strength of that work gave them confidence that, in that area at least, he would not be missed – indeed hadn't many of their strongest musical moments in the past come from the nucleus that remained? They were also suitably buoyed by the memory of the nightmarish sessions for *The Lamb*, inspiring the hope that future recordings would be made in an atmosphere free from the tensions that had attended that album.

Once they had decided that they would continue, the band quite consciously began to set the scene for their next album in press interviews they gave throughout 'The Lamb' tour, at a time when no one but they were aware of Peter's impending departure. Even more than before, they were keen to play up the 'group factor' in Genesis, emphasizing that they made up the majority of the team that was producing these acclaimed records and as such deserved respect for their achievements. Barbara Charone was one of the few writers willing to give them a hearing and in a piece she wrote for *Zig Zag*, Tony stressed that they were a true group, pointing out that during their live show attention wasn't constantly riveted on Peter. 'There are places when the show turns into a slightly different thing with just the band playing. It's nice that the atten-tion is on you even if it's more conventional.'[48] Typically, Phil was more animated in putting across the frustrations of the band: 'What annoys us intensely is when people come backstage after a gig, go up to Peter and say, "Amazing show, man – really dug your music".'[48] Mike then hammered the point home: 'The thing that bothers the band most is when people assume Peter writes all the numbers. I'm not so proud as a player, but as a writer I don't take criticism well!'[48]

The tour in support of *The Lamb Lies Down On Broadway* finally closed in France after 102 shows and Peter Gabriel went off into his self-imposed retirement in Bath to 'grow cabbages and make babies'. Tony, Phil, Steve and Mike agreed to take a couple of months off to recuperate and come up with some new ideas prior to meeting again in July to begin writing a new album, following which they would commence their search for a singer. They were very clear that the music would be written by the four of them rather than finding a new frontman and then trying to write with him, recognizing that having so many strong individual writers in the group was a contributory factor behind the tensions at work during the previous album.

The first piece of activity came from Steve Hackett, who booked himself into Kingsway Studios to record some of the backlog of material that he had been busily accumulating during his time with Genesis, particularly through the writing and recording of *The Lamb*. 'We were so bogged down with the bulk of the stuff that any spontaneous ideas I had couldn't fit, so I put them to one side.' There were many reasons why Steve decided that the time was now right for a solo venture. He was clearly looking after his own interests in establishing himself as a solo artist at a time when Peter's departure was still to be announced, ensuring he had something to present to the public when the news broke – if Genesis did fall by the wayside, Steve would have a higher profile and a new product to indicate that he had been an important contributor to the band. The album also provided him with a forum for some of his more experimental instrumental work that would never have found a home within a more traditionally song-based band such as Genesis, relieving his frustrations without him having to take the ultimate step of leaving the group. His ideas and those of the rest of the group had drifted apart during the making of *The Lamb* and *Voyage Of The Acolyte* acted as an antidote to those elements in Genesis which *The Lamb* had showcased and which Steve found less palatable.

Making the album acted as a great boost to Steve's own confidence, illustrating to himself as much as to anyone else that here was a prolific and talented composer who had the ability to carry off an entire album on his own. He had offered to leave Genesis some three years earlier because he felt he wasn't writing enough for the group, and freely admits that when he went in to do the album, 'I'd never even done a single let alone a whole album on my own before, so I didn't know if I could carry it off. I really didn't know if I'd come out with a bunch of out-takes or a full album, so I had this air of trepidation!' In order to give himself a sympathetic environment in which to work, he did recruit Phil Collins and Mike Rutherford to play on the album with him – Mike co-writing the album closer 'Shadow Of The Hierophant' – as well as his brother John, a flautist, who co-wrote 'A Tower Struck

Down'. Having a number of friendly faces around the studio waiting on his instructions gave Steve the necessary faith in himself to complete the album: 'I gradually gathered strength each day as I went in and the other people came in.' The fact that the album had been written over a period of a year gave Steve a wealth of material to choose from – had he simply decided to make a record without any songs behind him, he might have experienced more difficulties with the project, as he acknowledges: 'The problem with creative ideas is that you start on a project and it has to finish by a certain date, on the very last day all these ideas come along, part of the subconscious incubation period.' Steve circumvented the problem on *Voyage* by amassing his ideas over a prolonged stretch of time, using his entry into the studio as a cut-off point.

In July he finally emerged from the studio with *Voyage Of The Acolyte* completed. The finished product betrayed Steve's enthusiasm for the project and was an album brimming with invention, an ingenious blend of styles ranging from the classical to the jazz-tinged, from quiet lyrical passages to powerful rock assaults. His playing had never been so assured, so creative, so witty, as he revelled in the spaces he opened up in the music by concentrating largely on instrumentals and by using the keyboards as a secondary instrument instead of a leading force as they were in Genesis. The musical tension that existed between Steve's guitar and Tony's keyboard work, Genesis' strongest musical trademark, was notable not so much by its absence but by the multifarious ways in which Steve plugged what could have been a yawning gap, relying on his ability to use the guitar as a synthesizer. The challenges that this offered were accepted with relish, taking risks that he would never have done within the band format, though at times he did get carried away with his freedom and some of the songs were too busy to be completely satisfying. Likewise, lyrically the album was rather weak, bogged down in over-ornate pseudo-poetry which marred fine vocal contributions from Sally Oldfield and, most intriguingly, Phil Collins, making it clear that Steve's interests and strengths lay very much in instrumental work. Of that work, 'Ace Of Wands' and 'A Tower Struck Down' stood out: the former owing a debt to Robert Fripp in its manic opening guitar blast, the latter using effects to the full to create an impressive musical landscape that both conjured up elements of the sound pictures from *The Lamb*, yet still distanced Hackett from Genesis.

Quite rightly, Steve was delighted with the outcome of his début venture. 'I felt that I didn't have a duff track on it, the whole thing

took off and I was on a high. It was great to have a whole album of
things I wanted to do, largely instrumental, it was wonderful!'
The album reflected a buoyant period for Steve as he had recently
embarked on a long-term relationship that remains strong with
Brazilian artist Kim Poor, whom he had met in New York during
'The Lamb' tour. Happier with his personal life than for a very
long time and confident that he had a new outlet for his music, he
returned to the Genesis fold ready to start work on their crucial
next album, though by the time he had completed *Voyage*, the
other three members were already hard at work and refreshed by
their respective sabbaticals – Phil working with Brand X, which he
described as 'me letting off steam in another area just because I
don't like being in one hole,'[49] Mike working with Anthony
Phillips, and Tony having installed his own central heating! Mike
recalls that 'in the first three days with the three of us, we did
"Squonk" and most of "Dance On A Volcano". It was great!'[4]
Although at the time nothing was said, perhaps not even sus-
pected, the seeds of another personnel change were already sown.
Tony, Phil and Mike built further on their improvisational work
together, operating well as a self-contained unit within which
Steve did not function so efficiently, tending, as he did, to work
more independently and bring bits of music into the group to be
worked on by one or more of the others, although sections of
both 'Dance On A Volcano' and 'Los Endos' evolved from group
jamming. In spite of the distance that sometimes existed between
Steve and the others, the band put together a selection of new
material very quickly.

   With Peter gone, there was obviously far more space available
to each individual since there was one less writer battling to get
his ideas on to the record. This was heightened by the fact that
Steve had little material in reserve since his stock had already
found a home on the *Voyage Of The Acolyte*. As Phil was still very
much a fledgling writer, Tony and Mike had an opportunity to
stamp their authority on the group to an even greater extent.
Relishing the challenge, both responded well, dominating the
writing for *A Trick Of The Tail*. Throughout their careers, particularly since the departure of Anthony Phillips, Tony Banks had
probably been the most important guiding voice within the band,
more determined than anyone else that Genesis should continue
and reach as many people as possible, not by dint of any short-
term fixes but by virtue of hard work and dedication, a gradual
build-up resulting from regular album releases of the highest quality and from extensive touring. Hit hard by Peter's departure on a

personal level, Tony must have been concerned that he would lose the band too unless they came up with an album of such excellence that it could not be ignored. A band losing a member as charismatic Gabriel can find itself in serious trouble with fans and press alike, and must immediately come up with something special to weather the storm; it cannot risk taking some breathing space to forge a new identity. Well aware of this, Tony used the time between the tour and rehearsals to amass material that he could present to the group, some as complete songs, such as 'Mad Man Moon' and 'A Trick Of The Tail', a Beatle-type melody that had initially been around during *Foxtrot*, along with some shorter sections that were used in the improvisational sessions or were linked to other pieces, as was the case with 'Ripples', Tony's piano part being added to Mike's opening twelve-string section. The amount of material that he provided – he is credited as a writer on every song on the album – indicated that he wasn't going to let Genesis go down without a fight, a feeling echoed by the rest of the band.

Mike was equally fierce in his determination that the album should work and he arrived at the sessions with a number of different sections of music, re-introducing the twelve-string sound which had been far less prominent on *The Lamb* in the form of 'Ripples' and also kicking off 'Squonk' with a guitar riff that 'I really didn't think much of!'[16] Mike's faith in the group was affirmed in the opening days of rehearsals as they worked on that riff: 'It just shows how much the group helps me as a writer. I hadn't seen it how they had, I really didn't think it would come out like that.'[16] With some group work on the arrangement and the introduction of a softer middle section written by Tony, Mike realized that working with Genesis gave his music an edge that he couldn't achieve by writing in isolation and provided him with an added incentive to keep the group intact.

In retrospect, Steve missed a golden personal opportunity to take a more forceful role within the band and challenge the inevitable ascendency that Mike and Tony had as founder members and prolific writers, as he had fewer pieces of music to offer. His commitment was unquestioned and he responded to their new circumstances with some beautiful guitar work, but his contribution to the songwriting process was rather less than it could and should have been.

Phil again contributed significantly to the arrangement of the material, helping to link sections of music and giving different feels to various tunes. Working almost concurrently with Brand X, he was keen to inject some of their looser playing into the 'staid wife' that was Genesis, which he did to great effect on 'Los Endos'. The opening section of that track came from a softer piece called 'It's Yourself' which finally appeared in the UK in 1977 as the B-side of 'Your Own Special Way'. Lifting its chords and fusing it to a rhythmic idea of Phil's, the track developed into what he described as 'American music vaguely in the mould of Weather Report,'[16] helped along by breakneck sections written by Tony and Steve into a closing reprise of some of the other songs from the album.

The rehearsals went very well, all the band absorbed in the new songs, Mike averring that 'making *A Trick Of The Tail* was fun, very easy – recording *The Lamb* had been difficult when Pete left and came back, but this time we were going in the same direction.'[4] The only black spot on the horizon was that they were still without a frontman in spite of an anonymous advert in the music press requesting a singer for a 'Genesis-type' group. In the region of four hundred tapes were finally sifted through, including a motley selection of candidates singing along to their Genesis records, some who couldn't hold a tune in a bucket, and some wearing odd masks and dresses à la Gabriel. According to Mike, 'People started sending us these pictures of costumes they wanted to use. There was a guy wearing a red dress and he looked like some sort of hooker!'[47] The management offices went through the tapes and whittled the list down to around twenty, who were auditioned over the rehearsal period, without success. Mike remembers the process: 'When we auditioned them, Phil would sing the song to show them how it went, but he always sounded better than they did!'[4] With this demonstration of Phil's talent as a singer, it was thought that he would perhaps take a greater share of the vocal duties, certainly taking the lead for the softer songs like 'Ripples', but their intention was still to find a new frontman.

Then the bombshell dropped. The press had got wind of Peter's decision and the front page of *Melody Maker* for 16 August 1975 carried a picture of him resplendent in batwings with the headline 'Gabriel Out Of Genesis?', coupled with the appropriate denials from Tony Smith. The following week, the cover story was 'Genesis Seek New Singer', as Peter's departure was confirmed.

The breaking of the news shook the new team quite severely, isolated as they had been from the press – to them, Gabriel's departure was yesterday's news, but suddenly the full glare of the media was on them with a particularly devastating piece from Chris Welch in *Melody Maker*, where he 'Recalls A Great British Band'. Genesis without Gabriel did not exist in the jaundiced eyes of many a critic who had chosen to ignore the music in favour of the visual feast despite the protestations from the band that Peter was not Genesis, just part of the team. Despite already having virtually an album's worth of strong material, the press' blanket dismissal of the group as a viable entity did upset them, as they admitted when they went out to face the music journalists in early September.

'We'd been rehearsing for three weeks when the news broke,' Mike told *Sounds*. 'Suddenly the photographers came down and it brought a lot of things home to us. Then we got the shakes!'[50] The mood within the band was one of quiet confidence and, on hearing the fruits of their labours on *A Trick Of The Tail*, it is not hard to understand why; the problem was how to communicate that assurance and play down Peter's departure. Tony opened discussions with 'for us, it's no big deal'[50] while Phil pointed out regularly, 'Peter's leaving isn't the blow that some people seem to think it is. Mike and Tony write nearly as much and very much in the same style – it's a band style of writing, not Peter's alone.'[51] He went on to say, 'Peter's leaving is just as much a dent as if any of us left. There's never been that Rod and the Faces situation within this band. People have actually said to me, "Peter's left the band, are you still gonna be called Genesis?" That riles me!'[50] There was a general acceptance that the idea of 'All Titles By All' which had been introduced to avoid ego problems had backfired – since there were no individual song credits on any of the albums, people tended to assume that Peter had written everything. 'You end up saying, "Well, I wrote this and that," '[50] admitted Mike, Tony adding a note of confidence to proceedings and simultaneously castigating the prevailing newspaper attitude with 'We never doubted ourselves. We know what's been strong in Genesis and only a part of it has been lost. Everything Genesis has written has been created by the five of us. One person leaving will change that one-fifth.'[50] In order to re-affirm that all the members were important contributors, individual credits were given on the new album, showing that each had had a hand in at least some of the songs.

The group also lost little time in stressing the positive aspects of the split. Tony: 'Anyone leaving is a setback but it can provide new ideas, new stimulants . . . the audience becomes more aware of the group. The whole situation got out of control. We'll steer clear of that trap because when visuals overshadow the music it's upsetting for any band – with shitty music you won't get anywhere.'[50] Mike also took up the attack: 'The music is just as strong as ever. It's more harmonious now – there's still that healthy friction but we seem to be moving faster.'[16]

In spite of the positive responses from the band, one question remained uppermost in the minds of the journalists, one which Genesis could not answer: who replaces Gabriel and how? They admitted that they had already booked studio time for November and were keen to record then whether they had a new singer or not, but they did make it clear that they had no one in mind at that time, announcing that there were tentative plans for Phil to take the reins at least for this album as they were so keen to maintain the schedule they had set themselves. Phil spoke to the *NME* at the same time and revealed, 'I do most of the singing actually – there's just the four of us. We may feature one or two singers, as guest vocalists on a few tracks.'[51] The general feeling was, however, that they needed to get a full-time singer to work with them if they were to have a long-term future. The key problem was finding someone who was good enough for the job and who would have his own musical and visual identity. 'We've no intentions of looking for a replacement for Peter in that [visual] sense, a direct imitation. Just someone we can work with who can sing'[50] was Tony's view, Mike adding, 'We obviously want to find another good musical force.'[50]

Following these interviews, there was still doubt as to whether Genesis could come up with the goods, the only real support from *Sounds'* Barbara Charone who again gave them a fair hearing; picking up on their air of confidence and on Tony's leadership of the group, she closed with 'as much as I liked them before, I am just as willing to like them now. The band will undoubtedly be different but they will undoubtedly be as good,'[50] a clarion call to objectivity that was a far cry from the obituaries prepared by other journalists.

Charone received initial confirmation of her suppositions in October when Steve's *Voyage Of The Acolyte* came out to a warm response. The album was the first pointer as to how Genesis would survive and proved that at least one important writing force remained in their ranks, a surprise to the press who had Steve marked down as one of the lesser lights. The album charted at number twenty-six, proving that there was still a market for Genesis-related music and that interest in them was still high, a welcome confidence-booster as they went in to record the new album. Phil was already on a high since 27 September had seen him get married to Andrea Bertorelli, whom he had originally met at Barbara Speake's Stage School and whom he had regularly dated during the intervening six years.

Press chores completed, Genesis returned to the tasks of finding a singer and completing rehearsals ready for their date with Trident Studios, where Phil had just spent a month making the first Brand X album *Unorthodox Behaviour*. Hopefuls included Nick Lowe and Manfred Mann's Mick Rogers who, as a singing guitarist, received pretty short shrift from Steve! They still found it difficult to fill the role that Peter had vacated and ultimately entered the studio in November as a four-piece group. They hoped to draft in a singer as the project went on, auditioning as they recorded.

With the new line-up, they wanted to open a completely new chapter of their career and to set a new agenda for the group, so to break more of the ties with their past, they drafted in David Hentschel to produce the album. Having worked as tape operator on *Trespass* and then as engineer on *Nursery Cryme*, David was already familiar with the individuals in the band and with their music, so there were no awkward initial moments of getting to know one another. Following his work on the early Genesis albums, he had gained some critical acclaim for his 1975 album *Startling Music*, an interpretation of Ringo Starr's *Ringo* performed almost exclusively on ARP 2500 synthesizer, and which had also included Phil on drums. Phil was very happy with the drum sound that Hentschel had given him on that record, while Tony was attracted to his knowledge of synthesizer technology which he wanted to explore in further detail. All these factors made him the obvious choice as producer.

Hentschel remembers that the recording process was a very enjoyable experience, very relaxed in spite of the problems regarding a singer. He recalls that they started to record without one sorted out and that it slowly dawned on everyone that perhaps they weren't going to be able to track one down in time. The final straw came when they took Mick Strickland into the studio. Recalls Collins, 'We took him in to sing "Squonk" and it was in the wrong key for him, it sounded awful. When he left, we were sitting around very depressed, so I said, "Can I have a go tomorrow when we come in?", so I went in and did "Squonk" and it sounded all right so we finished that and then I knocked the songs off one by one. Suddenly, I'd done the album!'[4] Tony remembers, 'We just couldn't find anyone to do it, so it became logical for Phil to do it. It seems so obvious with hindsight, but we had no idea how he'd cope with the hard songs and it wasn't until he'd tried "Squonk" that we realized he was good at it.'[4] Mike's verdict is, 'He became the singer without us knowing it!'[4] He agrees with Tony that the main reason nobody had considered Phil before was

because he had no reputation as a singer of harder edged songs –
'We thought we'd have to get somebody else to do the raunchier
stuff!'⁴ Almost by accident Genesis had found themselves a singer
with whom to make their new record and by the end of November,
right on schedule, it was complete.

A Trick Of The Tail was their most consistent album to that point
in time, one without any real weak links. The sound quality had
improved exponentially since their previous album – the partnership with David Hentschel a roaring success – and that greater
level of technical expertise was echoed in what was their most
accomplished musical outing. Tony was just as much to the fore
instrumentally as he had been in the writing stage, synthesizers
of various types shaping his sound although he did return to the
piano, which he utilized with great taste. His passionate belief in
the band and their music shone through his work as never before,
this album placing him way beyond the keyboard heroes of the
day. His work with Steve was incredibly effective, the two combining and contrasting superbly on 'Entangled', where, Mike remembers, 'Steve started writing verses which were very airy-fairy and
then he came down with a bang.'¹⁶ This was one of Steve's main
writing contributions to a record on which he operated far more
as a player, albeit a very inventive and original one. Mike and Phil
were a solid driving rhythm section, particularly on numbers like
'Squonk' and 'Los Endos', Mike also adding some beautiful
twelve-string passages, perhaps prompted by his recent collaboration with Anthony Phillips. But it was on Phil the singer that
most of the attention fell. Would he be able to cope with the songs?
Would he be able to cope with the shadow of Gabriel? What sort
of voice did he have?

To call Phil's performance on A Trick Of The Tail a triumph would
be an understatement. On the evidence of the first track, 'Dance
On A Volcano', there was never any question that he would be
able to carry the whole record. In the past, he'd been known for
the purity of his voice on songs like 'More Fool Me', a characteristic
displayed here on 'Entangled' and 'Ripples', but the power that
he brought to bear on 'Dance On A Volcano' was a revelation. He
proved that not only did he have a technically impressive voice,
but also one of character, one with its own personality and rich-
ness, illustrated by 'Mad Man Moon', a song which it's hard to
imagine Gabriel performing so strongly. He injected his own ideas
into the melodies, giving them a punchier, more rhythmically
orientated sound, rather different to the way Peter had wrapped
himself and his persona around previous lyrics. Peter had given a

more emotional reading to the earlier songs, whereas Collins was more proficient at offering a musical interpretation, giving the music a different slant. This was heightened by the contrast between their vocal tones. Peter's voice often had a very thick, husky quality to it which would eat up the sound frequencies and give the instrumentation less space to make its mark. With Phil that problem dissolved, giving the music room to breathe, something which contributed in great measure to the new dynamism show-cased on the album – there was less of an internal battle between voice and instruments. Also the lyrics were honed to fit the music more than had been the case previously, when Peter would pre-sent his ideas to strap on to songs that had already been written. 'Mad Man Moon' and 'Ripples', in particular, both benefited from this new approach, Mike explaining, 'We worked closely with Phil, whereas Pete used to like to record the vocals by himself before he played them to us.'[52]

Although most came to lay plaudits at Phil's door, some prof-fered backhanded compliments, insisting that he had succeeded simply by duplicating Peter's voice – even Tony Stratton-Smith stated, 'He sounded more like Peter Gabriel than Peter Gabriel did!'[5] Granted there were some superficial similarities, but the accusations of plagiarism were ludicrous. The major reason for the likeness was that Phil's voice had been heard in the past far more than was realized, particularly on stage, as Steve explained: 'Pete and Phil used to link up, so what people used to think was one voice was often a composite voice of the two, so you've got half of that still.'[53] He admitted, however, that 'they do have very similar vocal tones, though Phil's style is more melodic than Pete's'.[53] Phil, understandably, was more adamant: 'I get fed up reading that the only way we're gonna be successful is for my voice to sound like Peter. The vocal sound of Genesis has always been Peter first and me sort of A-minus. My voice was always there in the backing harmonies. I am my own master,'[54] something clearly proven by his performance on 'Robbery, Assault And Battery' which he sang superbly and in character. To bury the argument, Mike weighed in with the information that 'a lot of the singers we auditioned had very different voices than Pete, [but they] wound up sounding like him when singing our songs because our note melodies made them sound that way. The material pushes the voice in a certain direction.'[47]

The direction they now had was a confident one, responding to the new challenge with music of self-assured eloquence. The harbingers of doom who had surrounded them since August were a very positive source of inspiration, as they made clear, Mike stating, 'The challenge has been good for us. Suddenly it was fresh and pulled us together, it's good fun to push yourself harder.'[55] The ultimate test came in their ability to come up with lyrics that were the equal of Peter's finest moments. 'Squonk', 'A Trick Of The Tail' and 'Robbery, Assault And Battery' were very conscious, indeed self-conscious, attempts to fill the lyrical gap that Peter had left. The humour in some of his best work was a crucial element in setting Genesis apart from some of their competitors with their readings of Shastric scriptures, their chronicles of the fight for survival within the music industry and their convoluted allegorical cosmic fairy tales. Gabriel had always walked the fine line between the surreal and the pretentious, the revealing and the self-absorbed, with consummate skill, injecting his lyrics with witty asides, agonizing puns or good old-fashioned stupidity. This was a standard that had to be maintained and although 'Squonk' saw them return to myths and legends, it was handled with a sufficiently deft touch to survive its subject matter and bring a wry smile to the seasoned Genesis-watcher. Tony's title track also worked nicely: based on William Golding's book *The Inheritors*, it told of an alien's arrival in a modern city and the reaction he receives. The humour was further enhanced by a promotional film they made for the song featuring a miniaturized Phil essaying some dance steps and Steve playing guitar with a claw-clad hand. 'Robbery, Assault and Battery' was less successful – though its accompanying film was more satisfying – betraying the fact that its lyrics were mostly put together by Tony in the recording studio. It was too contrived to be totally convincing in spite of Phil's attempts to save it with the adoption of his Artful Dodger persona.

Those few qualms aside, and taking into consideration the immense pressure the group were under, *A Trick Of The Tail* was an unqualified success, a resounding raspberry in the face of those who had said it couldn't be done. It held a nice balance between the romantic and the absurd, their aggressive playing and their softer acoustic moments, an exposition of all the things that Genesis were best at. Its weakest point had little directly to do with Gabriel's absence but was more a result of their new circumstances. Perhaps inevitably, there was little musical progression on the album, representing as it did more of a consolidation of all their better ideas to date – it had the lyricism of approach that had characterized much of *Selling England* combined with the more ballsy directness of *The Lamb* – something implied by the album sleeve which returned to their tradition of song illustration, this time featuring all the rich characters that populated the album. Preoccupied, as they had to be, with thoughts of producing a good record, of ensuring that people would not miss Peter's contribution and with releasing an album that would disappoint no one, the adventurous spirit that had fuelled earlier recordings was less noticeable, with the exception of 'Los Endos' which took them into new territory, almost into the realms of jazz-rock. Although Peter's last album with Genesis was *The Lamb Lies Down On Broadway*, that era wasn't over until the completion and release of *A Trick Of The Tail*, the final cohesive statement on that period of the group's development, a summing up of much of what was best about Genesis, pieced together in a simpler fashion that was, to many ears, much more palatable. Although they were satisfied with their achievement – waving a fond goodbye to Peter and the past with a quote from 'Supper's Ready' in the closing seconds of 'Los Endos' – it would take a tour to develop this new identity in the minds of their audience and lay Gabriel's ghost to rest.

That tour was set to open in March in Canada, but the band still didn't have a singer. As far as they were concerned the album had given them an initial breathing space, but they needed a singer to take the music on the road. After all, singing drummers never worked, did they? Mike remembers: 'We considered not going on the road at all, because the four of us had been together so long and no one was quite suited to just pick up with us.'[47] He and Tony did wonder if Phil might consider the job but nobody wanted to ask him simply because no one thought that he'd ever give up his precious drums. As time passed, however, there was still no solution. Phil remembers, 'One night, my wife suggested that I become the singer, but the thought horrified me. I've always thought that the singer was the cheapest gig in the band – all they had to do was look good and wiggle their bum. I never wanted to be a singer, I was a musician!'[4] After some thought, and recognizing that it would be hard to get hold of anyone else who would fit in, Phil decided to put the idea to the band, mainly because he could at least rely on himself to do a good job. 'They were surprised and a bit dubious at first, but they agreed.'[4]

Before he took up the role, however, Phil wanted to sort out a few things. 'I felt the music had suffered because of all the costumes, so I said I'd do it if I could just stand there and sing and present the music.'[4] Ironically, while there was absolutely no personal animosity between Peter and Phil, it had really been Peter's departure that had kept Phil in Genesis. 'The theatrical side was being talked about a lot and the music was very much secondary. That's when Brand X came on the scene and made me think about leaving. Then when Peter said he was leaving, it suddenly changed my attitude. I thought that maybe the theatrical side would have to go.'[20] The music was again top of the Genesis agenda, so Phil was happy to continue with the group and was pleased to have the chance to complete the circle by returning the live emphasis to the music. With that settled, Genesis faced a very supportive press – displaying the archetypal English affection for the underdog – on the release of the new album in February 1976.

The reviews for *A Trick Of The Tail* were universally positive, everyone bewildered that they could return in such form having lost their mentor. Displaying commendable tolerance in talking to these previous unbelievers, Genesis slowly, patiently explained why they were still around. Mike began with the gambit that they had used since time immemorial: 'For years, we've been telling people that we're primarily songwriters,'[54] at other times adding, 'I see myself primarily as a writer, not a player. We're more concerned with our songs than our playing.'[47] He also confounded those who felt that recording must have been a real struggle. 'It was very easy to make the album. When someone's unhappy and wants to move as Pete did during *The Lamb*, I'd much rather they did it and leave the rest to get on with what's left.'[4] The band were very happy to set the record straight after years of neglect – they could write songs perfectly well without Peter, this was no one-man band. Phil was particularly invigorated by his and the band's success, saying that 'during *A Trick Of The Tail* I felt like I was doing something constructive. Before I felt like I was marking time,'[54] a clear indication of his delight that the music was once again their priority, taking pains to point out that while their live show would still be an impressive spectacle, the band and its music would be the focal point – he would have no truck with the promotion of himself at the expense of the others. 'The show will be very exciting, but I'm not going to out-Pete Pete. I'm not gonna be wearing costumes.'[55] As they looked toward the challenge of playing live, Tony stated, 'There's more excitement now. Our stage show was getting kind of easy. Everything would be appreciated. Now we've got to establish ourselves again as a live act.'[55]

In order to get the show on the road, the band needed a drummer for the sections when Phil was singing, and he insisted on making the choice himself. Over the course of rehearsals with Brand X, he had got into conversation with Bill Bruford, veteran of both Yes and King Crimson, and admitted that he was having problems finding a drummer he was happy with, at which point

Bruford offered his services. Since Bill was one of his favourite musicians, Phil accepted the offer with alacrity, saying, 'Bill playing tunes that I thought were only OK and saying, "That's really nice" makes you think it's all right after all.'[54] Having Bill in the band was healthy not only from the point of view of his musicianship, it also bestowed a certain amount of recognition on the band. Phil explains: 'His being in the band impressed a few people who didn't think we were respectable. He's given us a breath of fresh air.'[54] Tony also refuses to underestimate Bruford's worth to Genesis on that vital first tour. 'He had a strong personal following which helped us and musically his work with Phil meant that we sounded better than ever.'[4] Phil supports this: 'In the States, people were saying, "Bruford's joined this group. Something must be happening!" '[49]

With the line-up finalized, Genesis went to Dallas for some vigorous rehearsals before the tour got underway. Steve remembers, 'We spent on the lights to compensate for Pete . . . Phil did incredibly well. He carried the spear for the rest of us and I felt we had to change – you couldn't just sit down on stage any more.'[4]

With an impressive set of backdrop slides and film, lasers, state-of-the-art lighting and the best stage sound that they had had, they were ready to meet their audience face to face. Phil was nervous before the gig, not because of the singing but because he had to communicate with the audience between songs. 'Pete was seen as a mysterious traveller and he held people's attention that way. He talked to an audience very well, it was a definite link and so I wanted to carry on the tradition but in a different way. I knew that the singing was OK, but I didn't know how to communicate with them, and you can't rehearse that, you just have to do it.'[4] Mike remembers that Phil was 'more worried about the talking, so he wrote some notes of what to say and he was trying to read them, but his hands were shaking!'[56] Indeed Phil was so concerned that he drafted Mike and Steve in to help with the on-stage announcements, just as Richard MacPhail had helped Peter in the very early days. Like the others, Tony also had a few lingering doubts before their first show in London, Ontario. 'Peter had so many things that went with him, but the audience immediately seemed to like Phil. From halfway through I knew it would work, he had a great rapport with the audience.'[4] Phil approached this new role by trying to get people on his side through laughter: 'If you make them laugh, they relax and then they absorb the music. I became "friendly", which gave it a different feel, made Genesis a friendlier animal.'[4] Phil developed this 'one of the lads' approach further in an attempt to involve the audience more and more, going so far as to talk to foreign audiences in their own language to increase their participation in the show.

The band breezed through the concert which was an undoubted success in every respect. Phil unquestionably had a major advantage as a new vocalist in that he had been recruited from within the group – none of the audience were keen to criticize someone that they already admired and respected. Many bands have tried to replace singers from external sources – Black Sabbath and Yes spring to mind – only to be greeted with howls of derision from fans loyal to the previous incumbent. With Genesis, at least they'd be willing to give Phil a chance – and that was all he required, although Steve can recall an odd incident at that first show. 'There was a guy dressed exactly like Pete used to dress in "Watcher", he had batwings, a cloak and he was standing in front of the stage all through the gig, he wouldn't sit down!'[4] Despite that, 'The audience reaction was incredible,' says Tony, 'we didn't get any heckling, presumably because Phil came from within the band.'[4] Phil's verdict at the time was 'I do have an advantage because the audience will trust me whereas they wouldn't trust someone off the street,'[55] remembering later that 'the audience were willing it to succeed'.[4] Worries about talking to them were forgotten: 'Once I'd done one gig, I knew what to do!'[4]

There were other reasons, of course, for the success of the show, Phil's performance notwithstanding. Tony feels that their choice of material was crucial. 'After "The Lamb Lies Down On Broadway" tour, people were relieved when we did a show that involved lots of different songs like "Supper's Ready", and A Trick Of The Tail had also been well received.'[4] Old classics that hadn't been played for many a long day, such as 'White Mountain', were dusted off and given an airing and the set remains one of the most balanced they've played.

Starting their tour in America was excellent thinking on their part. While America had begun to wake up to the band over the previous couple of years, they were still largely unknown there before the release of Trick and Peter Gabriel certainly hadn't attained the legendary status that he was accorded in the UK and the rest of Europe. Genesis had the advantage of playing to a largely first-time audience, drawn in by the new music – music better suited to radio than before simply because of the improvement in the production – and who had few if any preconceptions as to what they were about to see. The group were able to build up their confidence in front of enthusiastic audiences before having to tackle the potentially harsh home waters. In order to ease their homecoming, *Sounds* ran a piece on their American tour in mid-May where Barbara Charone set the nation's mind at rest, commenting on the 'aura of success [that] surrounds this revitalised Genesis'[54] and letting everyone know that 'supper is definitely ready!'[54]

The American tour progressed serenely, the band selling all 7000 tickets for an appearance at Burbank's Starlight Bowl within a couple of days and regularly out-doing the top concert draws of the time. The tour was such a success that plans were made to record concerts in Paris for a possible live album and to film the show at Stafford New Bingley Hall in England for cinema release. Their return to England culminated in appearances at the Hammersmith Odeon in London where they grabbed all the headlines, Chris Welch calling the concert 'a show to remember and savour . . . Genesis returned with a sense of purpose and confidence that drenched all sceptics in pails of cold water.'[57] Barbara Charone in *Sounds* unleashed a thesaurus of superlatives (including some of her own, pronouncing that the country was to be swept by Genesisteria!). As the front page of *Melody Maker* screamed, Genesis were indeed 'back in triumph'!

For those who had predicted the demise of the band, family-sized helpings of humble pie were on the supper menu, although no one, except perhaps the band themselves, could have anticipated just how adroitly and successfully they were going to handle their new status. Tony states, 'It was very satisfying for us to show that we could carry on. We were confident, but you can't tell how other people will react. It was great not to have to involve another person too,'[4] something which was very important for their longevity. The key element right through Genesis' professional life has been the chemistry between the group members, something which would inevitably have been disrupted by the introduction of a new singer. By the same token, Peter had left, at least in part, because there were too many strong writers in the group – by involving a fifth person, they would again be limiting the space available to each writer, which would have been potentially destructive, especially as Steve and Phil were beginning to produce more material. Tony also agrees that the band did benefit from being underdogs, struggling on in the face of adversity in the eyes of a press from whom they got a very fair deal. 'A lot of people re-evaluated us when Pete left which was useful.'[4] Although some were entranced by Peter's costumes, many were put off by what they felt was a bizarre presentation. With that

gone, a lot of people heard their new album without any preconceptions and found, to their considerable surprise, that Genesis
were far more accessible than they had previously given them
credit for.

By the close of their 1976 tour, Genesis had done the seemingly
impossible. They had coped with the loss of a distinctive frontman,
written their most consistently impressive album to date, pleased
the faithful, converted some sceptics, topped the year-end music
polls for best album and best live act, had a number-three album –
equalling the performance of *Selling England By The Pound* – made
great strides into the American market and even become fashionable with the English music press. Fighting shy of actually turning
water into wine, the band could look back with pride on an incredible year, one which ended with the only questions about Peter
Gabriel being 'Peter who?'

When they returned to the fray with their next album, the
musical climate would be rather different and Genesis would be
facing another major challenge.

CHAPTER TWELVE

'This is the end of your road'

'I actually agreed with what was being said by punk – most of the bands being slagged off as dinosaurs and boring, I thought were boring as well. I never thought of us as being like Yes, ELP, Tull or Floyd, so when they came along and said, "All that lot are crap, they're boring, they're old farts," I was agreeing with them and then found that they thought we were like that too, which was a drag. I saw different things in us – a lot of humour, we were more open and direct, we never fitted with those other bands. I just thought punk was a great idea – like someone shaking an apple tree until all the bad ones fell off and you'd just got the good ones left.'[4] (Phil Collins)

As 1976 moved towards its close the press again reverberated to cries of 'NO FUTURE!'. This time they weren't talking about the prospects of Genesis without Peter Gabriel but quoting the gospel according to the high priest of punk rock, Johnny Rotten of the Sex Pistols, the representative of disenfranchised youth, disenchanted by an England that offered them no opportunities, no hope, no future. This rage found some kind of focus in music as they tried to tear down its establishment, hoping to inspire apathetic youths into anarchistic action across the country while making a few quid for themselves. Ignoring the social/political aspirations of punk, if ever there were any, its musical viewpoint was certainly valid – people had tired of watching monumental egos drag themselves around the world to play hollow music in cavernous barns, making the greatest amount of money with the least possible effort, pausing only to indulge in drink/drug/sex rituals on the way, as their fans looked on with mounting disgust. Music, it seemed, had been sewn up by these inspiration-free technicians who flaunted their musical posturings to all and sundry, taking, taking, taking, but rarely, if ever, giving. Tiny little figures on some distant stage churning out passionless doodlings in an orgy of self-gratification, contemplating their navels – if they could still see them – all the time ignoring those who had put them in their inflated position was not what the original rock and roll experience was about, was it? Punk didn't think so. The time had come to tear down the walls of the pomp citadel and, since that was this week's thing, the papers tagged obediently behind, slinging mud at anyone and anything that had existed prior to June 1976. So it was that Genesis, the heroes of '76, became the unwitting lepers of '77, a stigma that has lived on.

OK, the idea of Genesis claiming to be anarchists and anti-Christs is fairly ludicrous – although they were little different in terms of age and background to many of punk's leading lights, some of whom could hear London calling and many of whom saw the blooming punk and new-wave movement as a tremendously useful career-enhancing pose – but they had never had any pretentions to be the voice of youth, neither had they been pretentious in their music or staging unlike some of the antediluvian rock monsters that were being attacked. Genesis were entertainers with a capital E, not artists with a capital A, and while their brand of entertainment wasn't to everyone's tastes, it was a bit much to accuse them of being part of the rich, fat, bloated face of corporate rock, particularly as they had only recently broken even after many years of debt!

It was to this background that their next album, *Wind And Wuthering*, was released. The band had decided to record in September 1976 at Relight Studios in Hilvarenbeek, Holland, where they had rented a house to work together and recapture some of the communal spirit of their earlier albums. By now, the desire to prove themselves as individual songwriters after Peter's departure was having serious consequences regarding the battle for space. Tony, Mike and Steve had each written almost an LP's worth of material for the sessions which they had already decided would yield a single album. The friction began to tell over the course of recording. 'We got into arguments about songwriting,' remembers Steve, 'because I knew that the lion's share would not come my way.' Fired up by the success of his début solo record, he had hit a rich vein of creativity and was constantly coming up with new ideas which he obviously wanted to release. Almost all of the songs that he wrote were put forward to the group for possible inclusion on the album, but they met with resistance from the others whose tastes veered more towards the material that Tony, in particular, was submitting. Additionally, their view was that Steve had already put out a solo record giving him an outlet for his material and so perhaps he should have less space on the forthcoming Genesis record, though no one else was keen for Steve to do another album on his own. 'I had pressure to give up my solo career – they perceived it as a threat to the group. I agreed to give up if a percentage of what I wrote was done by the band, but they refused, saying that everything should be done by the committee vote.'[4] Phil explains, 'He thought that the one hundred per cent of space should be divided equally, but that wasn't how we worked – we just wanted to use what we agreed was the strongest material, irrespective of who wrote it.'[4] The others having put their viewpoint across, Steve 'swallowed that for a bit and made the album with them.'

Wind And Wuthering was completed at Trident Studios in London in October, ready for its release in January 1977 when it reached number seven. In many ways it's the most under-rated album of the entire Genesis canon coming as it did between the twin peaks of euphoria that were *A Trick Of The Tail* – the proof positive that there was life after Gabriel – and *. . .And Then There Were Three. . .* – the source of their first big hit single. That this was the case is particularly sad as it's home to some of their greatest moments and is a potent, coherent piece of work, bound together by the thematic continuity of its musical content. The lyrics were far sharper and a considerable improvement on its predecessor as the band appeared to take strength from their great triumphs of 1976 and were able to approach their new work with an air of relaxed confidence. No longer making the conscious effort that characterized *A Trick Of The Tail* and which gave it a bookish, rather earnest atmosphere at times, they were less concerned to please all of the people all of the time and the album benefited immensely as a result, regaining the majestic sweep of the past, the melodramatic approach that had released the epic power and passion at the root of such emotionally affecting music as 'The Musical Box'. Their certainty of step allowed their collective imagination free rein, culminating in an album rich in storytelling, unashamed in its romantic escapism.

As with *A Trick Of The Tail*, *Wind And Wuthering* saw some consolidation of older ideas – 'Wot Gorilla?' building upon the success of 'Los Endos', for instance – but the record was also defined by a renewed spirit of adventure, of wonder, embodying a greater sense of advancement and of experimentation than its

predecessor. There was more scope for the band to stretch themselves as musicians just as they were doing as writers with the
instrumental sections on the second side, 'Unquiet Slumbers For
The Sleepers . . .' and '. . . In That Quiet Earth', which contained
some marvellously atmospheric playing, each phrase having its
place with no superfluous embellishments. Likewise, the simple
emotion captured on 'Afterglow' represented a very important
step forward for the group, a concise love song free from any
unnecessary ornamentation – it gave notice that Genesis could
edit themselves and were able to boast an increasing grasp on the
art of brevity, a talent they have continued to refine with great
success. 'Afterglow' is as sensitive, emotional and ultimately as
powerful a song as anything among their previous work, yet it
lasts little more than four minutes rather than the ten or fifteen
minutes of past 'epics', losing none of its impact as a result. Written
off the cuff by Tony in virtually the time it takes to play it – that
spontaneity being the key – it was an indicator to part of their
future direction and it has gone on to be one of their most enduring
tracks, the passionate intensity it generates still forming a stunning
climax to live performances.

Tony also offered 'All In A Mouse's Night', a delightful piece of
comic whimsy with a cartoon-like *Tom and Jerry* feel to it, again
very relaxed, not trying to prove any points or plug any gaps, a
song that exists for its own sake. He also provided the most
interesting musical fantasy on the record with 'One For The Vine',
a song that had been a year in the writing, a complex tale of an
ordinary man put forward as a Christ-like figure and forced to lead
a people convinced of his invincibility into battle, a situation from
which he had just fled. The lyric is imaginative and intriguing,
the music springs from a melting pot that bubbles with dynamic
invention, quite the most exciting concoction on the album,
crowned by a sensitive vocal from Phil. Admittedly the album had
some weaker points too – Mike's otherwise excellent ballad 'Your
Own Special Way' meandered rather aimlessly through an instrumental bridge section of little apparent relevance – but the overall
quality of the songs was such that any minor irritants were soon
forgotten.

Having made much of the running on *A Trick Of The Tail*, Tony
maintained a position of eminence on the new album, having a
writing input into six of the nine songs, contributing also to the
three other tracks that were completed for a later EP release. It is
hardly surprising, therefore, that he often refers to it as his favourite album, agreeing that 'I would hark back to that album more

than some of the others.'[58] Again, his tastes moulded the music and the increasing maturity in his writing pushed Genesis gently towards a more equal split between the 'epics' and the more traditional song format in terms of length (but which still managed to subvert the conventions of orthodox pop song construction), which is rather ironic since Tony's tastes are inclined towards the more complex and involved side of the group, something demonstrated by his solo offerings. It was to be another four years, and take the emergence of Phil Collins as a solo artist, before Genesis were to be accepted as a group that wrote and performed pop songs suitable for the singles market, but the decisive move – though certainly not a contrived one – in that direction began with *Wind And Wuthering*, with Tony taking the lead, although it was Mike's 'Your Own Special Way' that was released as a single, reaching number forty-three. As the band have said many times over the years, it has simply been a question of getting better at writing shorter songs, Mike admitting that it's often 'harder to write a complete "logical" song than to just do bits – it's a doddle just to join bits together. If you've got a piece that lasts for a minute and a half, you can't possibly turn that into a song, but to put that bit there, followed by another bit here is actually very easy. With short songs, the whole piece is developed.'[59] Tony was the first to get fully inside the idea of the shorter songs, something which they hoped might prompt journalists to give greater credence to their oft-repeated protests that they were songwriters first, musicians second.

Tony's quality and quantity of material allied to his implied leadership of the group was something that added to Steve's frustrations, restricting his input. Although Phil maintains that the band liked a lot of Steve's songs, Tony's tended to win the popular vote. Even so Steve did make a number of important contributions to the album with 'Blood On The Rooftops', co-written with Phil, being a particularly lovely song which opened with a beautifully executed classical acoustic guitar piece and which contained some sharp satire on the invidious influence of TV, coupled with a number of political references, something of which they'd previously steered clear – a sign of the times? The chorus, in musical terms, was something which Phil had come up with earlier and which Steve fused on to his other sections. 'The lyrics probably glued it together, the idea of a central theme of all the levels of action happening on the TV,'[16] is his memory of it, the lyrics undergoing last-minute alterations having started life as a love song! 'When I heard the other lyrics on the album, there was a bit of a romantic tinge anyway, so I decided to go right the other way and make it as cynical as possible,'[16] and as such it acts as a very nice contrast.

In all, *Wind And Wuthering* was another album that illustrated the constantly evolving and maturing Genesis sound, a furthering of their musical fantasy that proved that they weren't going to stand still and reap the commercial rewards by becoming a pale imitation of themselves. The album did not employ the primitive gutteral snarls of the surrounding punk hoards but it was unquestionably a more potent offering simply because the band refused to hide behind pretence – what you saw was what you got. Sadly, the critics could only see the new clothes of the new-wave emperors and *Wind And Wuthering* was savaged by those who had acclaimed *A Trick Of The Tail* less than a year earlier.

Despite the critical bile, the release of *Wind And Wuthering* and the accompanying UK tour saw the completion of Genesis' rise to prominence at home. Prior to the release of the album, Genesis had been asked to re-open the Finsbury Park Rainbow Theatre, the scene of some of their earliest triumphs with Peter, beginning a series of shows there on 1 January 1977. When tickets went on sale for their three-night stint, the box office was besieged by 80,000 applications for the 8000 tickets – no sign of a punk backlash there! Throughout the country there were overnight queues for tickets, fans in Newcastle sleeping out through heavy snowfalls.

Before they could fulfill those concert obligations, however, there were further difficulties in the air for Genesis. Bill Bruford, who had always been regarded as a temporary member of the live troupe, was in the process of rehearsing some new material with John Wetton and Rick Wakeman in what was to evolve into UK. Working as just a session musician had never been Bill's style and he had found touring with Genesis rather difficult simply because he had little creative input, adopting as he puts it 'a cynical attitude towards the band which they were really sweet to put up with'.[20] *Melody Maker* heard about these rehearsals with Wakeman and Wetton and branded them the latest in a long line of 'super-groups' that dated back to Blind Faith, causing Phil to give Bruford a call to enquire as to his future plans. With another world tour looming, Bill decided that he couldn't give Genesis the time they needed and so Collins went searching for a drummer again. Still in the studio mixing the new album, he used the rest of his time to listen to as many records as possible in an attempt to find an English drummer who was available and with whom he would be happy to work. All he succeeded in doing was eliminating everyone and leaving himself with a giant headache.

As tour rehearsals approached, there were still no likely English candidates for the drum stool so Phil had to widen his net. At the end of 'Afterglow' he had doubled up to play a drum lick that he'd adapted from a track called 'More Trouble Every Day' from Frank Zappa's *Roxy And Elsewhere* album, a double drum part played by Ralph Humphrey and Chester Thompson. Phil had seen Chester play with Weather Report earlier that year and was suitably impressed. On hearing that drum fill again, he decided to ask Chester if he'd take over from Bill Bruford. That drum part 'floored me completely, so I rang him up and said, "I've heard your stuff, would you like to play with Genesis?" He came over as a member, he didn't even audition!'[33] Phil was amazed that Chester was so keen to join the group, thinking that he'd probably never heard Genesis anyway! In fact, Alphonso Johnson had been playing *A Trick Of The Tail* constantly on the Weather Report tour bus, so Chester was well versed in their recent work. As Phil recounts, 'When he said he'd like to do it, I thought, "This is a turn up for the books – we must be pretty good!" It was a vote of confidence to have him in the group.'[60] Even more than adding Bruford to the band, the introduction of Chester – someone with an impeccable pedigree and a CV to match anyone in the drumming world – showed that Genesis made music with the emphasis firmly on feel and emotion, music that could appeal to a wide range of tastes and sensibilities, not merely the fans of 'art-rock'. To boast in your ranks an ex-member of Weather Report – Phil's favourite band and one of the most revered acts in the world at that time – was the final seal of approval. While Phil was on a high, informing all and sundry that the double drum sections would be much improved, Chester had the problem of learning the music and adapting his style of playing. If before the tour he'd said that he was always keen to play different kinds of music from different cultures, he had just nine days' worth of rehearsal before the Rainbow gig to cope with this particular culture shock.

Initially, Chester found it hard to get to grips with the music, having to take out the swing from his playing to meet the tight arrangements of some of the songs, admitting that Genesis was 'the most different thing I have ever had to adapt to, the most difficult. Genesis was a lesson in discipline. They're real different, very unorthodox even for the English!'[5] He added that, 'In the beginning it was almost the opposite to everything that I was used to do doing!'[33] To make matters worse for the American, when Genesis finally stepped out at the Rainbow, he and the band were panned by Chris Welch in *Melody Maker*. Under the heading 'Cold Genesis', Welch steamed into Chester: 'The missing ingredient

was in the percussion department. [Chester] failed to inject personality into his playing . . . one seriously missed the unexpected
twists and dynamic fire of Bill Bruford who equalled Collins in
inventive attack. Without either of them, the band fell strangely
limp . . . Bring back Bill Bruford – at least he can be relied on to
help cast out demons!'[61] Such a review might have frightened
away many a musician, but Chester quickly got to grips with the
job, so much so that the band decided to record their Paris shows
with him in June that year for inclusion on the live album that they
had begun with Bill on the previous tour. The band agreed that
Chester had introduced a new dimension to their music and that
songs like 'Eleventh Earl Of Mar' were granted a whole new
perspective on stage by his presence.

Their UK tour complete the band set off on another world trek,
taking in venues such as New York's Madison Square Gardens for
the first time, although not everything was sweetness and light.
Steve, in particular, was feeling increasingly frustrated, later conceding that at that point in time he had no interest in touring,
being more attracted to making a solo record – like Peter before
him, he had other things that he wanted to pursue, activities that
were sabotaged by Genesis' intensive work schedule, a situation
that was not improved by his American record company,
Chrysalis, demanding a new album. As the band prepared themselves for the States, the ABC Cinema on Shaftesbury Avenue in
London saw the opening of the film of their stage show, imaginat-
ively entitled *Genesis In Concert*. The Royal Première in support of
BAFTA and in the presence of HRH Princess Anne and Captain
Mark Phillips took place on 31 January as one half of a double-bill
with *White Rock*, the official film of the 1976 Winter Olympics
which boasted a Rick Wakeman soundtrack. There is no official
record as to whether or not the Royals were Genesis fans, but
attending the première was an act of supreme endurance which
justified their Civil List payment for the year as they were required
to sit through a dreadfully tedious film that not even the most
rabid Genesis follower could defend. Part live action and part
other footage – including some from silent movies and a piece
featuring a young girl dancing through sand dunes to the sound
of 'Entangled' – it was so inordinately dull and pretentious, it
could have been an ELP film, although happily it never achieved
the heights of preposterousness which Led Zeppelin scaled so
effortlessly during the ludicrous fantasy sequences, used in 'The
Song Remains The Same'. Seemingly filmed without any on-stage
lighting, director Tony Maylam appears to have had little

understanding of the group's dynamic and less of their instrumentation, flitting from one individual to another with no real plan of attack – wisely the band have never sanctioned its release on video, presumably in order to protect the innocent! Miraculously, some very strong musical moments did emerge, notably 'Los Endos' and the closing sections from both 'The Cinema Show' and 'Supper's Ready', which illustrated just how easily they had picked up the threads after Peter's departure, but that aside, this was an example of 'rock cinema' at its indulgent worst.

The wheels were starting to fall off the Genesis wagon as far as Steve was concerned and when Genesis returned to Earls Court in June, towards the end of their world tour, there was some doubt as to just how much longer Genesis would remain a four-piece band. England was delighted to see the group again and the three dates sold out immediately, emphasizing the magnitude of the group. Their popularity was further borne out by the success of the 'Spot The Pigeon EP' released to coincide with the tour, spending seven weeks on the charts and reaching number fourteen. It comprised three songs that hadn't made the *Wind And Wuthering* album, 'Match Of The Day', 'Pigeons' and 'Inside And Out'. The first two were lighter fare than one was used to from the band, both very bright, sunny sounds, written by the trio of Tony, Phil and Mike. They illustrated perfectly their improvement in writing shorter songs which, happily, also appealed more to the casual record buyer – three-minute tracks had always been a part of the group, which prided itself on the diversity of its landscape, but songs like 'Harold The Barrel' or 'Counting Out Time' were too wilfully obscure, too odd to capture a wider audience. Musically 'Match Of The Day' wasn't that different from some of the tunes on *The Lamb Lies Down On Broadway* and was made in the same spirit, but the lyrics about football were something which people could pick up on, encouraging them to listen to the band regardless of the press who described them as irrelevant and redundant. 'Inside And Out', a group effort, provided a glimpse of another facet of the band. A tale revolving around wrongful arrest on a rape charge and the subsequent social prejudices faced by the ex-prisoner, it showed that they weren't afraid to tackle issues, as 'Blood On The Rooftops' had already made clear.

Concluding the 1977 tour with a brief visit to the USA, the next item on the band's agenda was the mixing sessions at Trident Studios for the live album. The initial task was to decide which songs should be on the record and then whittle down the material that had been recorded to the best versions of those songs. Some preparatory work had already been done on that front. Steve commented in June that 'some of the tapes we've already mixed and there are versions of things which far surpass the recorded versions in terms of just spirit . . . just feeding off the audience'.[53] Sadly, Steve's initial enthusiasm for the project did not endure. Phil remembers, 'I was driving to the studio to mix *Seconds Out*, and I saw Steve on the street and asked him if he wanted a lift but he said, "No, I'll call you later." I got to the studio and told Mike and Tony I'd just seen Steve and they told me he'd decided to leave! He called me at the studio later and told me he was going, so I said, "OK," put the phone down and carried on working!'[4] Though disappointed that the band was losing an important member, the remaining trio continued to work on the live record without undue concern – having coped with the departure of Peter Gabriel, Steve's, while a loss of equal importance in terms of the band's internal structure, would cause less uproar among fans and critics and so was less worrying.

Steve's reasons for leaving were as varied and complex as Peter's had been a couple of years earlier. Having done a solo record, 'I did find it difficult [to step back into Genesis]. I agonized about the decision for two years.' The taste of sole control and total freedom had obviously appealed and *Voyage Of The Acolyte* was a source of great personal satisfaction for Steve, purely because he had been almost entirely responsible for its success. As he was becoming more excited about working in another format, the others felt that they should concentrate their efforts on continuing to establish the group. Only recently financially solvent and still very much feeling their way into America, there remained a collective belief between group and management that Genesis should maintain a prolific output and keep the pressure on – after eight years' worth of constant work, the end of the rainbow was in sight and so one further concerted effort seemed little to ask. Steve disagreed and insisted on the solo outlet. 'They were very much anti-solo album at the time so I didn't have the backing. It just seemed that it might be years before I did another one and I had all these ideas which I was coming up with which I didn't want to stick on the shelf. I wanted to record them and I wanted to use other people on them too, I thought that was very important – when you're working with the same people all the time you know what will please them, but the radical ideas are sometimes the ones you want to do, you don't always want to go for the lowest common denominator.' The fact that Steve had other people in mind to work on a number of the songs he was writing obviously precluded him from offering them to the group and he went on to give notice of his intentions in the press. 'I would like to see the band working with other musicians as individuals and corporately because I do feel that's really where it starts to happen or else it becomes insular to the point of being incestuous.'[16] One song which he had in mind was 'Hoping Love Will Last', leaving no one in any doubt as to his views by saying, 'I felt the band were incapable of performing it!'[26] (It was eventually recorded by Randy Crawford.) With this and other numbers like 'How Can I?', written specifically for Richie Havens, it was clear that Steve would have to make solo records: 'I felt that some things couldn't be done in a group context.'[4] That being the case, he admits, 'I really felt that I needed the safety valve of doing my own albums or else I was going to go crazy.' When it was clear that no one else found this acceptable, Steve was pushed towards leaving, despite Phil's protestations that 'He could have stayed with us and done as many solo albums as he wanted.'[20] The others agreed that they had thought the problems had been ironed out and that Steve was simply going to do a solo album, re-joining the band for their next record.

The other area of difficulty was internal friction. The share of the songwriting cake had become an especially contentious issue during the making of *Wind And Wuthering*. Unlike *A Trick Of The Tail*, when Steve had less material in reserve for the sessions, this time he arrived with virtually an album's worth, as did Mike and Tony. Once again there wasn't sufficient space on the vinyl for all the material that was available and Steve was particularly upset that much of his music was dropped, mainly in favour of Tony's contributions, though this is something that Phil plays down, pointing out that 'We'd always worked on songs that motivated everybody, rather than "I want a quarter of the album".'[20] Nevertheless, Steve felt that some of his offerings were left out arbitrarily, with 'Please Don't Touch' being dropped in rehearsals when Phil found that he couldn't get behind the song. Realizing 'My development as a writer created a difficult situation – within the group there were so many writers that we couldn't contain it,'[4] Steve could no longer commit himself to Genesis without a guarantee that his material would be used, a guarantee which was not forthcoming, something he found particularly galling as he was less happy with what he saw as the band's latest direction. 'I was interested in instrumental music and the balance was shifting more to songs, to simplifying, and I felt that the wackiness was being toned down, maybe in search of a new audience, maybe less élitist and I was maybe more purist than that!'[4] In defence of the band, however, *Wind And Wuthering* contained some of their most impressive instrumental moments ever.

Following the recording of the album, Steve continued to contemplate his future while on tour, often seeming to be detached from the rest of the band. By nature a quiet, polite, introverted man, his frustrations were turned inwards, rarely confiding in the others or letting off steam, causing Chester to observe, 'Steve often wouldn't say anything which always leads to problems. If somebody's not talking then there's going to be tension.'[20] Had there been more communication things might have worked out differently, but the tensions continued to simmer under the surface until, during the mixing of *Seconds Out*, Steve decided that he'd had enough of the group. 'I did feel it was under-mixed, everybody wanting to be louder than everybody else.' Having already worked as a producer on his own record, he had an abundance of ideas that he wanted to bring into play to liven up the album even though the idea of doing a live record didn't overly excite him. 'I felt that once we were starting to regurgitate things like "Supper's Ready", the band was very much repeating itself.' Keen that the group should avoid unnecessary self-plagiarism, he had said to the *NME*, on the release of *Wind And Wuthering*, 'I want to change the band, just for its own good. If it really did appear like concrete then . . .'[16] In retrospect, this was an ominous warning rather than an empty threat and when he felt trapped by the group he bravely walked away from it.

More than anything else Steve had reached a point where he could no longer take a back seat within a group situation and where he had to become master of his own destiny. 'I think it's quite natural for people to grow out of groups, it's very hard to keep the co-operative spirit going all the time. Normally someone has to have the controlling say and that's why you find that most groups are not democracies and don't pretend to be. It's he who shouts loudest or he who was the founder member.' He no longer wanted to participate in what he saw as a quasi-democratic process feeling that he was ready to call the shots himself. Implying that Genesis had almost become imprisoned by their success, he stated, 'It was like leaving home, but I wanted that challenge.'[4] Having reached the level they had, having survived Peter's departure, there seemed to be no new mountains for Genesis to climb. Once they'd played Madison Square Gardens in New York, the group had, for Steve, achieved its goals and had nowhere to go, nothing new for which to strive, something with which the others strenuously disagreed.

In many ways Steve had always been an outsider within Genesis which had meant he was able to give their music a new perspective but which prevented him from becoming as obsessive as Tony, Phil and Mike about the group and its future. Tony says, 'Right from when he joined, I always had a feeling he wouldn't stay – our tastes didn't quite join perhaps as much.'[4] Phil often recounts the story of Steve's leaving and seems bemused at his own lack of emotion over the split, though Mike rationalized it by recalling that they had sensed his comparative lack of commitment so his decision came almost as a relief, adding that, 'The three of us had already sat down and discussed what we'd do if Steve left – we had a bit of a crunch on the American tour where things came to a head.'[62] It was a piece of news they were expecting and less of a shock to their collective system when it came.

The loss of Steve was, from a purely musical point of view, as severe as that of Peter. His disturbing, dreamy, ghostly guitar playing which could be by turn soothing or disorientating, placid or aggressive, had lent a very distinctive quality to the Genesis sound. Phil calls him, 'A very original, natural creator of sounds',[4] and his interplay with Tony in particular was a constant source of fascination and excitement. Mike also picked up a great deal from Steve, adding an extra dimension to his playing, an aggression that hadn't been there before: 'He was a very original player – I always felt his strongest point was as a guitar player rather than as a writer because he came up with such original sounds.'[4] Indeed, Steve was very much the opposite of Tony and Mike, being a player first and a writer second. Where they had begun to play in a band simply because it was the only way they could air their songs, Steve had started as a player pure and simple, which in many ways created the ultimate breakdown with the group – by 1977 Tony and Mike were very experienced, mature writers, used to having the lion's share of the albums and who had shaped much of the band's music over the years. In contrast Steve's material, though at times more challenging, was less suitable for a song-based band format. As he was less forceful in the presentation of his ideas it was difficult for him to eat into the space previously reserved for their songs. It's interesting to see how differently the two sides saw the same situation – while Steve thought that he hadn't got enough of his material on to the album, Tony was surprised that he chose this time to make his break. 'On *Wind And Wuthering*, I felt that he'd made some of the best writing contributions he'd done to that date – when Peter was with us, the old school tended to dominate but when he left Steve took a stronger role – 'Blood On The Rooftops' which he wrote with Phil is a lovely song, so I was very surprised, I thought he could have come through more.'⁴ As the two sides of the argument saw things so differently, it's obvious that something had to give, though Tony is unstinting in his praise of Steve's work with Genesis. 'He was a very valuable contributor, especially soundwise. He'd often take us into areas we wouldn't have otherwise explored which was nice.'⁴ In spite of some barbed press comments from Steve just after the split, it was reasonably amicable and he looks back on the group as 'my formative period. I had a lot of good times with Genesis'.⁶³

With Steve gone, *Seconds Out* came to represent the end of an era, acting as a very good pocket history of the band for the newer fans they were attracting, presenting a number of songs that were ready to be laid to rest, principally 'Supper's Ready' and 'Firth Of Fifth'. Ironically in agreement with their defecting guitarist, the trio felt that the band had to move on to new ideas but that they could not do so until they buried some of their past – 'Supper's Ready' remained a potent piece of music and something of which they could be justifiably proud, but while it was still in the live set it towered above all else, rooting the band to 1972 and visions of Gabriel and his costumes, a snare from which they needed to escape. *Seconds Out* stands as one of the better live albums of the rock era – it's that rarity, a live album that gets played more than a couple of times and one that acts as more than just a souvenir of a particular tour by virtue of its presentation of superior recordings and different interpretations of a number of the songs. Mike confirms, 'A lot of the things hadn't been heard done by Phil and a lot of the old recordings were so much weaker – we were producing better versions.'⁶⁴ Many improved with the advent of the double drums which emphasized the rhythmic content of some numbers – 'Los Endos' was transformed by it – while in purely sonic terms, songs such as 'The Cinema Show' were infinitely better than the original album versions, a result of improved production values. Wisely the album showcased songs that held less of the Gabriel ghost, the exception being 'Supper's Ready' which did not suffer by comparison, thanks to the conviction of the playing and Phil's intense vocal performance. While he didn't equal the emotional impact of Peter's interpretation, his greater musical understanding meant that he could treat the song as a whole piece, adjusting his reading of the song to complement the instrumentation rather than simply focusing on the lyrics alone.

The release of the album was clouded by Steve's announcement, and it didn't receive the acclaim it deserved, although it did chart at number four, illustrating just how fast their army of followers was growing. Genesis now had an audience as big as virtually any band in the UK and at last their album sales were starting to reflect that fan base. All that was missing was a hit single.

CHAPTER THIRTEEN

'A firmly laid and simple course'

When Genesis regrouped to make their next album, they faced a familiar challenge – recording following the departure of a key member of the band. As Tony jokingly remarks, 'By now, we were getting used to it.'[4] Displaying a nice line in self-depreciating humour, preparatory work progressed under the working title of . . .*And Then There Were Three*. . . . The band did, in fact, return to the fray almost immediately after completing the mixes for *Seconds Out*, never doubting that they could continue without Steve.

Similarly there was no real question of bringing in a new guitarist for studio work as Mike had decided he was happy to take over the lead playing – having coped so well in replacing Peter from within, there was concern that introducing a new force could upset the delicate balance and chemistry of the group, and might also lead to the old problem of having too many writers and not enough space. It was felt that working as a three-piece gave Genesis a self-contained structure with very clear demarcation lines – Phil would deal with drums and percussion, Tony with the keyboards and Mike the guitars. This lack of cross-over gave everyone additional room and responsibility, with a consequent reduction in internal strife.

The essence of the band was still very much intact: the empathy between the remaining trio had always been strong, all three understanding the value of the group ideal and being prepared to involve themselves in the necessary give and take and the compromises that group life imposes. Phil says, 'We enjoy working with each other because we all complement each other. I may go in with an idea . . . and it will get the stamp of the others on it.'[65] The sanctity of the group product opposed to an idea wholly realized by an individual is a quality recognized by Phil, Mike and Tony – the belief that a special group is greater than the sum of its constituent parts – and one borne out time and time again throughout the history of rock music. It's very rare that solo records can match the excitement and consistency that the band can generate – compare Lennon and McCartney's individual output to that of the Beatles, for example – and the trio were keen to maintain that group interplay, while agreeing that future solo records were on the cards. 'The idea of a group is to pool your ideas,' explained Phil, 'but that's not to say that we're all faceless individuals and we can't cope on our own. I dare say everyone will be using up their excess material in the form of solo projects.'[65]

The writing and performing they could approach with confidence. They had regularly worked together as a unit in Genesis and the results had been both prolific and prodigious – the closing section of 'The Cinema Show' and 'Apocalypse In 9/8' were major musical moments for which they'd been responsible, as was a large portion of *The Lamb Lies Down On Broadway*, added to which the three had kicked off the vital sessions for *A Trick Of The Tail* while Steve was working on his own record. Rutherford and Banks had forged a partnership responsible for a sizeable chunk of early Genesis material, while more recently Tony had proved himself to be a formidable individual writer and Mike had increased his profile on *Wind And Wuthering*. Added to this, Phil was still just as keen to set the group in motion for improvisational sessions, so there was little doubt that there would be as many ideas for the new album as there had been for the previous one – indeed, hadn't Steve left because there was too much material around?

Everyone was satisfied that Mike was a very accomplished guitarist, well qualified for the job – having defined the twelve-string basis for the group along with Anthony Phillips in the early days, he'd gone on to play rhythm guitar. Just as people hadn't realized Phil's contribution to the group's vocal sound before Peter left, so they were unaware of Mike's input on guitar. Obviously the idea of tackling an entire album of lead guitar parts was fairly daunting, but Mike felt that the challenge would bring out the best in him, and so it was to prove, allowing Genesis to further develop their sound and give their music a very definite shift away from some of their past efforts.

The brief for this next album was to experiment with shorter songs so that the record could include more musical ideas (and, coincidentally, form a response to the new-wave catcalls that charged them with being long-winded and incapable of concise writing. As Mike explained: 'When a band's been going for a long time, it's hard for things to stay fresh – every year you try to get a fresh element into the group, the way you do an album, the way you write, that's one of the hardest things after ten years.'[66] The restless urge to avoid repetition and to continue to try new ideas has always been at the heart of their work ethic and this year's model, the attempt to produce a series of shorter songs, was the latest in a line of methods they had employed – new producers, concept albums, writing as individuals – to make the current Genesis sound different from the previous one. This time the result was a large number of individually written songs rather than songs which evolved from group jamming – of the eleven tracks on the finished album, seven came from individuals (Tony's four to Mike's three). Tony and Phil collaborated on another, leaving only three group-written tunes on the album.

Pleased with the facilities on offer at Relight Studios in Holland when recording *Wind And Wuthering*, the group again set up camp there in September 1977 to record the album plus two further songs that were to be future B-sides. According to Tony, 'Making . . .*And Then There Were Three. . .* was a very pleasurable experience. We weren't in each other's way because we had such definite roles – we felt very complete in the studio.'[4] It's certainly true that the album has the feel of a group of people getting on well together and revelling in their environment. It captures a very warm period and, in that respect, it's a success, soulful in the way it catches that emotion and yet it doesn't really begin to meet the demands the group had set themselves, failing to achieve the variety it was hoped the short-song format would provide. Part of the problem lay simply in the personnel change. Steve was a highly gifted guitarist with a very individual style which he had worked on and adapted over a number of years and which was an integral part of the Genesis sound. Mike, while a perfectly able guitarist, had never before been faced with the prospect of playing all the lead parts and it was something he had to get to grips with quickly, so some of the guitar parts did not have the fluidity that Steve had brought to the group. Mike was also very much his own man and had no intention of being a pale imitation of Steve Hackett. He aimed to put his imprint firmly on to the music and so was keen to produce his own distinct voice, but on . . .*And Then There Were Three. . .* it was a slightly faltering voice, one in its infancy. Naturally for his first foray into the territory of lead guitar things were kept relatively simple although there were intermittent impressive flourishes, but it would take a full tour with the new material before Mike really felt confident in the new role, going on to give a revelatory performance on his first solo LP *Smallcreep's Day*. Consciously deciding not to stray too far from the basics had reduced the amount of interaction between guitar and keyboards, the Genesis trademark. As guitar was taking more of a back seat on this outing, Tony's keyboards came through stronger than ever and it was his sound that moulded the music. Though Tony employed his customary taste and restraint, the dominance of the keyboards occasionally jarred, giving much of the material a very similar kind of feel.

. . .*And Then There Were Three*. . . was planned as something of a reaction to the previous studio record. The band felt that whereas *Wind And Wuthering* had been top-heavy with swirling atmospherics, melodramatic pieces and short on musical light relief – a problem that might have been alleviated with the inclusion of 'Pigeons' at the expense of 'Your Own Special Way' – this album would endeavour to employ some 'nice songs that stood up',[5] as Phil described them. With so many individual songs, the ideas were less expansive, less mutated by the influence of the other members than their past work – although Mike and Tony both had catholic tastes and were always keen to broaden the scope of their writing, a collection of songs written by one person in isolation within a short space of time will inevitably reflect the writer's tastes and ideas at that time and thus seem similar. Excellent though the songs were, there is a sameness to much of the album that goes against the grain, an uncharacteristic homogenization that lacks the spark of eccentricity or magic which had come to define Genesis. In retrospect, Mike admits that by the time they made the album 'we'd forgotten why we were doing it'.[4] Although they enjoyed being in a group and recognized the attendant strengths, they'd fallen into the trap of being Genesis almost out of habit. They were writing, recording and touring under the group moniker but were missing out on that crucial element which gave the group its *raison d'être*, writing songs together – if they weren't fulfilling that part of group life, they ran the risk of simply acting as session musicians on one another's tunes.

Dispensing with the customary cross-pollination of ideas between the three, save at the arrangement stage, was not the sole reason for the similarities between the songs, however. Fairly obviously, if a record is to consist of around a dozen different tunes, their length will, by definition, be restricted and so as

writers they faced the challenge of stating their cases more concisely. A keynote policy in the Genesis manifesto had been to
bring a little more imagination to bear on rock music than most of
their contemporaries, which generally meant that in order to
convey all the necessary emotions and ideas they exceeded the
traditional three-minute format several times over. Though they
had proved they could cope with short songs very successfully
through the likes of 'Counting Out Time' – indeed much of *The
Lamb Lies Down On Broadway* – 'More Fool Me' or 'A Trick Of The
Tail', they had never tackled a whole album of such pieces. By
endeavouring to do so, they were required to address themselves
to brevity and ruthless self-editing. Mike and Tony had thus
refused themselves the full freedom of expression and imagination
which they had employed in the past, and the music illustrated
this, some songs suffering from being cut short – 'Undertow' was
a prime example of a stunning piece of music which would have
scaled Olympian heights had it been stretched further, an irony at
a time when critics were castigating the progressive bands of the
day for extending the flimsiest of themes way beyond breaking
point. (Tony did, however, return to a theme from this song on
his album *A Curious Feeling*, also employing it on a soundtrack for
The Shout which he co-authored with Mike once the recording of
. . .*And Then There Were Three*. . . was completed.)

The album struggled as much as a result of what wasn't on it as
what was. The time constraints around which they constructed
the record had undermined the writing process, giving rise to a
suppression of creative invention – ideas that screamed out for
longer treatments were shelved simply because they didn't fit in
with the concept of the album. With regard to studio albums, the
release of . . .*And Then There Were Three*. . . was sandwiched
between *Wind And Wuthering* on the one side and Tony and Mike's
début solo albums on the other. All three of these albums featured
longer, more instrumentally based pieces, and they are generally
more satisfying as a result. While there is no justification for
stretching ideas beyond their limits for the sake of it, it is just as
foolhardy to edit a song to fit in with a pre-determined time
allocation. As Genesis quite rightly refused to do this, the more
experimental and radical ideas could not reach the finished product and therefore the album has an oddly unadventurous quality
to it.

Another reason for that lack of adventure was rooted in Phil's
domestic situation. Since he and his wife had moved into their
house in South Ealing with their two children, it was very difficult

for Phil to find the opportunity to play drums – they're not the most sociable of instruments, so in deference to the finer feelings of his neighbours and his children, he chose not to play except when he was working. 'Not being able to play when I'm off duty, I can't really come up with so many ideas. I usually come in with rhythmic ideas and a very basic chordal idea, give it to them and we all thrash it around and it becomes something like "Los Endos".'[65] As Collins brought little to the sessions Genesis lacked the musical looseness and freedom from tight arrangements which they had explored so successfully on the previous couple of albums, and so were required to concentrate on the scrupulously arranged, relatively straightforward melodic pieces that Mike and Tony had prepared earlier. Phil agrees that in terms of rhythm Mike and Tony didn't write that way and regrets that the group hadn't spent more time writing together to achieve a wider picture: 'I'd rather Genesis do what Genesis does best, which is me coming in from my area and clashing straight in the middle with what Tony does so you get a compromise which sometimes can be a lot stronger.'[65]

Ultimately the laudable aim of getting more music on to the album by the use of short songs backfired on the group, though some sections of the press considered the record a success simply because it featured eleven songs rather than the customary eight or nine. Had they ever listened in the past they would have discovered that many individual Genesis songs contained a greater range of music than some acts had recourse to during their entire careers. For a piece of music to have just one title didn't mean that it contained only one idea. Perhaps the group themselves might have done better to bear that in mind to balance the scales more effectively.

Criticisms as to balance and form dealt with, what of the individual songs? . . .*And Then There Were Three. . .* , for all its faults, did illustrate one thing very clearly – Genesis was as vibrant and relevant as any band in the world, punk or otherwise. Mike, Tony and Phil were still questioning themselves and the reasons for their continued success, boldly refusing to set Genesis in concrete and becoming a lumbering cabaret act – the music never stood still but it remained their only message. Some of the songs were quite outstanding, Mike writing his first solo classic with 'Say It's Alright Joe', a bluesy, three-in-the-morning bar-room drunk song that was lifted higher on stage with Phil donning an old raincoat and acting out the song, using Tony's keyboards as a bar! In some respects 'Joe' was the album in microcosm – an atmospheric but simple song, breaking into a more traditional Genesis instrumental surge that was ended prematurely. It marked a clear-cut change in lyrical style too, the fantasy toned down or replaced with more matter-of-fact, day-to-day ideas.

The greatest level of invention and excitement was to be found on 'Burning Rope', tellingly the longest song on the record, though one which had been reduced from its original length. Mike gave his most impressive guitar performance during the long middle section, integrating beautifully with Tony's work; an extended instrumental passage which allowed the band the opportunity to spread the wings that had been clipped elsewhere. Looked at in isolation, every song stands up as a solid, if sometimes unexceptional, piece of work – 'Deep In The Motherlode' is a rockier number and one on which Mike thrived, 'The Lady Lies' is a splendidly witty slab of melodrama that wouldn't have been out of place on *Foxtrot*, 'Scenes From A Night's Dream' an endearing childhood dream sequence (with some backing harmonies from Phil that send shivers up the spine) and 'Many Too Many' the most gorgeous ballad that they've ever committed to vinyl.

. . .*And Then There Were Three*. . . retained the bright warmth of the 'Spot The Pigeon EP' but, where it had worked so well in EP form, the LP was too long for one predominant feel and at times one yearned for the orchestrated sweep of an 'Eleventh Earl Of Mar'. In the final analysis there wasn't a bad song on the record, as one had come to expect from Genesis, but it was too lightweight, without the sharp contrasts and the telling use of colours that was their stock in trade.

The song that attracted the most comment was the single 'Follow You Follow Me', their first to crack the UK top ten – finally reaching number seven – and the song that introduced the group to a totally new audience. Having a hit with a three-minute pop song caused apoplexy among hardcore fans, leading to cries of 'sell out!' which the group were understandably keen to play down. Initially Phil pointed out that it was the only truly group-written song on the album, the only one written from scratch in the rehearsal room. 'There's no devious thinking behind it,' he said. ' "Follow You Follow Me" was written in exactly the same way as "Los Endos". We sat down with a riff and we worked on it. It went through loads of different changes before ending up as a three-minute song. It could have gone on for eight minutes, we just thought it sounded better ending after three and since a three-minute song is a lot easier to get played on the radio we put it out as a single.'[67] Stung by some of the unfounded criticism, he added, 'Genesis is a band of composers. If a song sounds good at three minutes long, then we leave it . . . "Follow You Follow Me" is one of the hippest things we've done, just out of improvisation, the attitude was totally on the level.'[66] Much of the problem centred around the fans themselves – having had Genesis as their pet group for years, been able to get gig tickets and bask in the kudos of espousing a group that few had heard of, suddenly the nation's, then the world's, pop kids knew about them too. From a selfish point of view, many fans want to keep their group secret and so lose some of their passion when the band become successful. Phil accepted that the group had changed but argued that from one album to the next they'd always done different things. 'Groups have to develop but fans like what's safe. It's all very well treating a band like a toy, but the people that level those criticisms at us don't read the same books, eat the same food or wear the same clothes they did ten years ago, so why should we?'[68]

There were several contributory factors behind the success of 'Follow You Follow Me'. At the core was the song itself, a very straightforward love song with none of the bizarre elements that harmed the profit potential of 'I Know What I Like' or 'Counting Out Time'. The band noticed that the balance of their audience was beginning to shift, as Mike declares, 'Suddenly they all brought their girlfriends. All those years these blokes had been unsuccessfully trying to persuade their girlfriends to come and see Genesis. After "Follow You Follow Me" your predominantly male audience was filled with girls. Wonderful!'[69] It is also clear that the group were now better at writing convincing short songs, the result of years spent honing their songwriting skills, guaranteeing them the required radio airplay. More than any of that, however, it was just time for Genesis to have a hit single. After a decade of hard slog, gradually accumulating an audience largely through live work, they were one of the biggest bands in the country, if not the world, and were a very newsworthy item. With the release of their first single in almost a year as a taster for a brand new album they were ensured a high profile – the press reported it and radio stations wanted to play it, so people were well aware of the single's existence before it came out. With their dedicated fan base, which had taken on the status of a very large cult following, it was inevitable that the single would achieve excellent sales figures in its first week of release, as fans clamoured to hear the new music and to discover how Genesis sounded without Steve Hackett. A good initial response meant a national TV airing on *Top of the Pops* of the promotional video before an audience of millions, thus staking out a claim for a whole new collection of fans. Here was a lovely little pop song that still managed to sound very different from anything else around it – 'Pop music done with more subtlety'[70] is Tony's description of most of the Genesis catalogue. The 'Spot The Pigeon EP' had shown the way with its very impressive chart placing the previous year, so it was really little surprise to find 'Follow You Follow Me' infiltrating the upper reaches of the charts. Tony, however, was amazed: 'I never thought we'd have a hit – even things like "The Carpet Crawl" which I thought were good singles never were hits, so I just thought we'd go on like that with the albums doing well.'[4]

Nevertheless, the hit single ensured a doubling of sales for . . .And Then There Were Three. . . , in turn scuppering hopes of a hit for the follow-up single 'Many Too Many', the more casual audience refusing to buy a song they already had on LP, though the more dyed-in-the-wool Genesis supporters picked it up for its two unreleased tracks, 'Vancouver' and 'The Day The Lights Went Out', allowing it to graze the lower reaches of the charts.

Tony recognizes the crucial part that 'Follow You Follow Me' played in the band's future. 'It came at a very key point in our career and was the only reason Genesis were able to exist in an era when singles became more important. We managed without singles up to the late seventies but after that there were very few groups who could get anywhere without a hit single and I don't really think Genesis would have been the exception.'[71]

With the album finished, Genesis made plans to go on the road. The tour was scheduled to begin in April 1978 in America and was to encompass almost a hundred dates with three separate visits to the States, six gigs in Japan, some arena shows in Europe as well as a series of concerts at assorted European open-air festivals in the summer, including their only UK date on 24 June at Knebworth Park. This solitary UK gig was a further source of disappointment for the home contingent of fans who felt they were getting a raw deal and that their heroes were deserting them now they had found fame and fortune elsewhere. The truth was that as the rest of the world woke up to Genesis they needed to put in the same kind of intensive effort on foreign soil as they had in the UK to consolidate these advances – 'Follow You Follow Me' had broken into the American Billboard top thirty, the album becoming their first gold record there. In addition, it was only by touring the massive halls in America that the group could recoup the enormous cost of keeping their show on the road, a cost running at a reputed $25,000 a day. Tony points out, 'After A Trick Of The Tail

Above: Genesis 1972. Phil Collins in foreground, Peter Gabriel, Mike Rutherford and Tony Banks in second row and Steve Hackett sitting at the back (*Pictorial Press*). *Below left:* 'You foxed me with that one, Sandro.' Peter Gabriel performing 'The Musical Box' 1972 (*Retna*). *Below right:* Flower power. Peter Gabriel and 'Supper's Ready' in 1973 (*Rex*).

Above: 'Tense, nervous headache?' 'Supper's Ready', 1973 (*Retna*). *Below left:* 'I'm not old, I'm thirty-seven.' Peter Gabriel, 'The Musical Box', 1973 (*Retna*). *Below right:* Steve Hackett (*Rex*).

Above: Back in New York City, February 1976. *From left to right:* Steve Hackett, Phil Collins, Bill Bruford, Tony Banks, Mike Rutherford (*Retna*). *Below left:* Peter Gabriel maps out his career strategy (*Rex*). *Below right:* Chester Thomson (*Rex*).

Above: Would you buy a used car from these men? On the set of the 'Illegal Alien' video, 1983 (*Rex*).
Below left: 'From Milwaukee, the fabulous Mr Daryl Stuermer' (*Retna*). *Below right:* Anthony Phillips contemplates the potential commercial success of a series of Swedish cycling songs, London 1985 (*Carole Willis-Impey*).

Above: *Spitting Image* puppets used on the 'Land of Confusion' video, 1986 (*Rex*). *Below:* Sax and drugs and rock and roll. On the set of the 'Anything She Does' video, 1986 (*Retna*).

Above left: No jacket expired. Phil with his wife Jill (*Pictorial Press*). *Above right:* Tony Banks (*Retna*). *Below:* Mike the Mechanic (*Rex*). *Opposite page:* They seem to have a platinum touch. Giants Stadium, New York, May 1987 (*Retna*).

Above: Silent running! On uneven ground. Mike Rutherford at the country home of the Who's Kenney Jones (*Rex*). *Below left:* Peter Gabriel in New York, January 1990 (*Retna*). *Below right:* Phil Collins and Hugh Padgham gra a Grammy (*Pictorial Press*).

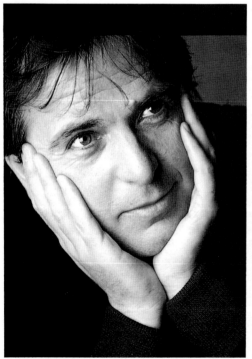

we started to sell smaller places out but it wasn't until . . .*And Then There Were Three*. . . that we got the audiences we needed for the shows we were mounting.'[4] For this tour, they employed a set of six hexagonal mirrors which were computer-controlled and which rotated above them, reflecting the already impressive light show on to the group, another on-stage innovation but one which wasn't cheap!

The cost wasn't the only problem regarding the tour. Phil recalls that after a meeting to finalize the schedule, he had informed his wife Andrea of their plans for the coming year. 'By then she'd had already become tired of me not being around. She said, "If you go away, I won't be here when you come back." '[72] Sure that he would be able to patch things up on his return and that things weren't so far gone as she'd implied, Phil decided that the tour and the band came first, if for no other reason than they were finally making a commercial breakthrough and reaping the rewards for which they'd worked so hard.

With the tour approaching fast, Mike found himself in the same position Phil had a year earlier – trying to recruit a new member for the forthcoming tour. Initially the group had toyed with the idea of asking Alphonso Johnson of Weather Report to step into the breach, but he was primarily a bassist whereas the new man would have to handle Steve's guitar parts on the old material since Mike had decided to play lead guitar only on the tunes from . . .*And Then There Were Three*. . . While Johnson did rehearse with Mike, it soon became apparent that things weren't working out, so Johnson suggested that they audition Daryl Stuermer, another American who had spent several years working with Jean-Luc Ponty. Stuermer was looking for a change of scene and, crucially, was already well aware of Genesis, being a great admirer of their work of the previous few years. Mike auditioned him in New York and after just two songs, 'Down And Out' and 'Squonk', was impressed. Within hours Stuermer was offered the tour with Genesis, which he was delighted to accept, not least because he already knew Chester Thompson and could thus slot into the line up much more easily.

Like Chester, Daryl found that playing Genesis' songs was more difficult than had appeared on the surface, partly because his roots were in jazz-fusion, an area that Genesis had merely dabbled in from time to time. He quickly got to grips with his role, however, accepting the reduced freedom that Genesis' music initially gave him – testament to his personality as much as his technical expertise – and soon became adept at injecting his own identity into the

songs. Inevitably, on this first tour Daryl was required to play
mainly lead guitar since the Hackett material made up most of the
set and just as they had when Peter left, the group took the
opportunity to bring out a few old songs that hadn't been played
for some time – 'Fountain Of Salmacis' took a bow for the first
time in six years and gave Daryl the perfect opportunity to win
over the audience by taking on one of Steve's trademark solos and
making it his own. Again there were no problems from the crowds
– no one shouted for Steve, although with so many new fans in
the audience, especially in America, they may not have known of
him anyway!

The group had spent long periods on the road and away from
home in America over the years so they devised a plan for this
tour which they felt would give them more time to spend with
their families, Mike having joined the ranks of married men in
November 1976 at his Knightsbridge wedding to Angie Downing.
By the time they were ready to tour . . .*And Then There Were
Three.* . . , Phil and his wife had a son, Simon, and an adopted
daughter Joely, the Banks family now included their son, Ben, and
Mike and Angie had a young daughter, Kate. With their young
children in the forefront of their minds, they wanted to devise a
tour which would allow them as much time at home as possible.
Rather than spending three solid months in the States, they
decided to play three one-month stints over there. Unfortunately,
this meant that while there were short breaks in between the tours,
they had only just begun to wind down when they had to go back
on the road again. 'It made it seem much longer,' recalls Mike.
'The last tour tended to be in places where we hadn't made much
of an impression which was depressing for us.'[20]

The tour did, however, prove that after a decade of hard work
and fine music, Genesis had reached the very top of the rock tree,
selling out the biggest venues all over the world. Having proved
themselves equal to every challenge that had been thrown at them,
be it the changes in personnel or the vagaries of musical fashion,
the future for the band looked rosy. They began to formulate ideas
for their next batch of concerts, intending to do an extensive UK
tour late in 1979, returning to theatre venues to recreate the intimate atmosphere of the old days, as opposed to the huge open air
shows and ice hockey stadiums they'd been playing on this tour
and of which they were tiring. Phil, rather prophetically in terms
of his own future, caught the mood of the party when he said,
'We've definitely come to an end of an era. We've been touring so
much and that's the way we've always viewed things, going on

tour promoting the albums, but because of the situation we're all in, with families, kids and stuff, we don't want to flog ourselves to death any more.'[65]

The tour had also brought other ideas to the fore regarding the way in which Genesis should operate in future. As the tour progressed, they came increasingly to the conclusion that the songs they'd been writing more recently as individuals didn't give them the collective enjoyment they gained from group-written songs – it was noticeable that they played relatively little of the new album compared with their previous tours where the new music formed the centrepiece of the set – and there was a general intention to return to the original premise of using the rehearsal room as a writing rather than arranging forum in the future.

Before they could address themselves to making another record, however, the band needed a break to recover from the year's heavy workload. Only after that period would they meet again to make any concrete plans with regard to touring and recording.

CHAPTER FOURTEEN

'Just one more step ahead'

Abacab to many marks both an artistic and commercial watershed in Genesis' evolution, and it is true that it saw them consolidate and then build on their worldwide popularity while also showing a marked musical departure from their previous releases. However, the seeds of those changes had been sown with the recording of *Duke*, both in terms of the music that they were making and, most importantly, their approach to writing and recording.

Nineteen seventy-nine was a year when the continued existence of Genesis had never been in so much doubt, its future probably never so precariously balanced since the departure of Anthony Phillips nine years earlier. A year spent almost exclusively on the road, travelling across the world to capitalize on the new opportunities that the success of 'Follow You Follow Me' had given them, had taken its toll on the group as a whole, but for Phil its repercussions were especially traumatic.

In spite of his wife's warnings of the potential personal cost of the touring schedule Phil felt, correctly as events proved, that the band were on the verge of reaping some of the benefits of their incredible and sustained dedication over the years and that his loyalty to Genesis at this particular time outweighed the dangers to his marriage, dangers that he perhaps didn't fully appreciate. On returning home to his wife and children from the third and final American leg of the tour for a few days' break, prior to completing the year with some dates in smaller halls in Japan, he found their relationship in shreds. Rather than cancel the tour and disappoint the fans, Phil chose to go to Japan where, by his own admission, 'I spent ten days drunk. I hated every minute of it.

I couldn't sing and everyone was very concerned about my welfare.'[20]

By Christmas 1978, he was very clear that his major, indeed only, consideration must be to salvage his marriage and take care of his family. Genesis would quite rightly have to take a back seat – ironically a similar pull away from the group towards domesticity had led in part to Peter Gabriel's departure. By now, Andrea wanted to move out of their home and spend time with her parents in Vancouver which Phil saw as a golden opportunity to start afresh and he was happy to up sticks and move lock, stock and barrel to Canada. In a new climate, away from all the reminders of the pressures of the previous year, they both hoped there would be time to discuss their differences and piece together a reconciliation. The key to it all seemed to be Vancouver – a new life, a new start, a chance to become a family man again. At this point, his entire career as a musician seemed to have little bearing on anything, much less his position in Genesis, and so prior to his departure in the early part of 1979, he arranged to have dinner with Mike, Tony and Tony Smith. Over the conversation, Phil outlined his difficulties and his intentions, encapsulating everything in the simple message, 'If we can write and record in Vancouver fine, if not then I'm out of the group.'[4]

Though the others had been aware of Phil's troubles, this pronouncement still came as something of a bombshell. The ultimatum was obviously the source of some consternation which eventually gave rise to occasional dark murmurings within the music industry that Genesis had reached the end of their road. Common sense won the day – Mike and Tony were keen not to make any snap decisions that would rule out any hope of further Genesis recordings. They came back to Phil with the suggestion that the band take a break for a few months to give him the opportunity to sort himself out. If at the end of that time Phil was happily ensconced in Vancouver, they would then, and not before, deal with whatever problems that threw up.

This was to be the first really extended break the band had taken since they had begun their careers in earnest with their spell at the MacPhail cottage. It was a striking irony that the tour that had put Phil's marriage under such strain was the very reason that they were now able to put things on hold for a lengthy stretch. In the past Genesis had been a struggling group, desperately trying to establish itself as a worldwide force, hence the problems that arose when Peter and Steve wanted to give time to other interests away from the group – the band needed to maintain its intense work schedule if it was to achieve its goals. Now, with . . .*And Then There Were Three*. . . becoming a worldwide hit album consolidated by their tour, Genesis were an internationally renowned act, able to devote time to things other than the group. This had been Phil's hope when he first agreed to the tour – knowing that Andrea hated to be alone and would find the year difficult, his argument had been that this would be their breakthrough year and that when he returned he would never have to commit himself to the same rigors again and be able to spend far more time at home. As she had warned, the loneliness had become unbearable for her, but now, at least, Genesis' success gave him the time to try to patch things up between them.

As Phil was setting off for Canada, Mike and Tony were making their own plans as to what they would do during his absence. Solo albums had regularly been mentioned over the years but had been forsaken in favour of the group. This enforced hiatus, however, was the perfect time to delve into a musical world away from Genesis. Tony, the most prolific writer of the three, had already found that he was amassing a large backlog of material that hadn't made it through the Genesis selection process, or which simply wasn't suitable for their albums, and the previous year had been toying with the idea of making his own record. Similarly, Mike had compiled a number of short ideas, which weren't fully formed songs and which, because of the way they had written . . .*And Then There Were Three*. . ., hadn't been worked on by the rest of the band.

Tony was the first to enter the studio, using David Hentschel as producer. Following Genesis' example, he chose to record *A Curious Feeling* outside the country at Abba's Polar Studios in Stockholm, where Led Zeppelin had made *In Through The Out Door*. The trap that the majority of seventies solo albums had fallen into was one of self-indulgence – the drummer with a drum-heavy album, the guitarist with one featuring innumerable guitar solos, etc. – and this was something of which Tony was well aware, combating it with his customary preference for good songwriting over any musical histrionics. Pleased with the chance to put some of his extra songs on record he also saw it as a learning process that could benefit both himself and Genesis and he seized the opportunity for possible experimentation.

The bedrock decisions that he made before recording were with regard to personnel and instrumentation. Always a twelve-string guitar player, having sometimes used it in composition – the opening of 'Supper's Ready', for instance – Tony wanted to investigate his capabilities as a lead and rhythm player and was also ready to take on the bass duties, a real test borne out of his mistrust of session players. This left him to recruit a drummer and a vocalist. The drummer was easily found as he called Genesis cohort Chester Thompson into the fray, but the singer was another matter. As he had doubts about his singing voice, deciding that he was incapable of giving a convincing performance – although *The Fugitive* was later to give the lie to that claim – it was important that Tony didn't use anyone who had a very well-known name as that would detract from his 'ownership' of the record. His very real reservations regarding solo records which feature singers other than the artist himself – giving the record an identity crisis – had in the past put Tony off the idea of making his own record. Finally taking the plunge, Tony felt that Kim Beacon might fit the bill, having heard him with String Driven Thing and aware that he would respond well to the slightly R. & B. feel of some of the songs.

After the constraints of the last Genesis project, Tony gave himself a free run at his solo record with a greater emphasis on moods and atmospheres and introducing a higher percentage of instrumental passages than could be found on the recent Genesis album. These pieces were almost minimalist in parts, while other sections were so evocative, so vivid and dramatic they would have made superb film music. 'I sort of drift away from Genesis. We may have a done a minute's worth but I drew it out to about seven and went a lot further with the atmosphere I created,'[58] – a very rewarding but commercially limiting exercise! A number of evolving musical themes unwound over the course of the record, complementing beautifully a typically intriguing storyline which ran through it – the concept album strikes back! The lyrical idea was reasonably simple and featured the story of a man consciously losing his mind, a story which, Tony was at pains to explain, was in no way autobiographical.

Increasing his knowledge of production work was a priority of this first solo foray and there was a roughness to some of the music, though this was in part a result of Tony's lack of familiarity with some of the instruments – some guitar parts were done a number of times while Chester coached him through the bass playing. At the end of the sessions, Tony was able to put out a fine album that showed that he was more than willing to take musical chances rather than trot out the old Genesis sound. In spite of this there was criticism that the album sounded too much like Genesis, an accusation against which he was quick to defend himself: 'As the keyboard player of Genesis you do tend to define the sound of the group to a large extent.'⁵⁸ Clearly it was not a case of self-theft but rather an inevitability – he was one-third of the group, Genesis had just produced their most keyboard-orientated album to date and he was the band's major writer, after all! In addition, as he had chosen to play so many instruments, he deliberately kept the guitar parts simple which emphasized the keyboards in the way that . . .*And Then There Were Three*. . . had done, but these were superficial similarities and those prepared to listen to *A Curious Feeling* were soon aware of the differences.

Tony was clearly happy with the results and found it an educational and stimulating process. It also demonstrated that just because he had previously restricted his activities to Genesis, it did not mean he wasn't as musically ambitious as the others in the band, alluding to Steve and Peter's premature departures by saying, 'It was nice to do [my] own music while still being part of the group.'⁴ Tony also adds that the time was now right for solo work – 'a window appeared for me to do the album'.⁴ Attacked by the critics on the basis that it was (a) a solo record, (b) a solo record by a member of Genesis and (c) a concept album, the public at least gave it a chance and the album charted very respectably at number twenty-one, a similar position to Steve Hackett's recent *Spectral Mornings* release.

If Phil had the highest profile simply by virtue of being the band's lead singer and Tony received the greatest respect from the Genesis cognoscenti as a result of his extensive writing credits on their recent albums, Mike was rather more of an unknown quantity and could approach his début solo record with intrepid anticipation. Only recently coming into his own as a composer of complete songs, he had generally worked in partnership with one or other member of the band, bringing in bits of ideas and then fleshing them out in improvisation or by grafting his ideas on to theirs. To have to write a complete album from scratch was a stiff challenge, but as he has often said a challenge brings out the best in him. Nevertheless, he was rather less sure of an audience for his album than Phil and Tony might have been so this represented a voyage of discovery which in many ways couldn't have come at a better time. Having only just become a fully fledged lead guitarist on stepping into Steve's shoes, a solo record provided a convenient forum for him to develop his style further. 'My motivation was to uncover my own talents. I have never in the past had the confidence to plan a whole operation from beginning to end and do it.'⁷³

Hearing impressive reports from Tony regarding the facilities at Polar, Mike felt that would be a good place to record and ferried his team of session musicians out to Stockholm. He employed David Hentschel as co-producer, renewing his partnership with Anthony Phillips – taking a break from his solo career – who contributed keyboards and moral support! Simon Phillips (no relation) took over the drum kit and Noel McCalla sang, Paul Carrack (later to become a member of Mike and the Mechanics) having originally been pencilled in for the task. Legendary in Genesis circles for the collection of 'bits' that he had written, Mike needed a theme with which to tie them together. As a consequence side one took the form of a concept piece, 'Smallcreep's Day', based on a book by Peter Currell-Brown which Tony had suggested he read – a section of fairly short musical ideas glued together by the lyrics which detailed the story of a factory worker who didn't know what the end product of what he was making was and who was determined to find out. The second side of the album was made up of songs – some excellent, including 'Time And Time Again' and 'Every Road' – which dovetailed snugly with the more disparate musical ideas of the 'Smallcreep's Day' side, its lead off single 'Working In Line' carrying an infectious hook which made its lack of chart success rather surprising. On the more instrumental side of things, 'Out Into The Daylight' thundered along on a wave of axe-hero adrenalin(!) and can still rank with anything that he's put on record.

If Mike's songwriting had come along leaps and bounds, then his guitar playing was astonishing. Here were examples of an assurance that had been lacking at times on . . .*And Then There Were Three.* . . . The decision to involve Ant was completely vindicated as the two plotted and conspired to arrive at some enthralling keyboard and guitar combinations while Mike was able to coax superb performances from Simon and from Noel, who produced some very emotive vocals. At the end of the day, Mike had proved himself to all with a quite superb album very strong on well-rounded songs which was, one suspects, a surprise even to Mike himself. Charisma were concerned about his public profile, however, and to ensure good sales stickered the cover with 'A Genesis Solo Album'. While making people aware of just who had made the record – it reached number thirteen on its February release – this did little to establish Mike as a separate entity from the rest of the band, a point confirmed in Hugh Fielder's review of the album. Generally favourable in tone, noting that 'several of the instrumental passages had me swooning', his overall view was that there was 'nothing unexpected'[74] about the album, which is rather harsh on much of the 'Smallcreep's Day' section. As with *A Curious Feeling*, there were similarities with Genesis to which Mike happily admitted, but he rationalized that 'The first album that you do away from the group will be the closest to it – you have to put your feet down somewhere. Next time, I'll be braver and move away more from Genesis.'[64] All the same, 'it's an incredible boost to realize that I can do it.'[73]

While Mike and Tony were busy writing and recording Phil was, of course, in Vancouver. Once there, his first reaction was to look for a new house and then think about making his own record. Despite the initial optimism, he soon realized that the marriage was working no better in Canada than it had in England and that the situation was irretrievable. 'I came back after a couple of months but by then they were well ensconced in their albums. I was on my own and wanting something to do.'[4] Recording with Brand X in April was his immediate solution, working on their most commercial album, *Product*, which was followed later in the year by a tour; but even then, he still had a yawning gap to fill. In time-honoured fashion he went to work on some sessions, including one for Dave Greenslade and then for John Martyn on his wonderful opus *Grace And Danger*. John was going through similar domestic difficulties and he remembers the sessions vividly. 'We became really close friends. We were both going through divorces at the same time so we just got on. It was great fun, you know, like Heartbreak Hotel, taking turns on the phone . . . "darling please" . . . all that . . . everyone's the same!'[75] Another session was for Pete Townshend, shortly after the death of the Who's drummer, Keith Moon. 'I actually asked Townshend if I could join the Who at one point. I was doing these sessions and I said, "If you need a drummer, I'll make myself available," but he'd already asked Kenney Jones.'[76] Despite these sessions, Phil was suffering from itchy feet, and played some gigs with Peter Gabriel, including shows at Aylesbury Friar's and the Reading Festival which featured duets on 'Mother Of Violence' and 'The Lamb Lies Down On Broadway'. Phil agreed to do some drumming on Peter's upcoming third solo record and was booked to play a few sessions at the Townhouse in London. He was very excited by some of Peter's new ideas, thinking that he might be able to get things moving, and remarking that 'Pete, left to his own devices, will take for ever and he'll do something great, but sometimes he's too stubborn!'[4]

The Townhouse in London's Shepherd's Bush was a Virgin

Records flagship that had been built to house some of the latest technology. The engineer on Peter's album was Hugh Padgham who had been involved in the actual construction of the studio. Says Padgham, 'I was sick of hearing records that sounded like they were made in cardboard boxes, I wanted live sounds on records. We built a live room and over a period I evolved some ideas about recording drums there. Phil was the last part of the jigsaw, especially as Peter gave him the time to experiment.'[4] One of Peter's experiments was to record drums without any cymbals which gave a totally different sound and which immediately caught Phil's ear. 'I was sitting in the drum room just tuning the drums. While I was doing that Hugh and Steve Lillywhite [the producer] were starting to fool around with noise gates and compressors and the sound was starting to happen in the headphones so I started playing a pattern. Pete said, "That's great, do that for ten minutes." At the end of the session I told Pete that if he didn't want it, I'd have it – he didn't really have a song, he was going to find one to fit to the rhythm. He had this song called "Intruder" which he adapted.'[33] When Peter's third album eventually came out in the summer of 1980, 'Intruder' was a startling opener with a drum track unlike anything ever heard before, a spacy, ambient, live sound. The drum pattern was credited to Phil and was the birth of the 'Phil Collins Drum Sound' on which some of his later success was to be founded.

As there was still plenty of time for Phil to sit at home on his own, he began to involve himself in writing songs. He'd recently taken delivery of some eight-track recording gear – used to record both 'Wal To Wal' and 'Soho' on *Product* – as well as being the recipient of one of the very first Roland drum machines when Genesis visited Japan the previous year. With his own drum kit, piano and synth set up in his spare bedroom, he had a studio where he could come up with a collection of impressive-sounding demos, most of which detailed his state of mind at the time. This was the first batch of songs that he'd completed, following on from '. . .And So To F. . .' earlier in the year on the Brand X album, having in the past generally limited himself to collaborations. Now he had a whole album's worth of tunes available in demo form, most of which he intended to put forward for the next Genesis project. Some of these were given an airing in 1979 on Capital Radio's *Mummy's Weekly* presented by Nicky Horne, including 'Misunderstanding' and 'Please Don't Ask' which were later to appear on *Duke*. Though Phil was happy to play these tunes to the others, because of their very personal nature he had quite definite ideas as to how he wanted them to sound and would only release them if they were to his satisfaction. In essence, they were *his* songs.

There was a renewed air of excitement surrounding the band when they returned to work on their tenth studio album, a freshness generated by the break they'd had from one another. Right through their career they had been on the record-tour-record-tour treadmill with gaps of mere weeks between projects, the three living in one another's pockets and seemingly, by 1978, making albums almost from habit. By the end of the 1978 world tour there was a genuine sense of frustration in their public statements, largely regarding their workload, but there was also perhaps a personal staleness brought about by their enforced closeness. Absence had indeed made the collective heart grow fonder, but, just as important, Tony and Mike were keen to put into action the lessons they'd learned during the course of their extra-curricular activities. One of these lessons was not to take each other for granted. Mike admitted that in the past 'I have avoided lots of things because there was someone else around to do them,'[73] but the experience of having to decide on drum and keyboard parts, production values and vocal performances, gave him more of an insight into how important Phil and Tony were, and vice versa.

Rehearsals began at Phil's house in the autumn of 1979 when Mike and Tony visited to take a look at his new recording equipment that was set up in the spare bedroom. Mike recalls, 'The music room was great, but it was a bit small for all of us, but we kept walking past his bedroom which was a great size.'[77] Bowing to the inevitable, Phil moved into the spare room and put the gear into the main bedroom where Genesis began to rehearse what was to become *Duke*.

Initially they listened to the songs that were available. Phil had his batch over which he was very protective, while Tony and Mike were obviously short of material having just completed their own albums. As they had already discussed the idea of writing more material as a band, this paucity of songs was less of a problem than it might have been. Writing as a band, new songs came very quickly, Mike pointing out the benefits of the break: 'We've come back fresh for the group to do group material, it's given us a new burst of energy.'[77] The improvisations gave rise to some of the strongest work they'd done for a long while, illustrating very plainly the importance of writing together and the peculiarly individual quality this lent to Genesis. It also caused them to re-assess just how they should continue to operate.

For reasons of time as much as anything else, they agreed that each member should have two songs on the album, Tony having a third with the linking 'Guide Vocal' section along with 'Cul-De-Sac', a fairly traditional Genesis anthem 'about the demise of the dinosaur' (prog-rock perhaps!) and 'Heathaze' which represented the more complex side of the band. Mike contributed the powerful 'Man Of Our Times' and the beautiful ballad 'Alone Tonight', and Phil gave up 'Misunderstanding' and the almost painfully introspective 'Please Don't Ask'. In spite of the quality of the individual pieces, it was the group-written material that lit the fire under the album. It wasn't merely the quality and execution of the songs that was so exciting, it was the spirit and attitude behind them. The fact that Phil, Mike and Tony had got together to write in the way that had created so many of Genesis' greatest moments was sufficient to set fans drooling, but better than that, and more important for the band's longevity, they were loving every minute – 'It was a rebirth of Genesis,'[4] is Phil's summary, 'there's a chemistry in the band that works'.[78] Such an asset was crystallized in the making of the album. 'I've lived with Mike and Tony for ten years and the relationships have grown up. We don't need to play games any more, we just get on and do it.'[79]

The three were united in their approval of the new work ethic and the ease with which it operated. 'We hadn't done much group writing since *A Trick Of The Tail* whereby we sit down and jam for hours and a bit develops until it becomes a song,' said Mike. 'I think that's very often our stronger stuff. With me and Tony having done solo albums, it means that you don't come to the group with millions of songs thinking, "This is all I can get out this year, let's get a lot of them on." You're a bit freer to use some bits which start from nothing but often become the best things. It really benefited from that and I think we should do that in future.'[64] In many ways, it was a sensible return to the group ideal – it is logical that that group should reflect the tastes and ideas of all its members, something which can best be achieved by them working together – the return of the songwriters collective! In that simplistic sense, the album marked a return to their early days, feeling like a real 'band album' yet irrefutably a modern record reflecting the unique fusion of styles and tastes that they'd always worked towards.

The songs came together under the blanket working title of *Duke*. 'At the end, we felt that the album was a lot more direct and harder-edged than for a while and we thought "Duke" summed up that mood, so we used it as a title,'[77] Mike explained. This material did make up a pretty impressive return to business – it was as if they'd never been away, so assured was the music. The playing side of the group had not been stretched to such an extent since Peter's time but Mike was now thoroughly at ease with his dual role following the consolidation that *Smallcreep's Day* had provided, and Phil's singing was improving with every outing. The new songs were designed to use these growing talents to the full. The beauty of improvisation was that whatever elements were especially strong in the group at the time would naturally come to the fore and each song would contain input from all members, rather than, say, a song by Tony being short on rhythmic punch or perhaps one of Phil's excluding ideas that a more gifted keyboard player would bring to it. The music on *Duke* very definitely played to the group's strengths but there were still surprises a-plenty, not least the pounding aggression that was on show.

'Behind The Lines' opened things up with a pungent instrumental burst before 'a Supremes feel crept in',[20] as Tony put it. The song then went straight into 'Duchess' which was built around a very soft, almost disco-style drum-box pattern, the first time Genesis had used a drum machine. The song was constructed from there into a huge wall of sound and it remains one of Tony's favourites, despite, or perhaps because of, its failure as a single – 'It was an important song, it's very simple but it has almost as much emotion as "Supper's Ready". We'd learned to abbreviate things by then!'[4] Next of the group songs was the first UK single 'Turn It On Again', which featured a simulated brass section courtesy of Tony, and which indicated Phil's desire to further loosen Genesis' music, introducing a funkier dimension à la Earth, Wind and Fire. On release it became a big hit (number eight), allowing them to appear on *Top of the Pops* in person for the first time – history shows that they did not repeat the black and white clothing theme they had chosen to wear had 'The Silent Sun' catapulted them on to national TV – but more importantly bearing witness that the UK hadn't forgotten them during their sabbatical. The album came to a climax with a 'fabulous, simply fabulous', instrumental, 'Duke's Travels', an appropriate title for a piece that incorporated Scottish, Arabic and English elements. Of these archetypal Genesis blow-outs, ranging from 'Los Endos' through 'Second Home By The Sea' and parts of 'Domino' towards the most recent 'Fading Lights', the 'Duke's Travels' and 'Duke's End' passage remains the most affecting and impressive, sadly missing from their live sets of late. It was a fittingly tumultuous conclusion to an album that was to become Genesis' first UK number one.

It was clear to those who were interested that Genesis had bounced back refreshed and with a wardrobe full of new ideas, but the press were dismissive, seemingly drawing on the same reviews they'd used for the last four or five albums, simply substituting the song titles. They dismissed Genesis as artless art-rockers, pompous prog-rock bores and calculating clever-trevors. Even Hugh Fielder in *Sounds* was less than enthusiastic, concluding that *Duke* showed 'no radical changes, but you don't expect that by now'.[80] The music had gone in a new direction (considerably more belligerent, if nothing else) but many were fooled by the surface sheen applied by David Hentschel's production – aided further by the high-tech surroundings at Polar – an undeniable point of reference between this LP and its predecessors. Phil reacted with some anger to the lazy journalism that abounded, explaining the changes in attitude at length whenever possible. Owing to his personal circumstances he had invested a great deal of his time in the album and told *Sounds*, 'I do feel very close to *Duke*. It's the first album we've done that I've had the time and inclination to put myself into completely.'[79] As a result, he wasn't going to let anyone put it down lightly. 'There are a lot of new areas that we never covered before, soundwise and psychologically. It's looser than anything we've done.'[73] Dismissing the constant comparisons with their contemporaries, he said, 'I do feel that Tull are redundant, I can't think of anything Led Zeppelin have done in recent years that's progressed them. I find Floyd very boring – there's more substance in what we're doing.'[62] While Phil's views may not have won him too many friends, there was a great deal of truth in what he said; Genesis were the only band to go the distance with their artistic integrity intact.

In mitigation of some press comment it was an album of two halves, as the group material put the other songs somewhat in the shade. They toyed with the idea of having the group material on one side with the solo songs on the other but quickly decided against it. 'We found it made a very badly balanced album,' reasoned Mike. 'All the more driving, powerful stuff came from the group compositions and group playing and the other side would have been softer songs so we decided to split it up.'[64] It also neatly side-stepped the problem they'd faced with *The Lamb Lies Down On Broadway* where no one paid attention to the songs but rather to the album as a whole. There was no such problem, however, when the album was presented in concert, playing all the group songs together plus Tony's 'Guide Vocal' in the same order as on the album. When one remembers that the tour began just before the album came out – shades of America 1974 – the 'Duke Suite' was a monumental success, carrying all before it, becoming as integral a part of the set as hoary old favourites like 'Dancing With The Moonlit Knight' or 'The Carpet Crawl'. This was the final confirmation that the magic of Genesis did indeed lie in the three of them working together as a unit.

Returning to the concert stage was the centrepiece of the year. True to their word after the last tour in 1978, they decided to tone down their show, go back to basics and to play the UK. Mike, with classic understatement, said, 'We felt we owed England an extensive tour, a thank you to all the fans.'[64] That thank you comprised some forty-odd dates, taking in venues such as the Lyceum Ballroom, Birmingham Odeon, Aylesbury Friar's Club, Newcastle City Hall, Liverpool Empire and the Theatre Royal, Drury Lane. Visiting every corner of the UK, this was the hottest ticket in years with every venue besieged by punters who queued overnight in the February cold to get a glimpse of their heroes. Unlike the previous UK gig at Knebworth Park where 100,000 had seen them, this time the biggest venue was London's Hammersmith Odeon with a capacity of less than 3000. The shows were triumphant, the band, which still included Daryl and Chester, firing on all cylinders night after night. The production was designed to fit the venues but it still comprised 367 lights of which 80 were aircraft landing lights. The gigs were intense, emotional events on both sides of the stage as Phil described his approach to them: 'I find it difficult to do anything less than better than I did the night before just because it's an on-going thing. You have to think of the set in the same way, dare I say it, as you would titillate a woman – you have to reach some kind of climax. Hopefully!'[66]

The Genesis year reached its climax in the summer as they returned home from another tour of the States which had seen them again play at the Roxy in Los Angeles as well as Madison Square Gardens. America welcomed them with arms as open as their British counterparts, having put 'Misunderstanding' high in their singles chart. Phil, Mike and Tony had skilfully re-invented the idea of Genesis and were keen to continue, laying a longer term strategy than was usual, including the purchase of their own recording studio in deepest Surrey. Plans were afoot for them to begin work on their next album in November, the following few months left free to pursue individual interests. For Phil, that meant returning to work on his demos, fleshing them out into a fully-fledged début solo album. For the short unspectacular man with the beard, things would never be quite the same again.

CHAPTER FIFTEEN

'Like it or not'

Unlike Mike and Tony, Phil was adamant that he should open his solo career on a very distinct footing, placing clear daylight between himself and Genesis. There were obvious reasons for so doing, not least in terms of the music itself. Much of what was to become *Face Value* had little in common with what the group was doing: it was musically simpler and lyrically more personal. Consequently Phil was sure that it could reach a wider audience than the one which religiously bought any Genesis-related product. It was very important that he be portrayed as a separate artist since so many people already had set views on Genesis. If the marketing and overall presentation of the album could help them to shed their preconceptions about him as an individual, so much the better.

One of the cornerstones of his strategy was to get a new record company – since *Trespass*, all of Genesis' records had been released by Charisma as had Tony's and Mike's albums and even those by Brand X, Peter Gabriel and Steve Hackett. By 1981, Charisma Records meant 'Genesis Records' so it was vital that he got a deal with someone else to illustrate his break away from the fold. To achieve the necessary distance, he signed a long-term contract with Virgin Records – who, ironically, were to take over Charisma Records in 1983! He told *Melody Maker*, 'I think *Face Value* has great potential to appeal to more people than those who like Genesis – I thought for the casual buyer it would help if it was on a different label.'[76]

Those casual buyers also found many other elements to attract them on a musical and lyrical level – there were few of the intense instrumental passages or long songs that turned some away from the band and there were plenty of catchy hooklines. That aside, the tone of the lyrics struck a particularly strong chord with thirty-somethings around the world – ' "If Leaving Me Is Easy" and "You Know What I Mean" are a conversational thing, people who've heard them say, "That's what I feel!" '[81] It opened up to the audience a whole new side of Phil's personality. Though Genesis had recorded some intensely emotional and passionate music over the years, little had been on a one-to-one level; *Face Value* was the complete antithesis of this: 'I spent two years going through the divorce just writing and recording and the songs came out of that period. It did serve as a feeding ground – I almost started to thrive on being depressed. I wanted to call it *Interiors* but Woody Allen did the film and I wanted to call it *Exposure* but Robert Fripp did the album, so Jill my girlfriend came up with the title which seemed to say what the album's about, an exposure of my ideas and feelings.'[81] He also agreed that 'My solo career was the direct result of being thoroughly miserable!'[82]

That baring of the soul gave rise to other new departures for Phil. Unwilling to go through an 'interpreter' he produced the record himself. 'I did my album at home on eight-track which I transferred to twenty-four-track later. It was very relaxed with a bit of spirit and emotion as opposed to clocking in and clocking out, so I had the spirit, the foundations on tape and then got the right people to come in and add their bits.'[81] The right people included Eric Clapton, Stephen Bishop, Shankar, Daryl Stuermer, Alphonso Johnson, Ronnie Scott and, most strikingly of all, the horn section from Earth, Wind and Fire – something hinted at on Genesis' last album with its occasional simulated brass sections. 'I was very flattered with the horns. They do EWF, the Jacksons and the Emotions but they don't do anything else. And here I was, young white boy, and they're playing with me. I was really chuffed!'[76]

Phil's approach to the record was 'You can listen to it and if you like it, you like me – if not, you don't really like where I'm at.'[81] His involvement with the record was total, playing as many instruments as possible, producing it, handwriting the sleeve notes and deciding on the cover – 'It's a very stark photograph of me, as close up as you can get without seeing up my nose!'[81] – to get across the intimate message of the record. There was little question that Phil's album would fare better saleswise than Mike's and Tony's – he was a better known personality, he performed the vocals and the material was blatantly (though not calculatingly) more commercial. 'It's an album of music I like to listen to. I listen to a lot of diverse styles from Steve Bishop to Weather Report,'[81] he protested when accused of aiming purely for a hit album. Nevertheless, he could look forward to its release with confidence, having compiled a thoughtful and open début album which traced some of his musical roots – an off-the-wall cover of the Beatles' 'Tomorrow Never Knows', through the fusion of 'Droned', past a dance version of 'Behind The Lines' to the John Martyn feel of 'This Must Be Love'. There wasn't a duff song but much depended on how the press reacted to it, a fate he awaited with some trepidation as he returned to work with Genesis in November 1980.

One of the problems that has beset artists down the ages is studio time and, more directly, its enormous cost. Once studio time is booked, you have to pay for it whether it's being used creatively or not, which tends to force artists to finish tracks even when there's no spark. The solution is to own your own studio – once you've built it and equipped it, there are only the running costs to worry about, negligible when compared with the fees of major commercial studios throughout the world. If you have your own studio when nothing's happening, you just stop and go on to something else without that pressure of time and money. Having recorded their last three albums out of the country for largely financial reasons, Phil recalls, 'We decided to live here, record here, pay the taxes, to hell with it,'[56] adding, 'We'd always wanted to have a place where we could rehearse, record and write and not have to worry about booking ahead.'[83] Since Genesis were finally in the black in a big way, the time was right to purchase their own facility.

Fisher Lane Farm in deepest Surrey is almost on the doorsteps of the three band members. In 1980 the farmhouse boasted an adjoining cowshed which immediately caught their eyes, deciding that that was exactly the spot for a new high-tech studio! The property took some time to convert and wasn't ready when the band started work on their next record, so they set up in the farmhouse and began to rehearse.

Rehearsals went very well until they suddenly found themselves on a musical road to Damascus. Mike: 'We wrote a lot of songs and we looked at them and we found that we'd written songs like ones we'd done before. We were becoming a caricature so we threw all that away and worked on the ones that were a little different. Our only conscious change was on *Abacab*, I think we broke with the past then, it was an important moment in our career when we moved on.'[4] Phil, undeniably more confident than ever before and having a greater input recalls, 'We deliberately said, "Would we normally do it this way? Yes? Right, we're not going to do that." '[84] Tony agrees that 'on *Abacab* we consciously tried to avoid our clichés',[85] insisting that even thirteen years after 'The Silent Sun', 'we didn't want to repeat ourselves, we wanted to expand ourselves'.[85]

Following the renewed group-writing process on *Duke*, *Abacab* completed the change with each individual having just the one track, the rest were Banks/Collins/Rutherford efforts, thus the album was the first where the input was precisely one-third from each member. The spark of creativity that was unleashed by their new attitude to writing, to Genesis and to one another, let loose a torrent of ideas and soon they had a double album's worth of material, despite throwing an hour of material away! They decided to hold back some songs for a later EP release, conscious that a double record of brand new music was a lot for people to assimilate, especially when it marked such a radical change.

While writing the new songs, Phil's début single, 'In The Air Tonight' came out to mass approval. The 'paleolithic thud'[76] of the drums – a similar sound to that he'd used on Gabriel's 'Intruder' – and the 'ghost of a melody [that] slipped its hands under your shirt buttons and on to your heart'[76] placed the single comfortably into the upper reaches of the singles charts, paving the way for the album release. Picking up on Phil's ideas, Virgin cleverly advertised *Face Value* with the slogan 'If you thought you knew this man . . . think again' and journalists and public alike complied. Allan Jones in *Melody Maker* warned his readers that 'preconceptions tend . . . to blur the image, distort the outline: it would be easier for us both if you left yours at the door.'[86] If only he himself could apply that enlightened liberal attitude to Genesis, 'notoriously soporific pomp-rock megastars', as he termed them. On Phil's solo version of 'Behind The Lines', Jones admitted, 'I don't have a clue about the way this tune sounded when Genesis first recorded it on *Duke*, but I suspect it pales comprehensively beside this version.'[86] No preconceptions there! When limited to the tunes, Jones' review was that of the most zealous convert – 'You feel like someone's just burgled your heart' and 'Your heart would have to be built like a brick shithouse not to feel stirred by it'.[86] Those kinds of review were echoed around the world, *Face Value* went to number one and Phil had become a solo star. Apart from a week away to do the required press, TV and radio interviews, however, it made little difference to Genesis – at this stage they were so immersed in and excited by the making of *Abacab*, it would have taken an act of God to stop them.

The songs for the album now complete, they were ready to enter their new studio and begin putting it on to tape. Following on from Phil's experience, they decided to produce the album themselves using just an engineer for the technical side. As they'd intimated after *Duke*, the time had come to move away from David Hentschel's style of production, which had given the music a very lush, polished feel but which did little to refute press claims that they were totally removed from 'real' music-making. There was no animosity in the split, Mike describing Hentschel as a 'very important and valuable contributor. [We have] a very compatible way of thinking'.[64] Phil reinforced the new motivation and style behind Genesis with 'We wanted a change from David, just new blood,'[4] believing they had got too involved with production techniques in the 1970s. This time 'We tried to recapture the "spirit of the moment" idea, like in the sixties.'[87] The choice of engineer was fairly straightforward – it had to be Hugh Padgham. Phil had been very impressed with his work on Gabriel's third album, crediting him with the co-development of the drum sound that was such a part of 'Intruder', and had asked him to engineer *Face Value* where he again acquitted himself well. The logical extension was for him to go to work on *Abacab*, an ambition realized for Hugh: 'I was a huge fan at school and then after I left, I kept up with their records, so it was a real honour to work with my heroes!'[4] Though recording was initially fraught with technical teething problems, everyone quickly got into their stride and began to produce a Genesis record totally different to anything that had gone before.

The method of self-production signalled a shift in the texture and colour of the album and the songs themselves. Where before the band had been at the centre of a swirl of sound, *Abacab* cut them adrift in an empty landscape, leaving them to fill in whatever gaps they chose. The record was, according to Mike, all about 'sounds and feelings. It's got a lot of space, it sounds more like we do in the rehearsal room.'[84] Having dispensed with the services of a trained producer, Genesis were no longer slaves of technology: 'It's our least technical album,' enthused Banks. 'The strength is in the basic feel of the tracks, not the playing.'[85] The songs had a far harsher, rougher edge to them with, as Phil joked, 'less gloss, more emulsion!'[84] While Genesis weren't quite a garage band yet – unless it was a double garage with a couple of new cars in it – they had a bite to their new material that many artists ten years younger might have coveted. Hugh also brought a breath of fresh air to the proceedings as, unlike David Hentschel who had been 'very keyboard-orientated, I was more interested in rhythmic things'.[4] Coupled with Phil's increasing input to the band – 'It's always been a democratic thing but maybe my two pennyworth might be worth more now'[88] – the balance shifted very much away from the synth washes that had dominated Genesis albums over recent years, and the group aggression that had been straining to break through on *Duke* was finally unleashed.

Arrangements were less complex too, songs being written from scratch and built up gradually, arrangements forming almost by osmosis. They key to it all was the writing, however: 'We made a very conscious effort to do things together,' reiterated Tony. 'We did more group writing which is what we feel we do best. With . . .*And Then There Were Three*. . . so much of it was written before recording and in some ways it was the least satisfying album – writing together gives the group a reason to exist and it gives you a stronger feel for the album.'[4] Owning the studio was also a help – since they were going far more for feel than technical execution, if there was no emotion, there was nothing. As they no longer had to force ideas, a lot of material that would have previously been lost prevailed. 'We did lots of different versions of "Who Dunnit?" and we did a really nasty version of it that everyone suddenly picked up on and we honed that into a song,'[84] says Phil of an idea that probably wouldn't have survived in a commercial studio. Even the mixing process was changed: rather than going for a definitive version of a song, 'We did lots and lots of versions of different songs and lots and lots of mixes and chose the one at the last minute.'[88]

Prior to the release of *Abacab*, there were rumours that this album was going to be different. In the interviews for *Face Value*, Phil had said, 'We're writing modern music . . . things are becoming more basic.'[89] Reflecting on the success of the marketing of his record, he added, 'I'd love Genesis to get a different record label. I don't want to upset Charisma . . . but there are people who should have heard *Duke* and would have liked it, but they weren't really given a chance. They need an excuse.'[89] Phil indicated in his parting shot that Genesis were a brand new proposition – 'I can't really expect anyone who liked us in 1972 to like us now'[89] – a pronouncement that caused much wailing and gnashing of teeth among the Genesis faithful awaiting the new album, an anguish heightened by gossip that a potential name change for the group was on the cards to further erase preconceptions.

The lead-off single, an edited version of 'Abacab', didn't cause too many tremors – the latest in a line of sharply crafted pop songs with a very definite sixties feel, it sailed into the top ten. The real test came with the release of the album and to make sure there would be no misunderstanding as to the profound metamorphosis that they'd undergone, new cover artwork was commissioned to distance *Abacab* from their other work. While the *Duke* cover had been simplistic to indicate a shift in mood, this was something else again! Rather than the classically descriptive artwork on albums such as *Selling England By The Pound* or *A Trick Of The Tail*, *Abacab* came clad in a collage of colours. Tony expands on the idea of both sleeve and name: 'We used an abstract cover and title because there's an emphasis on the music rather than the lyrics.'[85] In a break with a tradition that went all the way back to *From Genesis To Revelation*, there was no lyric sheet included, though they did relent sufficiently to include one in the UK tour programme later that year.

Following Phil's example with *Face Value*, the group were happy to involve themselves in psychological games with DJs to ensure radio play for their new baby. Phil admitted, 'Sequencing the album is important, especially for America. You put your most accessible song as side one, track one because the DJ will play that first and if he likes that he'll play track two. It's frustrating but understandable that if a guy does a three- or four-hour show every bloody day fifty-two weeks a year, you can't expect him to even listen to bits of every track, he has to be lured into it.'[88] It was unusual to hear Genesis talking so openly about promotion and sales, but even Tony was heard to say, 'We're not talking about music that's supposed to be liked twenty years from now, it's supposed to be liked here and now. We don't claim to be any more esoteric than that.'[90] Coming from Tony this was incredibly revealing about the corporate state of mind, but as unexpected as hearing Van Gogh say that he was just going to knock up some sunflower pictures for Athena. Despite having received these warning shots across the bows, the punters were still to uncover myriad surprises.

Initial reaction was, to say the least, mixed. Old fans and friends in the press were stunned by the change in style and attitude and often didn't know what to make of it all. It's not hard to understand their confusion: while 'Dodo' and 'Like It Or Not' proved that some last vestiges of the old Genesis sound remained intact, a song like 'Who Dunnit?' must have caused apoplexy among the hardcore fans cowering beneath their faded *Selling England By The Pound* posters. If that wasn't enough, what were the Earth, Wind and Fire horn section doing on a Genesis album? Indeed, when Genesis dared to venture out on to the road in support of *Abacab*, in Holland they were booed – albeit good naturedly – for the first time since Peter Gabriel had asked the crowd at Friar's to boo them! By the same token, for every disenchanted old fan, there were two new ones buying a Genesis record for the first time, perhaps wooed by Phil's album and delighted to find high-quality songs of the order of 'Man On The Corner' or 'Keep It Dark'.

In hindsight, without the surrounding hysteria of the time, the album obviously represents a substantial shift even from *Duke*, but those that were offended were those that wanted to keep the band in a jar marked 1973, to be taken down for occasional inspection and for their eyes only. If they had opened their minds they would have found much to treasure, a music that was very modern but which still had a healthy historical perspective.

The title track opened with a nice encapsulation of Genesis as a writing partnership, beginning with a burst of drums, moving into a section where Mike's guitar riff was echoed by a keyboard phrase from Tony, then slipping smoothly into an extended jam where they were very definitely casting a glance over their shoulders to *The Lamb Lies Down On Broadway*. The title came from the way it was written, as Mike explained: 'The song was made up of three bits, bit A, bit B and bit C, and that was the order they were in at one time. It's not right now, but it was just a nice word and it stuck when we came to write the lyrics!'[84] For the traditionalists, 'Dodo' also offered some comfort, though even here Tony admitted, 'I wrote lyrics that sounded good rather than meaning anything – I wanted to use the voice as another instrument.'[85] Phil adds, 'We tried to rethink some of the more typical ideas like "Dodo".'[84] The constant questioning process also transformed 'Another Record', a song that had originally been kicked around during the sessions for *Duke* and which now surfaced as the album closer. The opening lulled listeners into a false sense of security with its Hackett-like guitar line before being kicked into life by Phil's drums and ending as a blues tune complete with harmonica.

The solo songs were illuminating too if one was looking for clues as to the source of the new shape. Tony's 'Me And Sarah Jane' was the most surprising of the three. 'Musically, it went through changes on a drum-box pattern which makes you play in a certain way, you can play with the tempo more. It's a lot of random ideas and then the name takes shape and a relationship develops.'[87] It is an intricate, demanding song – Tony's first dalliance with a reggae feel – that repays further investigation and which sent the album off on another tangent. 'Man On The Corner' was rather more predictable, a classic Collins ballad built around an insistent drum-machine pattern with a strong vocal but, though distinguished by Mike's lovely restrained guitar part, was a little too similar to some of the songs on *Face Value*. Finally of the solo tunes, Mike weighed in with a monumental ballad, 'Like It Or Not', another of the faint echoes of Genesis past but a superbly constructed one, the new production giving it a fresh aspect. As the song intimated, 'It was an old bit that I came across on a cassette,' but being slightly more traditional, 'it balanced the album.'[85]

The two flies in the ointment, the songs that polarized opinion, were 'Who Dunnit?' and 'No Reply At All'. There is little positive to say about the punk-rock anthem 'Who Dunnit?', except that the band liked it and that it showed they still had a sense of humour. It might have worked as light relief in the studio, and it did incorporate some of those odd noises of which Tony was especially fond, but listening to it now gives the impression that it was the tune for which the CD skip facility was invented. Originally scheduled for release as the second single from the album (a photo session being conducted with the band in convicts' suits) the idea was shelved when reason prevailed – sometimes you can be a little too different! 'No Reply At All' was a serious tune – even though it was accompanied by a tongue-in-cheek video – which featured some of the album's best work from Mike on bass and from Tony, but the lead instruments were courtesy of the Earth, Wind and Fire horn section which was seen in some quarters as proof that civilization was crumbling. It wasn't the best song they had, but it wasn't a disaster either and, having been softened up by *Face Value*, neither was it a shock. Having already worked with the horn section, Phil was keen to feature them on a Genesis record – 'It was different for the band and that can only be good. I loved doing it,'[85] he said, pointing out that 'it grew over rehearsal, written with a drum machine and crying out for a brass arrangement.'[84] Phil's enthusiasm, which contrasted with Tony's uncertainty, was picked up on by Mike who acknowledged, 'It was a big step. I was game, but it was Phil who provided the energy for it – it changed the song a lot, it really brought it to life.'[85] Mike and Phil flew out to America to supervize the session and the end result was a fine pop song and a top ten hit in the States.

In the final analysis, *Abacab* was a good album – transitional certainly and a little inconsistent, but by no means disastrous. If older fans disliked it, the reasons lay more within themselves, though Phil sympathized with their plight, remembering the resentment he used to feel when his favourite groups outgrew the confines of London's Marquee. Nevertheless this outrage indicated that they hadn't really been paying attention over the years, for as Cathi Wheatley astutely pointed out in *Sounds*, 'Post-Gabriel Genesis have progressed on every album since *A Trick Of The Tail* and *Abacab* is no exception.'[91] Genesis had never been afraid to take risks or experiment and if it didn't always work, OK, they'd tried. Indeed, fans could take great pride in the fact that Genesis were introducing a subversive element to the charts in the form of singles such as 'Keep It Dark', which was a track immensely more satisfying and challenging than the standard chart fodder. Mike recognized their dilemma: 'There's an art in keeping a band going. You either become a caricature like the Who or Status Quo or you move on which we've done and which has kept us alive. It's quite something to expect people to stay with a band for a long time – those who liked us in the early seventies probably like us less now, which is acceptable. We have to satisfy ourselves and do different stuff.'[68] Certainly making *Abacab* had given them the appetite and the energy for working together again – 'It was a very enjoyable album to make,' agreed Phil, 'that's why we keep doing it.'[84]

Concert chores were looming of course. The band restricted themselves to a three-month burst of arena activity across Europe and America, ending with seven heavily over-subscribed shows in the UK at Wembley Arena and the NEC in Birmingham just prior to Christmas. This added some fuel to the critical fire simply because a lot of the newer material didn't come across so well on stage, with 'No Reply At All' and 'Man On The Corner' palpably out of their depth in the cavernous stadiums – paradoxically, though, 'Who Dunnit?' worked splendidly, allowing Mike the brief opportunity to play drums! While 'Abacab' felt at home on stage, in general the new songs suffered the inevitable comparisons with 'Dance On A Volcano', 'Firth Of Fifth' or 'In The Cage'. Even then the introductions for Chester and Daryl received the largest ovations as Genesis fans had now come to regard them as old friends. Tony said, 'They add things to the music that aren't on the records.'[4] Chester and Phil had put together a formidable partnership over the years and Chester was giving as much to their music as he was taking from it – there is little doubt that his playing and attitude, along with that of Daryl, was a big factor in the changes that Genesis underwent. The looseness in both their playing and personalities rubbed off on Mike and Tony in particular, relaxing them and offering a different perspective on their own music.

As far as staging went, though, the tour was as staggering as ever. By providing both finance and some far-reaching suggestions as to what they required from concert lighting, the band had helped to develop a new system, Varilites, which was computer-operated, providing any number of colour combinations with unparalleled depth of colour and the ability to track like a manually operated spotlight. The sight of a bank of bright white Varilites swivelling to pick out Phil between the two drum kits during 'In The Cage' was unforgettable, though as they have now become widely available the effect has been diluted. Still, it was good to see that Genesis remained committed to the idea of giving value for money to the concert-goers and were still happy to fit in small shows. *Sounds'* Hugh Fielder caught them at New York's Savoy Theatre and gave notice that they were coming home on top form – 'While other big names have often used production gimmicks to hide their own atrophication, Genesis only use them as cream on the cake. Almost anything is possible – they have more fluidity about them now than ever before,'[92] which for a 'dinosaur super-group' was praise indeed!

The final stages of the tour were recorded and filmed for live video and album release the following year, but the Christmas shows marked an end to Genesis activity for the time being. Having answered a lot of searching questions over the course of the year, it was time for a break. Nineteen eighty-two was to be devoted, at least in part, to solo work from which they could return to Genesis, refreshed, at a later date.

CHAPTER SIXTEEN

'It's been a long long time'

Ironically, in view of 1982's dedication to mainly solo ventures, the first that was heard of any members of the group that year was the release of Genesis' '3 × 3 EP' – comprising tunes left over from the *Abacab* sessions – which secured them another *Top of the Pops* slot, the EP going to number ten. Since *Abacab*, the follow-up singles had both used unreleased instrumental tracks as B-sides, so this mopped up the remaining songs from the sessions. All three were easily good enough to have found a place on the album but had wisely been held back to make a well-rounded EP as the Beatles had done so regularly some twenty years earlier. The Beatles motif was maintained in the black and white sleeve shot which recreated the 'Twist And Shout EP', Genesis even calling in erstwhile publicity man for the Fabs, Tony Barrow, to write some sleeve notes. The main track, 'Paperlate', again involved the EWF horns with a sassy arrangement which provided a far more important contribution than on 'No Reply At All'. The song had its origins in a 1978 soundcheck, a rhythm idea arising when Phil, running through 'Dancing With The Moonlit Knight', constantly repeated the phrase 'paper late' from the song to help the sound engineers.

The other two tracks were classics. 'You Might Recall' featured an infectious jangly guitar hook with a sixties vibe and 'Me And Virgil' returned to the storytelling vein with a tale of the Old West, giving Mike the chance to play some heavier guitar than on the album. The EP even marked the reintroduction of bass pedals and twelve-string guitars. Not only was it a collection of good songs, it was also a smart marketing ploy, bringing Genesis back into the public eye just prior to the release of a double live album and a short world tour.

Three Sides Live came out to the general disinterest reserved for live albums, but sold enough to reach number two. Though it's not as strong as *Seconds Out*, it did provide yet more evidence of the way in which Genesis had reappraised themselves and were altering their stance live as well as in the studio. After the technical proficiency and note-perfect execution of the other two live records, this one captured the *atmosphere* of the gigs on the 'Abacab' tour. As *Sounds* pointed out, it was 'live in every sense – if Phil's voice wavers momentarily or Mike's guitar is a split second out, then so be it.'[93] This time Genesis were going for the bootleg effect, as the plain sleeve with stencilled title illustrated. Song selection was questionable, as was the track order, but the intensity that it generated brooked no argument. There was an added bonus for UK fans too; while the rest of the world had a final side made up of studio tracks – the '3 × 3 EP' songs plus 'Open Door' and 'Evidence of Autumn' which had been the B-sides of the *Duke* singles – the UK got a fourth side live which stretched back to ancient history with 'It' and 'Watcher Of The Skies' from the 1976 tour, 'Fountain Of Salmacis' from Knebworth 1978 – despite the sleeve notes which dated it as 1980 – and 'One For The Vine' from 1980, a real treat for the die-hards.

Better yet, the late summer saw Genesis returning to Europe and the UK for arena gigs following American shows that had featured the odd guest appearance from Bill Bruford and the EWF horns – if that wasn't enough, as they had no new studio product to promote, they used the tour to widen the scope of material they were playing, recalling such tunes as 'The Lamb Lies Down On Broadway', 'Watcher Of The Skies' and 'Supper's Ready'.

Meanwhile, in darkest Shepton Mallet, strange things were afoot. Since leaving Genesis, Peter Gabriel had been ploughing an increasingly idiosyncratic furrow, becoming heavily involved in 'world' music, a result of his increasing fascination with the use of rhythm in his songs, which he employed as the spine of the pieces as opposed to conventional melody lines. His earliest ventures, which came out on his third record in 1980 followed by the more adventurous employment of other cultures on the fourth album, pre-dated Paul Simon's *Graceland* by many years, with only David Byrne, Brian Eno and Talking Heads really delving into African music with any success at the same time. The unconventional sounds – to Western ears – that Gabriel uncovered had excited him more than anything else in years and, along with some similar enthusiasts in Bristol, he set about organizing a festival to showcase his new discoveries under the heading WOMAD – World of

Music, Arts and Dance. The festival was designed to mix traditional Western music with that from other cultures around the
world and headline acts included Peter himself, Simple Minds,
Robert Fripp and Echo and the Bunnymen who performed a
scorching set in collaboration with the Drummers of Burundi,
exactly the cultural co-operation that Peter had in mind, featuring
the Ekome Dance Company as part of his own set. The festival
showcased artists from around the globe that were totally
unknown in this country; it was hoped that Gabriel and company
would draw in the punters, who would then be turned on to these
different cultures. The festival was high on idealism and low on
realism – crowds weren't large enough, organization was chaotic
and WOMAD ended up £189,000 down. As the only 'name'
involved in WOMAD itself, Peter bore the brunt of the debtors'
complaints, actually receiving a death threat though he wasn't
personally liable for the money owed.

Hearing of Peter's plight through Tony Smith, Genesis immediately decided to help, initially agreeing to add an extra show to
their tour schedule as a WOMAD benefit to pay back the money.
Phil agreed that WOMAD 'was a brave attempt to gather together
so many acts. Unfortunately expense didn't seem to matter until
they got the bill!'[68] Keen to assist their old friend they had no
qualms in playing a show for him, but Peter wanted to get
involved. Feeling in some part responsible for the debts and desperate to get himself out of this all-engulfing hole, he offered to
take part in a reunion show. There were artistic reservations on
both sides – Genesis were trying to distance themselves from the
early seventies connotations and Peter still wanted to rid himself
of the 'ex-Genesis' tag – but it remained the only logical solution.
Milton Keynes Bowl was booked for a concert under the heading
'Six Of The Best' on 2 October, the promoters putting an unreason-
able amount of faith in the British weather.

As expected, the show caught the public imagination and
Genesis spent much of their time on tour answering questions
about the gig. Mike was very clear about the motives for it: 'It's a
charity show – great fun. It's a one-off that will work for those that
are there on the day, but we're not going to film it or record it
because it's wrong to try to make it live on.'[68] They were all quite
open that the show would be filled with mistakes but in the
atmosphere of the day it wouldn't matter – if they had to listen to
it later though, then the mistakes, the missed cues, the bum notes
would start to grate!

The other question was what would they play? According to

Collins, it would be a set of the old 'classics', which was proving to be a headache: 'Stuff like "The Musical Box", some fans might play it once or twice a week but we haven't heard the whole thing since Pete left! Fortunately, Daryl's very good at sorting things out, he teaches us the tunes!'[68] Mike agreed, 'We underestimated the workload – it's been a real crash-course to learn the songs again – there were four minutes in the middle of "The Musical Box" that we'd completely forgotten!'[68] Phil had the biggest problems to tackle, trying to remember how to drum on songs that he'd spent the last seven years singing – 'It's a lot of mental hard work to set the clocks back, I find it very hard for my hands to work the way they did then.'[68] After a couple of days' rehearsal at Hammersmith Odeon, Phil forecast, 'It'll be chaos – Pete could only just remember the words when he was in the band!'[68] As Gabriel was left at home to pore over the lyrics, Genesis let off steam by returning to their roots and playing an unannounced gig at London's Marquee where they were billed as the Garden Wall.

The morning of 2 October dawned wet – the high point of the day in terms of the weather, as from the moment the gates opened at Milton Keynes Bowl it poured with rain. The gently sloping banks of the Bowl were turned into an enormous mudbath as fans stood through the Blues Band and Talk Talk, then in their sub-Duran phase, John Martyn having inexplicably opened proceedings before two-thirds of the crowd had arrived. Although it had been wet and miserable all day, suddenly, at around seven o'clock, the sun came out – metaphorically speaking because the rain was still teeming down. Jonathan King appeared on stage to less than universal approval, then a team of pallbearers brought on a coffin from which Peter Gabriel emerged, clad in Rael's leather jacket, to belt out 'Back In NYC'. Promising to give the audience what they would expect from the combination, Peter had brought his full range of masks and had even brushed up on some stories to tell between songs. Despite the rain the 47,000-strong crowd was transported into a fantasy world as 'Six Of The Best' felt their way through 'The Musical Box', 'The Lamb Lies Down On Broadway', 'In The Cage' and 'Firth Of Fifth'; they even had time to play 'Solsbury Hill' and 'Turn It On Again', Phil and Peter embracing as they passed on stage, bringing a lump to the throat. The crowd also joined in with a rousing chorus of 'Happy Birthday' for Mike. Naturally, they closed the main set with 'Supper's Ready', as Peter donned his flower mask for one last time. In the opening passage, as Peter sang, 'It's been a a long, long, time. Hasn't it?', grown men wept and women fainted. The site was bordered with small fires, people began to sink into the mud, Peter forgot the words, nobody cared. A wonderfully warm, emotional evening was brought to a climax when Steve Hackett appeared for the encores of 'I Know What I Like' and 'The Knife' – 'The rock event of the year'[94] was how *Melody Maker* termed it. Better yet, the trendies in the press who had taken their customary élitist position over WOMAD were forced to concede that 'the patron saints of reactionary ol' rock 'n' roll'[95] had saved the day.

While Genesis had been on the road, Mike had been an indirect beneficiary as the tour coincided with the release of his second solo album, *Acting Very Strange*. He'd already gone on record as saying, 'I've got lots of bits I've not been brave enough to use – things with a rougher edge and a more basic style that I want to try next time.'[85] The music was undeniably different to *Smallcreep's Day*, more in the vein of *Abacab*. The songs were harsh in texture, using reggae, hard rock and straight pop ideas and were taut and tense, the *NME* going so far as to say, 'It bites, picks, pokes and occasionally blasts the ears as the bassist explores new uncharted area away from Genesis.'[95] The eight songs certainly weren't what you'd expect from Mike, hence the title, and though there was to be no single success the album performed respectably.

This time, Mike produced the record himself in association with Nick Launay, fresh from work with Public Image Limited and Positive Noise, and had chosen to use a number of different musicians rather than going for a band feel: Daryl helped out on guitars, Pete Phipps and Stewart Copeland on drums and Peter Robinson and Paul Fishman on keyboards. Noel McCalla maintained an involvement on backing vocals, but the lead singer this time was Mike himself. 'Being a writer, if you can sing, then you can write for your own voice which is much more helpful.'[97] In order to deal with the nervous tension arising from this dramatic step, Mike devised an unusual way of lubricating his vocal chords – two-thirds of a bottle of Remy Martin brandy a day. 'The whole album took years off my life, but I think the brandy helped! When you do sing, you just have to do it and learn by your mistakes – by the time we got to the end I wanted to start again because I learned so much. It was an interesting challenge, to be faced with something different.'[68] Mike's voice had a rough texture and it was no surprise that he'd been influenced by Pete Townshend's performance on the *Empty Glass* album, but he was adamant that 'Character is almost as important as the quality of the vocals.'[98] That character was best exemplified on 'Hideaway', a strong track, while on more up-tempo songs like 'Couldn't Get Arrested' the effect is less satisfactory.

As Mike was picking up some press coverage, Phil was probably the most visible member of the group, though in a rather unexpected guise. He had initially taken on the role of producer for John Martyn on his *Glorious Fool* album in 1981, but following the success of *Face Value* he was beginning to receive more and more offers. One of these came from Frida of Abba who wanted to make a solo record in early 1982. Keen to dip his oar into all kinds of musical waters, Phil agreed to give it a go, Frida having selected him on the basis of his first record – she'd just gone through a divorce and felt that Phil might have some sympathy for the way she was feeling and for the music she wanted to do. 'It was the first proper production I'd done in terms of being in charge of the budget, the musicians and the songs. I viewed it as a great challenge.'[99]

His next challenge was to prepare the follow-up to *Face Value* – this time all eyes would be on him, he couldn't take people by surprise any more. 'I wanted to do a record but I hadn't really written anything, so I just sat down at home and wrote specifically for it.'[68] The recording process for *Hello, I Must Be Going*, the title taken from a line in a Marx Brothers film, was largely similar to the first album – Phil made some eight-track demos at home which he then took to the Farm to complete, additional work being conducted at the Townhouse. Once again, Hugh was on board to engineer and assist with production, a partnership that has developed well down the years. 'He's a wonderful engineer and he has lots of ideas, but I am the producer more or less, it's a sixty-forty split. I see myself as a director rather than a producer, with Hugh as my cameraman, I just direct the music into certain areas that I like, though bringing in other musicians can change the direction of a song, you can suddenly hear new things in it.'[4]

As this record was to be produced to a deadline as opposed to the gradual compilation of the début, Phil chose to use a small clique of players rather than the wide selection he'd previously employed. Daryl played all the guitar parts, and bass duties were shared between John Giblin and Mo Foster, Peter Robinson contributing on keyboards, most of which Phil again did himself. The EWF section, now under the name of the Phenix Horns, was also much in evidence, which lent some of the music a *déjà vu* quality. There were strong similarities between the two solo records, though if anything the new material was stronger with a different lyrical perspective – Phil's personal life was clearly getting better as his relationship with Jill Tavelman grew stronger. By the time of the album's release, they had been living together for almost two years and so this was the first musical opportunity Phil had had to reflect on his new domestic situation. The glaring difference between the two albums was that *Hello, I Must Be Going* didn't have a signature tune à la 'In The Air Tonight' to distinguish it and so has generally been regarded as a lesser piece of work, even though it contained the cover 'You Can't Hurry Love' which went to the top of the charts – the first Genesis-related number-one single in the UK.

Tony also kept busy during the year, completing two albums. He had been offered the task of writing the soundtrack for the remake of *The Wicked Lady*, starring Faye Dunaway and Alan Bates (who had also been in *The Shout*, Tony's first taste of soundtrack writing). His music, played by an eighty-piece orchestra, was perfectly in keeping with the film and was an area of endeavour that Tony hoped he might be able to develop further in future, since there was less necessity to write that hit single and do the round of chat shows with which he was patently uncomfortable and which he attributed in no little part to the relative commercial failure of his second solo album proper, *The Fugitive*. The opening single from it, a classic pop tune, 'This Is Love', failed to get any radio play, presumably because of DJs' preconceptions. As Tony said, 'Perhaps I ought to change my name!'[22] This was particularly ironic when the following year Nik Kershaw, later to work with Tony, had great success with *The Riddle*, an LP which built on a lot of the ideas of *The Fugitive*. Things weren't helped by Tony himself: a quiet, shy person – characteristics Phil believes sometimes come across as arrogance – Tony agrees that he doesn't enjoy the videos, photo shoots and other image-making paraphernalia that increasingly surrounds musicians. Unfortunately, this means that he is a fairly faceless individual when it comes to solo work, something that these days works against record sales.

In an attempt to give the record a personality of its own, Tony followed Mike's lead and did the singing himself, handling things better. The delivery was rather aggressive on most tracks which did detract slightly but it was a good first effort with the later-period John Lennon being the most obvious reference point. Tony was still happy to stretch his audience, however, with two provocative instrumentals which were 'further down the road from what I do with Genesis, a little more bizarre,'[4] giving some obvious hints as to just what his particular input to the band sound was these days.

Solo outlets were obviously very precious to all three members, giving each an idea as to what it was like in the world outside

Genesis and breathing new life into a band that had, after all, been making records for fifteen years. The end of 1982 saw the start of a change in emphasis between solo and group work, especially for the hyperactive Phil who, having completed his second album, decided to take his songs on the road. Under the somewhat cumbersome heading of 'Phil Collins and the Fabulous Jacuzzis', he played shows in Europe and America, slotting in a few dates at London's Hammersmith Odeon before Christmas. So successful were the gigs that he returned to the States early in 1983. Tony and Mike saw their solo careers as outlets for their individual ideas and welcome chances to experiment away from the glare of publicity prior to returning to the more serious job that was Genesis, though that in no way reduced the commitment they had to their own solo work. Phil, on the other hand, perhaps as a result of his success and the increasing offers that were coming his way had a different perspective – obviously excited by the reaction to his own material and with the total control he could exercise over that aspect of his career, his activities away from Genesis were assuming more and more importance. He went on record as saying that he chose to dabble in many things and Genesis was just one of those. There was never any question of him leaving the band, but there was a definite feeling at that time that Genesis might have to fit in with his schedule rather than the other way around, and these live concerts only served to heighten that impression, the strong nightly feedback from the audiences amply demonstrating the esteem in which he was held.

As far as the group was concerned, however, he was as good as his word and by the spring of 1983 the three had reconvened at the Farm to 'dabble' in Genesis once more, with the proviso that this time there were to be no individual songs at all, and that they would begin with an entirely blank sheet of paper, no one bringing to the studio any half-finished ideas, chord sequences or guitar riffs. This album was to be all about Genesis, 1983 model.

CHAPTER SEVENTEEN

'Keep running, keep running'

Possibly the most appropriate name for any group in the history of popular music was that taken by the late eighties grebo rockers Pop Will Eat Itself. From its inception as a bastardization of jazz and blues in the 1950s, rock and roll has fed on its past, regurgitating it into an ever-so-slightly different style, tarted up with the new technology of the day and squeezed through a new, bigger, better (and more profitable) merchandizing hoop. How many imitators of the Merseybeat sound were there in the 1960s? How often and how faithfully were the Sex Pistols copied? What of the New Wave of British Heavy Metal (that's NWOBHM to you and me)? Just how many of today's 'alternative' rock bands believe that the world began with Jesus And Mary Chain – have these people never heard of the Velvet Underground? Genesis took relatively little from sources other than their own imaginations and even then they were influenced rather than plagiarists, embodying a relentless drive for innovation and originality that set them apart from the crowd. Since no one really knew what to make of such revolutionary thinking from a rock group, they were continually derided and deemed unfashionable.

Some people, however, thought that Genesis were really rather good and were inspired to form bands of their own. Some, such as the early Simple Minds, mixed that influence in with a host of others to come up with their own sound; some simply saved time by taking huge chunks of Genesis and copying them wholesale, grafting hollow theatricals on to their live shows to try to recapture the Gabriel days. Strangely, some sections of the press decided that they quite liked it and so it was that by the time Genesis were back in the studio in March 1983, they were teetering on the brink of becoming fashionable, something heightened by the acceptance that Phil had achieved in the early part of his solo career.

Though it seemed surprising to outsiders, Phil's wave of solo success had little effect on Genesis, other than increasing Phil's own confidence so that he could have a more equal say in the making of their albums, a point reached on *Abacab*. As casual listeners and the press expected a Genesis LP to be *Face Value* with louder keyboards, the group busily denied that Phil's solo career would make any difference. As Tony said, 'His success took us by surprise, but it didn't affect our working relationship. It's difficult to have illusions about someone you've worked with for so many years!'[4] It was also hard for people to grasp that Genesis were still together and intent on making an album – surely once there were solo records, particularly very successful ones, the band was past its useful life? Certainly not, was the reply, Mike Rutherford telling *Soundmaker* in early 1983: 'We do [solo things] before the frustration sets in so that we can return to Genesis with a fresh mind.'[98] Even then, there seemed little reason for Phil to continue as part of the band – little reason to anyone except Phil himself. 'I'm not a tremendous fan of what we've done, I like 40 or 50 per cent of it. With a group you carry on until you've got it right and then you leave – I still want us to get it right.'[4]

Their studio was now fully established and they were able to work there from day one which offered many advantages: 'As soon as we came up with an idea that was good, we could put it straight down on to tape and begin to develop it immediately. We've often found in the past that when you take two or three months to write before recording, you get some incredibly strong moments during the writing but which you can't recreate in the studio. It was important that we made sure that that didn't happen,'[4] states Tony, a view particularly true as Genesis continued to look towards atmospheres and moods rather than technical proficiency. One of the earliest songs that came out of the new process was 'Mama'. Tony: 'It would never have happened any other way because it had to be put on tape as soon as we'd started to write it.'[4]

In common with a number of the more recent Genesis songs such as 'Me And Sarah Jane' and 'Duchess', the character and mood of the track was established as soon as the drum-machine pattern began. For Phil, it conjured up a hot, steamy climate, providing visions of a Cuban brothel (though this image apparently did not come from any personal experience). The general thrust of the lyrics sorted, the cream on the cake came from the demonic cackle that Phil added. Engineer, and this time co-producer, Hugh Padgham remembers its inspiration came from a rather unlikely quarter: 'We were listening a lot to "The Message" by Grandmaster Flash which we all loved, which had a laugh in time with the beat of the song, which is how it evolved in "Mama".'[4]

'Mama' was a pivotal point in the making of the album and also in terms of people's view of Genesis in the 1980s. Its release as the first single from their album caused a stir because it was so far away from the norm at that time. In a chart filled with Culture Club, Wham, Spandau Ballet and similar pop fluff, it stood out a mile. The group had intended it for single release, but were surprised when it met with record company approval, being distinctly off-the-wall and six minutes in length. The single climbed to number four, their biggest UK hit, which Mike described as 'Fantastic . . . but by far the most important thing is that we've managed it with a song which is very much what we do. Our problem in the past has been that very often the best stuff we've done on an album hasn't stood a chance as a single, so we've put out songs that I've liked but have simply not been the best songs we've had at the time.'[100] Mike was surprised at the success, admitting, 'We don't make singles – it's pot luck if there's something suitable.'[64] 'Mama' was certainly suitable, the character of the song won out and it gained the success it richly deserved, which gave people the chance to reassess the band. 'Mama' was full of the sort of adventurous spirit that had seemingly disappeared from the singles charts – a powerful, passionate, challenging listen rather than aural chewing gum. Though a modern piece of music, it somehow harked back to elements of earlier Genesis, something that was ultimately true of the whole album. 'Mama' more than anything since 'Follow You Follow Me' opened up the band to a host of new followers, crucial for any group that intends to keep going. As Mike admitted, 'You lose old fans all the time – it happens with rock music, people just grow up and drift off it.'[66]

Following 'Mama', and its B-side 'It's Gonna Get Better', there was a genuine sense of anticipation for the new album. Called simply *Genesis* because it was the first to be entirely co-authored by the trio, it was released in October 1983 and contained nine new songs. Despite a lack of any real promotion – Tony was on holiday and Phil was in the States drumming with Robert Plant – the album nestled itself into the number-one slot almost as of right, an indication of just how much interest 'Mama' had generated. The consistency shown on *Genesis* certainly merited its lofty position too. If occasionally *Abacab* had smacked of being different for difference's sake, that wilful streak was kept in check this time – the songs were on the album because they had passed the group's stringent quality control.

This is not to say, however, that there were no new departures on the album. Inevitably opening with 'Mama', they then ran gleefully through a cornucopia of styles and ideas, tearing the rule book to shreds as they did so. 'That's All' was an archetypal country and western offering perfect for the local hoedown, there was a simple love ballad in 'Taking It All Too Hard', while 'It's Gonna Get Better' caught the band in sixties mood with the swirling instrumentation creating a delicious new variation on the Genesis wall of sound and the lyrics delving into the plight of the disadvantaged and the homeless (a piece of social commentary that Phil would return to years later).

The humour that has always been such an important part of the band surfaced most clearly on a couple of songs, 'Illegal Alien' and 'Just A Job To Do'. 'Illegal Alien' recalled 'Robbery, Assault and Battery' in its absurdity with a catchy hookline which attracted some ludicrous comment over its alleged racism – 'In fact it's meant to be sympathetic towards illegal aliens,'[101] Tony emphasized later. Phil's cod-Mexican accent on the song pointed the direction of the promo video, which featured the three attempting to bribe their way into America, Tony wearing an unconvincing false moustache, Phil in a remarkable wig which resembled a terminally ill hamster. The video shoot almost ended in disaster for Mike when he had to jump from a first-floor window into a moving car. 'Tony was driving and he's the world's worst. The first take, I was about to jump when he stalled the car!'[102] Staying on the wrong side of the law, 'Just A Job To Do' provided Phil with the opportunity to be a hitman for the day, Tony adding a simulated brass section as he had on *Duke*. The EWF section hadn't been asked to appear this time, the band feeling that they needed no assistance. Genesis was nowadays a reflection of the three individuals working together at that time, giving the record a character from which other contributors might detract. For the same reason, Daryl and Chester were not required for the album. Phil says, 'I would like to have two drummers on some of the tracks but when you come down to it it's much easier to go in and double track it than fly someone 5000 miles to play. Mike likes the challenge of improving and doing new things on guitar – we like to have challenges, it's good for us.'[88] Chester agrees, 'It's a pretty unique combination, it's as if there's some magic when the three of them get together.'[20]

Daryl has admitted to some initial disappointment in not having a closer involvement but has become more philosophical, conceding, 'I've played on all . . . of their solo albums, which lets me know they like what I'm doing.'[20] Indeed, the only 'outsider' allowed into the sanctum was Hugh Padgham. His relationship with the group had obviously developed and strengthened since *Abacab*: 'When we're working,' Hugh says, 'I feel like a fourth member of the group because we're working to the same end, I'm an invisible catalyst in a way.'[4]

A treat for the traditionalists arrived at the tail-end of side one of the album, an eleven-minute extravaganza in two sections, 'Home By The Sea' and 'Second Home By The Sea'. Telling the story of a haunted house, it developed into an elongated instrumental section that had all the hallmarks of the early Genesis, yet even here there were new twists – the drums were more of a driving force than in the past, the playing tighter. In Mike's view, 'It's a song we could have done five years ago, but we've done it in a newer way – the three of us jamming together always works.'[102] Though its appearance on the album was generally applauded there were suggestions that it had been included to placate the older fans who had been disappointed with *Abacab*, charges which Tony was quick to refute. 'We work on things which we collectively enjoy . . . it's important that we do things that have bite – you don't want everything to be easy on the ear. It's important to have something that's a bit more uncomfortable.'[4] Another track that was in that more awkward vein was 'Silver Rainbow', Tony's odd keyboard effects combining with the repeated thrashed drum figure which propelled the song, some abstract lyrical ideas matching the mood.

The album was a stern rebuke to those who thought Genesis were a thing of the past or a Phil Collins sideline. Artistically they were as challenging as ever, particularly when they avoided the ballads. Tracks like 'Mama', 'Home By The Sea' and 'Silver Rainbow' could only be Genesis, but 'Taking It All Too Hard' sent out invitations for Collins comparisons while 'That's All' might have been done by any number of artists – as Hugh Fielder put it, 'Their chemistry seems to improve with speed. With room to relax they start to sound less distinctive.'[103] On a fairly inconsistent album by their lofty standards, it was disappointing that Tony and Mike didn't give themselves the chance of a lead vocal each, though they were more prominent than before in the backing vocals.

Genesis did endeavour to keep the group and the solo projects very separate entities, avoiding overlaps, but during the American

'Mama' tour, Phil was asked to write a title song for Taylor Hackford's new movie *Against All Odds*. Time being short, he agreed to send a demo of an old song that had originally been destined for *Face Value* called 'How Can You Sit There?'. Hackford loved it, so during a few quieter moments on tour Phil wrote some new lyrics to fit the film. Unfortunately he didn't have time to do any more work on it and he flew to New York on a day off to record the backing track, leaving it to Arif Mardin, who had arranged the strings, to complete. He then sent Phil some rough mixes which Phil adjusted via telephone conversations. The result, 'Against All Odds (Take A Look At Me Now)' became his first American number one that April.

Meanwhile Genesis were on tour, with a light show that was astonishing. By this time, they had dispensed with ordinary stage lighting and were simply using 180 Varilites, the first time ever that such a rig had been set up. The available effects were incredible as not only did the lights have the capacity for movement, but the rig itself was able to come down to almost stage level, thereby seemingly changing the shape and size of the stage itself. Accused of going over the top, Mike defended the group with some common sense – 'If you play the big stadiums you do need something larger than life to make it work.'[1] The band played their only European shows at Birmingham's NEC, a five-night residency which captured the spirit of the new Genesis – relaxed and confident (even Tony allowing himself the occasional smile). Phil was by now a thoroughly seasoned master of ceremonies able to deflate the hugeness of the arena with some humour, mocking the traditional rock poses. 'It's very important. If you have dramatic songs that are lit that way, it's nice to preface it with a dirty story. I've always thought that by telling a few jokes and having a rapport with the audience, it takes the people off the edge of their seats and they relax and enjoy it.'[88] Well aware that a lot of old fans there wanted to hear 'The Cinema Show' or 'In The Cage', Phil played on their lesser enthusiasm for the new songs with a couple of routines – 'We're gonna play some new songs' (small cheer) and 'We're gonna play some old songs' (big cheer). Dramatic pause, then, 'And if you're really good, we might play some *really* old songs!' (cue uproar). Another favourite was the pantomime boo/cheer routine. 'When we go on tour, we have to decide what to play. So we get out all our old albums (cheer), then we put them away (boo), take 'em out (cheer), put 'em away (boo),' ad infinitum. As Phil has said, 'It's very difficult to introduce new material to an audience,'[66] so anything that made that process easier had to be a good thing. The band encored with a mutant version of 'Turn It On Again'. 'One night I just started singing a line from "Satisfaction" in it, a bit of "All Day And All Of The Night," ' remembered Phil. 'Everybody in the band was laughing, so then I got the John Belushi hat and shades and did the odd line from different songs and bit by bit people joined me and we took it to its conclusion with a medley!'[104] The medley grew nightly to the amazement and amusement of the fans to include 'In The Midnight Hour', 'Pinball Wizard', 'Every Breath You Take' and even 'Karma Chameleon'!

Genesis continued to play charity shows as they have done for WOMAD. The fourth night at the NEC was in aid of the Nordorff-Robbins Music Therapy Centre, a charity with which they've continued to be involved, as they have with the Prince's Trust, the beneficiary of their fifth show which took place in the presence of the Prince and Princess of Wales. Fingers were then pointed at Genesis as they were seen to be more and more 'of the establishment'. Naturally Phil disagrees, firstly illustrating the undeniably good work of the charities – if Genesis weren't doing such benefits, they'd be criticized for that too! 'If you change yourself to be on those shows, then I suppose you're becoming more establishment. I don't consider myself to be more establishment just because I'm a trustee of the Prince's Trust and I'm hanging out with barristers at meetings. I still go in my sneakers! A lot of those seemingly establishment things are coming over to us.'[69]

As a trustee, Phil has continued to maintain close links with the Prince's Trust. 'I get frustrated that I can't do more – I try to do their week of sport and leisure in Norfolk when I can, I teach the kids how to play in a band and we do a concert at the end of the week, I get a great buzz out of it. My commitment is very strong on a permanent level – my strong point isn't in the distribution of money and saying where it should go, it's the raising of the money in the first place.'[4] Phil's entirely selfless charity work was to play a large part in his career as the band went their separate ways again at the end of February 1984 with a firm agreement to get back together for a new album in eighteen months' time.

CHAPTER EIGHTEEN

'The torch is lit again'

'I was in England this afternoon. Funny old world, innit?' With those brief words from the stage at JFK Stadium in Philadelphia on 13 July 1985, Phil Collins became a bona fide member of the 'rock aristocracy'. The Live Aid concert, the 'Global Jukebox', was the brainchild of Bob Geldof, a natural progression from the previous year's Band Aid single and a desperate, defiant scream of anger at the governments of the world who stood idly by as people perished in Ethiopia. A worldwide phenomenon, watched by countless millions across the planet, it raised valuable money to help drought-ridden Africa. All the performers, the promoters, the technicians, the TV crews, the audience, etc., etc., can be justly proud of their efforts that day, whatever their personal motives – and some must have been questionable. It was an event that is still talked about as a Woodstock of the eighties, though its memory was tarnished by some artists who went to great lengths to get on the bill and then behaved like primadonnas, particularly in America where it was seen by some as a career-enhancing move. Most were there for the right reasons as their music and attitudes were to show – U2, Sting, Geldof's Boomtown Rats, Elvis Costello and Bryan Adams for instance, all known for their long-term commitment to a number of charities and worthy causes – and it was this that gave the event its integrity, despite the cash-in opportunities that the music business wasn't slow to seize on in its aftermath.

Among a galaxy of rock music's biggest stars, which included Paul McCartney's first live appearance in years, the reformation of Led Zeppelin, the Who, Bob Dylan, Mick Jagger and Tina Turner, one man, in addition to Bob Geldof, captured the

imagination of the public with his inexhaustible efforts for the
cause – Phil Collins. By becoming the only artist to play at both
Wembley and Philadelphia, he captured the headlines and the
hearts of millions. Not only did he play his own songs, he seemed
to be playing with everybody else as well – Sting in England, Eric
Clapton and Led Zeppelin in the States. Bemused by all the fuss,
for Phil it was no big deal just an extension of his normal tireless
work schedule, though originally he wasn't going to be the only
person to play both sides of the Atlantic. 'When I said yes to Live
Aid, Duran Duran were going to be in England and Power Station
in America so they were coming with me.'⁴ Like so many of Phil's
disparate projects, things finally boiled down to practicalities. 'It
was during the "No Jacket Required" tour and Sting got in touch
with me and said let's do something together, but for weeks I was
trying to find someone to play drums with because I'd only got
two songs I could do on my own at the piano. I wanted to sit in
with a band, but there was no one in England. I got a call from
Robert Plant because he wanted to get on the bill and he said,
"How about you, me and Page doing something?" I said, "Count
me in," but Robert was in America, so it became apparent if I
wanted to play drums, it would have to be in the States. By then
Concorde had reared its head and said they could get someone
over there, so I said OK, I'll do both. Clapton was playing there,
so I said I'd play with him, but then it was just a question of
making sure people went on at a certain time, otherwise I wouldn't
be there – the jockeying for position in the States was unbeliev-
able!'⁴ The logistical exercise sorted out, Phil's appearance on both
sides of the pond made the event even more memorable while
also implicitly posing a question of morality – if we're so clever
that we can fly people across the world so quickly, why are all
these people starving?

   If Phil Collins had been well known to the popular music fraternity before, he was now a household name. His *No Jacket Required*
album, released earlier in the year, benefited commensurately
from his performances at Live Aid and his subsequent tour. He
seemed to need no assistance as he played arenas on a scale similar
to those that Genesis had made their speciality. His new music
was entirely suited to larger venues – after the introspection of his
opening solo salvos, the third record was an upfront rhythmic
powerhouse that owed more to Prince than it did Stephen Bishop.
It was odd that such a well-respected drummer had made two
albums, that with the exception of a few songs, primarily 'In The
Air Tonight', had not significantly lent on his rhythmic drive and

inventiveness. He redressed the balance convincingly this time, however, with a string of songs that were sure-fire dance-floor winners – 'Sussudio' which caused trouble with its similarities to Prince's '1999', 'Who Said I Would?', 'Only You Know And I Know' and 'Don't Lose My Number'. Much of this upbeat up-tempo material was a reaction to his domestic situation – now happily married to Jill in a ceremony that took place on 4 August 1984 – the depressed ballads were a thing of the past and the slow songs carried much brighter, warmer feels than the tortured darkness of 'If Leaving Me Is Easy'. It was a useful album for Phil in that it gave an indication of another facet of his tastes and personality, bringing new people to his music. The title also gave him the opportunity to take a swipe at the Ambassador East Hotel in Chicago, which hadn't allowed him into its Pump Room res-taurant because he wasn't wearing the right kind of jacket. Game, set and match, Mr Collins.

Phil's social conscience came through again with his obser-vations on 'Long Long Way To Go' regarding the desperate politi-cal situation in Northern Ireland. He also voiced his concern for the mentally ill on 'Take Me Home', which featured a driving drum-machine pattern and a lovely melody line, the backing vocals including a brief appearance from Peter Gabriel, a man praised for his involvement in worthy causes while Phil is ignored. Now no longer just a rock drummer and singer, but a personality, during this period between Genesis projects Phil was like a persist-ent rash – he was everywhere. If he wasn't producing Eric Clapton he was promoting his own album. If he wasn't doing that he was duetting with Phil Bailey on *Easy Lover* – another number one – and producing Bailey's album, or singing with Marilyn Martin on 'Separate Lives', the theme tune to Taylor Hackford's film *White Nights*. When the music was on hold, he went back to acting, on American TV show *Miami Vice*. Playing a game show host, just as he had during breaks between songs in concert, he slipped comfortably back into his Artful Dodger role, borrowing a few mannerisms from Steve Martin. After the miserable experience that was *Calamity The Cow* almost twenty years earlier, Phil found that he enjoyed acting after all and resolved to delve deeper as and when time permitted, in the meantime fitting in a brief appear-ance on *The Two Ronnies*.

While Phil was in the ascendancy, Tony was having less luck. As solo success had so far eluded him, he was keen to work on film soundtracks, something to which he was ideally suited. As illustrated by the instrumentals on both his solo albums his music was very descriptive and cinematic in style. Given the necessary scope on a decent film, he would come up with the goods. He was approached to prepare the score for *2010*, the follow-up to *2001: A Space Odyssey*, a high-profile film, perfectly suited to his talents and an excellent vehicle to promote his name among the film moguls. Initially things went well but then internal politics and Hollywood's notorious capriciousness crept in and music that had initially excited the movie men suddenly wasn't what they wanted. Tony's eventual departure from the film was a source of intense frustration as he had invested so much time and excellent music into it and had turned down other film offers in its favour.

The situation improved a few months later, however, when he became involved in a low-key movie, *Lorca and the Outlaws*, which gave him the chance to revamp some of the *2010* material and to write two songs specifically for the film – he recruited Toyah and Jim Diamond to provide vocals and an EP later surfaced. Following work on this and having regained his appetite for film scores, Tony returned to Hollywood and Columbia Pictures' *Quicksilver*. In keeping with so many movies these days, the soundtrack was submerged beneath a series of attempts at the 'hit song' that would draw the punters to the cinema – Tony wrote one song with Fish from Marillion that wasn't used, 'Shortcut To Somewhere' – but the score contained some ambitious instrumental work that deserved a wider audience than the film would achieve. Thankfully Tony compiled some of this material for his *Soundtracks* album in 1986.

For the older followers of the band, Tony has come more and more to represent their favourite elements of Genesis, those pieces that help to take the group into uncharted waters – indeed one Genesis insider has said, 'If either Phil or Mike left the band there would still be a Genesis, but if Tony Banks left, that would be it.'[69] Whether that's entirely justified, and certainly none of the fans underestimate Mike and Phil's input, there's many a smile and a nod of approval when the band kick into a song like 'The Brazilian' – Tony's got his way again! He readily admits, 'My job in the group is to stop us just doing top-forty material'[105] and it's because both sides of the coin are so well represented in the band they are such a potent force. It remains a source of frustration to fans, as much as it does to Tony and the rest of the group, that his solo offerings are given such short shrift, though it is sadly indicative of the MTV/remote control age where anyone with an attention span beyond two and a half minutes ranks as an intellectual. Those with a desire for any depth in the artistic sense, be it in literature, music, TV or films spend their lives rummaging for the occasional diamond that has become harder and harder to uncover, so how much difficult is it for the artist to maintain his or her motivation in the face of such indifference?

Mike's sales figures did jump, however, during this 'away from Genesis' spell. Not fully satisfied with his earlier solo efforts, 'I just wasn't going to make any more solo records as such – I'd come to terms with the fact that maybe I wasn't meant to have any success at that kind of level outside Genesis and so if that's the case, don't be greedy. If all I've done is Genesis, then I'm very happy and proud of that.' Songwriting was something he couldn't simply switch off, however, so he compiled a number of tunes for other people – a return to the original Charterhouse idea – but soon discovered that 'The world of writing for other people isn't very nice, it feels a bit too commercial for me – getting publishers punting songs around, I don't like that very much. I can't do demos either. Just me and a guitar sound awful – unless you trust me that it's good, what you hear would terrify you!' Having written some material, Mike had a bunch of songs without a home so, 'I thought, "Sod it, I'll do an album myself." ' He then found himself back to square one with regards the presentation of the record: 'I didn't want it to be a "solo" album because I can't really sing and it's always a bit odd when you've got a solo record and you aren't the singer, so I decided I'd present it as a group.'

Acting Very Strange had set the scene for the next record as it had featured Mike writing in tandem with others. This idea was developed further as he wrote songs with B. A. Robertson – best known for his 1979 hit 'Bang Bang' – and Christopher Neil who produced the LP, Mike even choosing to revamp an old Genesis out-take. This largely stemmed from a realization that Mike preferred and got his best results when working with other people. The group was built up from basics: 'I went into it very much with Chris, do a bit, put the tracks down and see what happens. We did the basic music with Adrian Lee and Peter Van Hooke, but I didn't want to think about singers until I'd heard what the music was like, the mood instrumentally. We got a few singers down and the things Paul Young and Paul Carrack did felt very strong and I thought we had something that could be continued.' The backing tracks were recorded in Montserrat as Fisher Lane Farm was being extended, and the vocals added later.

When the album was released, under the eponymous title *Mike and the Mechanics*, the UK response was disappointing, but America quickly took it to its heart, with 'Silent Running' becoming a major hit single there. This gave the group a character which aided its promotion here and on its re-release 'Silent Running' reached number twenty-one. The album was very well put together, encompassing a wide variety of musical feels – there were some readily identifiable Rutherford bits, with the atmospheric 'Silent Running' or the mega-ballad 'You Are The One', but there was also a very clear attempt to widen his style, presumably a result from the input of the other writers. 'I Get The Feeling', for instance, was a bold, brassy upfront number that Hall and Oates might have covered, and the general mood was that of a good-time rock album which could claim one perfect pop single with wonderful melody and hookline, 'All I Need Is A Miracle'. Once released to a more sympathetic and open audience, the album was able to carve out a niche for itself, the contrast between the two lead voices giving it an extra diversity and the album carrying a warm band vibe. 'I needed something to build on, to feel I had a foot in the door, that I could go back to a project and develop it later. All I was really after was something I could feel I'd made a start at,' a belief that was cemented by a successful five-week tour of America just prior to touring with Genesis in 1986.

As the individual projects began to run their course, Tony, Phil and Mike were looking towards their next date together at the now fully refurbished Fisher Lane Farm studio in spite of a completely bogus announcement on Radio 1 to the effect that Genesis had split up. Ridiculous as this statement was, and totally contrary to the statements of each member of the group in the promotional work they did for their own albums, it did sum up the way Genesis was now seen. Few seemed capable of understanding that they were able to do individual things and then come back to do Genesis. Since Phil had started to have solo success, people had been sounding the death knell for the band and now with Mike and the Mechanics doing well in America and Tony having done more film work, surely it must mean the end of the group? In fact, quite the reverse – the solo activity had prolonged the group's life: there was no longer any frustration with the group's material, no more struggles to get material on the albums at the expense of the others' work. Solo records also offered a great deal more space for the music to come out, so anything that they wanted to do could be done, no matter how experimental or different to Genesis it was. Mike applies perfect logic when he points out, 'Being in a group is a bit unhealthy once you've got it going, just playing with the same three or four people all the time. You need new challenges and ideas.'[4]

Financial and artistic security was a major reason for the new flexibility – there was no longer that need to chase the worldwide commercial breakthrough which had forced them into a phenomenal work schedule during the 1970s. Genesis had become a name known and respected across the world and whenever they wanted to roll again, people would be waiting, in the same way that they had waited for the Who or Paul McCartney. Having fought their way through a long dark tunnel of seemingly never-ending tour dates, they were out into the light with time on their side. Perhaps the biggest change, and the reason they can juggle careers so well, is simply that maturity that can only come with time – having begun as intense, obsessive young men who ate, slept and drank the band, they were now much more relaxed with one another and with Genesis as a whole. Mike has said, 'We used to have rigid ideas about things, but these days I care less probably because we've proved a lot of things now.'[64] He continues, 'If I went to Tony or Phil and said I wanted to do something, however bizarre, they'd say OK and that feeling has kept us going.'[4] Genesis is no longer the trap which Gabriel and Hackett felt it was, no more the be all and end all of their lives. The open nature of the group avoids artistic frustrations and, importantly, offers personal satisfaction, giving them time to devote to family life. Mike: 'I've given myself more time off – I've neglected my family over the years because of Genesis tours, so that's very important to me.'

Beyond these arguments, the key to Genesis' continued existence is the music – all three recognize that the band offers them the opportunity to immerse themselves in a style of music which they could not create independently. They collectively enjoy the music that they make and also enjoy one another's company. Mike explains, 'Genesis is a combination of us working together and it's a very pleasurable thing. When it stops being enjoyable, we'll stop doing it.'[4] Hugh Padgham, from a perfect vantage point, has observed, 'There are no egos involved, it's very easy, democratic, it's very good humoured.'[4] The bond between the three has become strong enough to withstand the intense media spotlight that is concentrated on Phil, often to the detriment of Mike and Tony when they're working together. Many is the interviewer who has blithely assumed that Phil writes everything for Genesis and that the others are just backing players, a situation similar to that which caused problems prior to Peter's departure. Fortunately the internal chemistry is no longer so strained as to get upset about it, their humour going a long way to defuse any problems. Phil, for example, is sometimes referred to as Phil Collins A.R.E. – All

Round Entertainer – and Tony in particular is bemused by Collins' appeal to women: 'They all ask, "Is he as lovely as he looks?" I say, "Spare us!" '[69] Phil helps out with some self-depreciating humour: 'Drummers always used to be the fat, bald ones who sat at the back and got pissed. And I almost carry that off completely.'[69] On a more serious level, he is very quick to point out that it is a three-piece group with each member as vital as any other, also going on record as saying, 'Tony is the most important writer in Genesis closely followed by Mike, that's what people like about Genesis.'[4]

Just as Phil clearly appreciates the other two members of the band, they are just as happy with his contributions and give him much of the credit for having loosened up the band's personality as well as its music. If his solo success can sometimes divert attention away from the teamwork aspect of the group, the other side of the coin is that he has opened the band up to people who might never have otherwise given it a chance. The legions of followers that were turned on to his music by *Face Value* or by 'Sussudio' inevitably want to hear more from him, which has ultimately led them to a Genesis album. As Tony Smith has said, 'Each time to date whatever Phil's last LP sold, Genesis would sell the same or a little more and vice versa.'[30] At times in the last few years Genesis have over-simplified their music for some with a preponderance of ballads, though that's more a reflection of the way they are changing – Mike and the Mechanics also covering that field more now than previously – than a deliberate response to a particular section of the audience. It is undeniable, though, that this trend has further confirmed their popularity and drawn people to their records and gigs. In some ways, and without demeaning what are extremely good songs in their own right, they've been the spoonful of sugar that helps the medicine go down and if 'Taking It All Too Hard' or 'One More Night' is what introduces people to 'Home By The Sea' then it serves a secondary and very important purpose.

Whatever the initial source of their fascination with the group and whichever facets of it they enjoy the most, there were people the world over who were delighted to hear in the spring of 1986 that Genesis had a new album ready for release.

CHAPTER NINETEEN

'Asking all kinds of questions'

'When we get together to do a new LP, that's the point at which I say "Is it working?" and so far every time it has. If it doesn't work, I hope we'll stop.'[64] To Mike's satisfaction, Genesis 1985 was still firing on all cylinders, as they were to prove with the release of *Invisible Touch* in June of the following year. Maintaining their strict adherence to the group ideal, the songs were written together in the studio, though the album took on a very different character from *Genesis*: the sound was much sharper and there was far more consistency, as if there were a greater number of songs to choose from. If *Genesis* had sometimes sounded as though it comprised all the songs they'd written – something borne out by the fact that there were no unreleased studio tracks on the B-sides of the singles – *Invisible Touch* suggested they had songs coming out of their ears. Certainly it was their best album since *Wind And Wuthering*.

Hugh Padgham noticed a change in the music as the band 'were getting back to longer songs, to the time when, to me, they were a classic albums band.'[4] Possibly with the single success that Phil and Mike had enjoyed, they felt they could afford to try out some more involved music within Genesis, though this didn't prevent the band registering an astonishing five top-five singles in the USA. 'Invisible Touch' was their first number one there, reaching the top spot in the same month as Peter Gabriel's 'Sledgehammer'! If it was surprising that there was so much single success from the album, it was even more surprising which tracks became hits. If there was an obvious single, it was 'Anything She Does', which thundered along on a bass synth line with some brass added by Tony's keyboards. That it wasn't put out can only be because of its superficial similarities to some of the tracks on Phil's *No Jacket Required*, comparisons they were looking to avoid.

This album warranted proper consideration as a group project as it confounded preconceptions and kept the listener interested with its unexpected twists and turns. One of those twists was Tony's witty lyrics for 'Anything She Does': 'I'm sure people think we light joss sticks, wear white shirts and pray all the time for inspiration, but we actually cut out pictures of scantily clad women and stick them on the wall. We're getting quite a collection and this song is about the girls who do that or more pornographic things. The editors write these things about them – "Mandy likes to play tennis" – but the whole thing is obviously a fake and you can imagine these guys writing the stuff to create the fantasy.'[106]

The central piece on *Invisible Touch* was 'Tonight, Tonight, Tonight' which pulled together all the various strands of their career – in some ways a fairly basic idea, opening with a simple drum pattern, it built to an explosive crescendo topped with a searing, passionate vocal from Phil. Mike added some jagged guitar lines and the whole thing was held together by Tony's penchant for odd keyboard sounds. It has a traditional Genesis feel which still appears fresh: 'It's more of the old-style Genesis in that it covers a lot of ground musically and has a fairly involved instrumental passage in the middle,' explains Mike. 'We've done songs like this from the word go. The initial bit came from an improvised jam and the song and solo part in the middle were obvious from a longer section when Tony was just improvising sound over a rhythm being played by Phil and I and he just assembled a composed solo part.'[107] This is an excellent indication of how Tony in particular will stretch the others, Mike acknowledging, 'He's the most adventurous in terms of song format, he's always trying to not get stuck into a verse, chorus, middle eight, he'll always push us a little bit to question whether we couldn't explore a bit more.'[107] Just as they were improvising music, some of the lyrics were spontaneous too. During the writing of 'Tonight, Tonight, Tonight', Phil came out with the 'monkey' phrase from the song – its working title was 'Monkey/Zulu' – which quickly became an integral part of the piece, leaving him to write the lyrics around it. He had already used the 'monkey on your back' line in 'Man On The Corner', so Phil developed the idea, giving a thread of continuity for the band's train-spotters, the song detailing the dangers of substance dependency.

A similarly off-the-cuff lyric gave the album its title too. While working on another piece, 'The Last Domino', Mike hit on a guitar riff and Phil began to sing 'She seems to have an invisible touch'. Realizing they'd got a great hook, they turned the riff into a song.

Though in this instance the phrase stuck with the song, Mike admits that that isn't always the case: 'Quite often you try to avoid that because you feel that you should explore other themes, but this particular phrase always felt so comfortable being sung on that chorus.'[107] Tony agrees, 'We felt it was just a nice description of music so we used it for the album.'[56] Phil was delighted with the way the song turned out – 'I thought it was a great pop song. It encapsulated the whole record and it pushed Genesis into a bit of an R. & B. area, a little like a Prince thing.'[4]

While the band often describe songs as being like a certain artist – 'Abacab' having a Booker T. and the MGs section or 'Turn It On Again' being partly influenced by Earth, Wind and Fire – very few other people pick up on the similarities, largely as a result of the group being pigeonholed, but those influences are definitely there. For example, check the guitar riff accompanying the verses on 'Land Of Confusion' which owes a debt to Pete Townshend, subtly acknowledged in the lyric 'my generation will put it right', and more obviously in the Spitting Image video used to promote the single which includes an 'appearance' by the Who's leader. The Genesis songs that do bear such relatively blatant influences are as cleverly constructed as a good whodunnit – just as the clue appears, something else distracts the attention and you're left with the impression that you might just have missed something, but you're not quite sure what it was!

'Land Of Confusion' was Mike's first protest song. 'It just says that we live in a beautiful world and we're making a mess of it. When Phil came to sing it, I was actually in bed with flu and he came over to my house because they'd done all the vocals bar this one and he sat on my bed like a secretary, Miss Moneypenny taking a letter! I was in a kind of delirious state with a very high temperature and I dictated it to him and I remember thinking, "I think I told him the right thing", "Was it all rubbish or was it any good?"'[107] The lyrics did make a great deal of sense, considerably more, in fact, than the words spouted by the world leaders to whom it was addressed. It was a song that immediately indicated a direction for the video and Spitting Image accepted the opportunity to work alongside Genesis with alacrity, coming up with a savage attack on the world's statesmen, especially the bumbling Ronald Reagan. As Peter Gabriel's 'Sledgehammer' video had done a few months earlier, it offered concrete proof that the group had a sense of humour, a characteristic they'd been trying to get across for years in order to break away from the 'serious art-rockers' tag. Here was evidence that Genesis provided good fun

and entertainment while also offering a little more for those prepared to dig into it. Tony is happy to admit, ' "Land Of Confusion"
was our best video because we weren't in it. I loved my puppet
because it was so extrovert. Mike's was more of a caricature, but
then he is a caricature!'⁴

On *Invisible Touch* there is, more than ever, a group input to
each song, but on some there are obvious clues as to who takes
the lead – 'In Too Deep' was very much in Phil's field of excellence,
something Mike is quick to acknowledge: 'It's a feeling within the
three of us that there are different bits that one of us knows
about,'¹⁰⁷ so why deny their individual strengths? The lyrics were
written to fit the film *Mona Lisa* starring Bob Hoskins, an actor
with whom Phil was later to work on Steven Spielberg's *Hook*. If
Phil had his stamp on that tune, then 'Throwing It All Away' came
more from Mike's area, centring around a nice guitar phrase that
repeated throughout. It began life as a much heavier guitar song
called 'Zeppo', with Phil drumming in a John Bonham style, but
the middle eight and chorus then took the song off at a different
tangent and a much softer piece developed, matched by the simple
love-song lyric.

To complete the album there were a couple of pure Genesis
numbers. The album closer was an instrumental, 'The Brazilian',
which ranks with their finest music ever and which became an
instant classic on the subsequent tour. Illustrating the relaxed
manner in which a lot of their new music takes shape – the prime
importance of atmosphere over form – Tony began the piece by
sampling the room noise – Mike and Phil's playing – without
telling them, then forming a tape loop from part of it. When played
back it sparked some group improvisation over the loop, the odd
sound ending the album on a very individualistic note. But the
tour de force of the album had to be 'Domino', a two-part song in a
similar style to 'Home By The Sea', but far stronger. As the title
suggests, it's based around the 'domino theory' where one person's actions cause a reaction which affects someone else whose
reaction affects someone else, etc. The first section, 'In The Glow
Of The Night', is the tale of the victim at the end of the line who
has lost everything because of another party, the story of his anger
and frustration with whoever pushed the first domino. The second
part, 'The Last Domino', deals with the inevitability of his position
and the futility of fighting against it. Tony again had the lyrical
idea, Mike saying, 'He seems to enjoy most of all writing the
longer pieces,'¹⁰⁷ and Tony admits that they 'give you something
to get your teeth into.'⁴ Musically, the track opens in pastoral

mood before developing into an intense section which climaxes with Mike playing some thrashing guitar chords over a driving drum part from Phil. In Mike's view, 'It's an area we've done before but when you make it work, it's still very exciting. To me it's one of the best things we've done.'[107] It's also a track that cries out for concert performance and was one of the highlights of the 'Invisible Touch' tour of 1986/87, Phil belting out the vocals with frightening power.

On completion, the album took residence at number one in the UK, though strangely it did not reach that position in the States. After their slightly patchy previous effort, *Invisible Touch* marked a resounding return to form with one of the very best albums of the 1980s. It was an inquisitive and innovative record prepared to push back the artistic boundaries but free of unnecessary adornment or vacuous posturing. The band had been ruthless in the editing process, eliminating the chaff and leaving a concise and direct record full of well-turned songs. The chemistry between the three when in the studio had not diminished – if anything it was becoming stronger – and the writing process was still as fascinating and magical for them. Mike: 'We just play for a couple of hours on the first day, it's just long jam sessions – if someone came in at the wrong moment, it might sound horrible – but because we're completely unafraid of playing anything which is complete rubbish, or in the wrong key, that's how we find things. We don't mind branching off – very often we'll be playing and Tony will stab a chord or lead line that sounds fantastic and that'll lead whoever's following on to a new path. It's purely spontaneous improvisation when the three of us go in that produces this musical sound which is Genesis.'[107]

As Genesis clocked up dramatic sales figures, the world cried out to see them. This time the tour itinerary took in Japan and Australia as well as the States and Europe, featuring shows in Budapest and in the shadow of the Berlin Wall. The whole package comprised 111 shows, 59 cities, 16 countries and a total audience of in excess of three million. It wasn't all sweetness and light, however. There was some controversy in the USA when the group accepted tour sponsorship from Michelob Beer and agreed to allow them to use 'Tonight, Tonight, Tonight' in one of their commercials, a continuation of their previous involvement in tours by Phil and Mike and the Mechanics. The very issue of tour sponsorship is a thorny one with many artists making strong attacks on the very principle – Tom Petty has said that he'd feel like a joke if he took the dollar, U2 have regularly come out against it, while Neil

Young's 'This Note's For You' states his case very clearly. On
the other hand, numerous others, such as David Bowie, Paul
McCartney, Michael Jackson and even Lou Reed, have used sponsorship or done advertisements. The central argument is that, by
doing so, they can keep tickets at a reduced price, the revenue
received off-setting the immense running costs of their massive
show – the 'Invisible Touch' tour carried daily overheads of $90,000
whether they were playing or not. From a purist point of view,
the antipathy is understandable as for many the rebellious aspect
of rock music is still a major attraction, even if today it's generally
as rebellious as any of the largest banking institutions. Even so,
that perspective is very important to many, the freedom to play
that particular mind-game crucial to their appreciation of the
music. For many, to see rock taking the 'yankee dollar' is totally
repugnant, though if it really does lead to reduced ticket prices
maybe it's justified. As a fan it's easy to be precious without any
real knowledge of the financial niceties, to look at the fat cats
getting fatter when that isn't always the case.

Perhaps more disturbingly the deal was for a beer, Michelob
admitting that their rock-geared campaign, which had also featured the likes of Eric Clapton, had turned their fortunes around.
If not as grave a social ill as drugs (though many might disagree),
the promotion of alcohol must be questionable when one looks
at the figures for alcoholism, drink-related illness, drink-related
violence and drink-related accidents. While it's far too simplistic
to insist that if someone sees Genesis advertising a beer they're
immediately going to become an alcoholic, Michelob are clearly
using the group because they feel they will attract people to their
product. It seems particularly odd, if not insensitive, to use
'Tonight, Tonight, Tonight' as the music for the campaign – a song
about dependency selling a beer? Phil tried to explain their actions:
'We're not saying go out and get legless every night, we're just
saying a beer's a beer. Everyone has a beer, it's no big deal.'[108]
That may be so, but many still look to people in the public eye,
perhaps unfairly, to set an example for youngsters and though
difficult to prove, there is surely some correlation between attractive advertising and under-age drinking. While the group's
motives were innocent, their wisdom in taking part in such a
promotion is questionable. However, on the other side of the coin,
it should be stressed that Genesis were also heavily involved in
public information films for the Rock Against Drugs campaign,
and Phil has since done an advert that spells out the message
'Drink can wreck your life'.

The tour, which crossed the world over a period of nine months, was far less arduous than many might have thought – after all, this was a band that had done two hundred gigs a year through the early 1970s! The only real problem was Tony's dislike of flying, an absolute necessity for much of the tour, though he did try to drive between shows wherever possible. 'There's no real rule about it really, one day I feel bad about it, the next day better – I never come close to enjoying it, but the best time is straight after the show when I'm more relaxed.'[104] On tour, life for Genesis was also different from the norm, shunning the 'party party' syndrome. 'We've never been in the business for that, we're just in it to do the music,' explains Banks. 'A lot of groups that do that all the time tend to burn themselves out after a while.'[104] Taking care of themselves between shows has meant they've achieved an enviable level of professionalism on stage as each member is keyed up to do their job.

The 1986/87 tour was especially impressive for the amazing amount of material they had to draw on, including the vibrant new album. They opened with indoor arena shows in the States, then checked into Australia where, because of local regulations, they were required to employ local musicians for part of the show, augmenting 'In Too Deep' and 'Your Own Special Way' – a song they hadn't played in almost ten years – with a string ensemble. The tour closed with some open-air gigs across America and Europe, ending in the UK. The show at Glasgow's Hampden Park was staged in aid of Save The Children, and the four sold-out shows at Wembley Stadium helped assorted charities, the final gig on 4 July 1987 in aid of the Prince's Trust.

Though they had released live videos of the 1981 and 1984 tours, Genesis wanted to produce another to commemorate this latest tour. The first two, though employing state of the art techniques, hadn't really captured the Genesis experience, so this time they approached Sony for permission to use their newly developed high-definition film which gave the finished product a quite stunning quality, sound and picture so clear you felt you were at the gig itself. Unforgivably though, a section of the show didn't make it on to the final release, the 'In The Cage' medley which closed with 'Afterglow', one of the emotional peaks of the gigs. The release of the video was one of a number of similar moves which covered the period between Genesis albums, maintaining their profile and offering greater continuity, though fans might have been less than happy at times. The summer of 1988 saw the release of *Genesis Videos*, a compilation of all the promotional films they'd made since 1976. However, despite a total running time of around two hours, the videos were put out on two separate tapes at a significant extra cost to the punter, even more annoying since the tracks were not in chronological order, requiring the purchase of both even if you were only interested in one specific part of the group's history. To its credit, the compilation was exhaustive, though the flitting between periods was annoying at times. Worse was the fact that the tapes duplicated the six promos that had been released the previous year on the *Visible Touch* compilation – their omission would have facilitated a single tape compilation. The suspicion among fans that Virgin Video was taking advantage was increased the following year with *Phil Collins – The Singles Collection* despite the existence of two video EPs! A case of marketing gone mad after the terrible lack of promotion in the group's early days.

The final video release, in 1991, was much more satisfactory for fans. *Genesis – A History* gave an account of their career to date, featuring much unseen footage and including interviews with all the band plus Steve Hackett, Peter Gabriel and Anthony Phillips. Even though the gap between the respective releases of *Invisible Touch* and *We Can't Dance* was more than five years, these videos made it seem almost as if they'd never been away. Any further gaps were plugged by the prodigious solo output.

CHAPTER TWENTY

'Still it takes me by surprise'

A world tour is a rather more comfortable experience now than it was when the band took *The Lamb Lies Down On Broadway* on the road, but it takes its toll nevertheless. Touring is still something the band collectively enjoy, Tony remarking, 'There's no thrill like being on stage. I'm amazed by it sometimes, I love to see people get pleasure from the music,'[4] but nowadays touring is mostly 'travelling and talking and dealing with all the peripheral stuff.'[30] Mike, who had already spent five weeks out with the Mechanics a few months before Genesis went on the road, had some personal difficulties to endure on the tour: in particular the loss of his father and the complications suffered by his wife Angie during her pregnancy which nearly cost them their son. As the end of the road neared, it was clearly time to devote some energy to family life, as Tony said plaintively, 'You just want to go home and re-acquaint yourself with your family.'[104]

Almost inevitably, the first to emerge from this period of recuperation was Phil. Bitten by the acting bug once more, he had landed the lead role – starring alongside Julie Walters – in the film *Buster* based on the Great Train Robber, Buster Edwards. It was a love-story-cum-thriller-cum-comedy which told of the small-time crook who gets in on a major scam that will give him the money to provide his wife with 'the good life'. Originally intended for a Royal Première in aid of the Prince's Trust, the Prince and Princess of Wales were advised against attending following press attacks that the film of glorified crime (rather ironic since it was the media in 1963 that had turned the Train Robbers into anti-establishment heroes). The main point at issue was that the scene in which the train driver, Jack Mills, was killed was played down as far as possible. The director, David Green, was either evading the issue or applying great sensitivity, depending on your viewpoint. Buster was clearly the loser as a result of his felony, forced to do his time in prison so that he could finally return to his wife and child who had been unable to adapt to the high life in Acapulco.

The controversy tended to overshadow Phil's performance in the movie, taking some of the pressure from his shoulders. In fact he was excellent in the role, fortunate in not having to stray too far from the lovable villain he'd played to such good effect in *Miami Vice*. He'd also received staunch support from the others on the set, particularly Julie Walters who played his wife. Lacking the strong image that sits so heavily on the shoulders of Sting, Jagger or Bowie when they make films, Phil has always been perceived as an ordinary bloke and is therefore better able to submerge himself beneath whatever character he's playing – indeed once the initial flash of recognition had passed, it was easy to forget that it was Phil Collins, rock star, playing Buster. He distanced himself still further from that persona with his refusal to sing in the film, though he did provide two songs for its soundtrack, 'A Groovy Kind Of Love' and 'Two Hearts', both of which went on to be international hits. He wasn't up to Academy Award standards yet, but it was a promising big-screen début, though the real tests would follow if he accepted radically different types of role. Meanwhile, as had been hoped, the film proved to be a box office hit across Britain, increasing Phil's popularity still further. More significantly there was agreement among the moguls in Hollywood that Collins might yet prove to be a bankable talent.

Fortunately, just as Phil was reaching total media overload, Mike and the Mechanics unleashed their second album, *Living Years*. Their first had initially been ignored and this met the same fate despite the release of another brilliant pop single, 'Nobody's Perfect', which inexplicably failed to chart. In the early part of the following year, however, the title track was put out, an emotional piece written by Mike and B. A. Robertson, both of whom had recently lost their fathers. A song about the way in which we often don't tell the people who mean the most just how we feel about them, it struck a chord with the public and spent several weeks in the higher reaches of the charts in the UK, being kept from the number one slot by an unlikely duet from Marc Almond and Gene Pitney, 'Something's Gotten Hold Of My Heart'. Again the single rejuvenated the album which achieved sufficient success for Mike to be able to bring the band to Europe for a full-scale tour of theatres such as Manchester Apollo and Hammersmith Odeon.

The contrast between those gigs and the Genesis stadium shows was something Mike had wanted to achieve, having taken his children to see Michael Jackson at Wembley the previous summer: 'I was halfway back and I said to my wife, "Why does anyone come to these shows?" after I'd been round the world playing them!'

The shows worked well, the second album providing some stronger material than their début effort. Mike agrees that 'The writing got easier on this second record because I knew where I was going and the writing relationships with Chris Neil and B. A. Robertson had developed and got better.' If the individuals had succeeded in achieving a band feel the first time around in order to provide a cohesive sound, then by now they seemed to be a fully operative unit working together with a common aim. This impression is a tribute to their abilities as individuals for the record wasn't made as a band, as Mike explains: 'The Mechanics album was four months' solid work for me but the others just come and go to play their parts,' preventing the band ever actually playing together at any one time.

Tony had seen how Mike had managed to divert attention away from himself by forming a band, thereby throwing some of the spotlight on to other people, and tried a similar approach, giving his next album the moniker 'Bankstatement'. He had lost some of his interest in writing film scores, a result of the directorial interference and their insistence on a hit song, and now attached more emphasis to his solo album releases. As Mike had done, he decided not to sing all the songs – restricting himself to one lead vocal – which presented him with the familiar dilemma of projecting a personality on to the music. Having faced the problem without success on *A Curious Feeling*, the band title seemed the obvious answer this time around, also throwing off the dreaded 'solo album' tag that gives the counter-productive impression of a musician with time on his hands. Tony hoped that the use of other vocalists would not only provide better singing on the album but also that they would help in the image-mongering so vital to pop success these days. 'I have no public persona and that makes selling records difficult,'[4] so there was an intention that the others might take their share. In the end, Bankstatement came to represent Tony and two other singers, Jayney Klimek and Alistair Gordon, using assorted session musicians such as Pino Palladino on bass, and Steve Hillage, co-producer, on guitar.

Tony maintained his interest in using odd combinations of sounds and off-beat musical imagery to build an atmosphere,

which, along with his instinctive feel for melody, gave him a strong
body of songs. There were the more immediate tunes such as
'Throwback' and 'A House Needs A Roof' combined with the
typically atmospheric pieces such as 'Thursday The Twelfth'
(which bore a faint resemblance to Led Zeppelin's 'Kashmir') and
'Big Man' which Tony sang himself. Jayney Klimek was superb
on her three songs – 'Queen Of Darkness' was particularly
impressive, a reworked version of 'Lorca' from the 'Redwing Suite'
on the *Soundtracks* album – and Tony could have used her to
greater effect, while his own vocal was also very strong. Sadly
Alistair Gordon, possessing a good but not distinctive voice, gave
the songs he sang a pedestrian air that lacked individuality. Tony,
if not as gifted technically, would have been better suited to doing
the vocals himself, as he admitted later: 'In some ways people find
it easiest to take the tracks I sing because there's a personality to
go with it rather than being an unknown singer.'[4] The production
was competent if not startling, but again the record came out to
indifference. Tony says, 'I was very satisfied and was very surprised it didn't do anything. I'm surprised sometimes that people
don't give my solo stuff a chance.'[4] Unfortunately, in many
respects he was swimming against the tide, as he acknowledged:
'For me, composition is the most important thing. I may be one of
the few people who actually looks at things like that any more – I
think people tend to look at the final sound as what's important,
so production and rhythm have become the gods these days.'[109]
You've only to look at the singles charts to discover that cacoph-
onous dance records of one stripe or another are the sound of the
day and, unless you're an already established major artist such as
Genesis, there is no other way through short of the mega-ballad.
Even so, it's very surprising that with the worldwide success of
Genesis more of those record buyers don't seek out Tony's own
albums.

Phil might credit Tony as being the main writer in Genesis,
but there was little doubt as to who was the most successful
individually, something confirmed in late 1989 by Phil's appearance at charity performances of the Who's *Tommy*, where he took
the part of Uncle Ernie from the late Keith Moon. The real business
for the year began with the release of his fourth album, . . .*But
Seriously*. It was preceded by a single, 'Another Day In Paradise',
a straightforward treatment of the emotive subject of homelessness and the way in which countless governments across the
world ignore the issue, largely because the disenfranchised can't
vote and so don't matter. The single reached number one around

the globe, putting the issue on the political map, especially in America. 'I wrote it very easily, I was playing the piano, the words came out and that was the song. I never thought anyone would pick up on it until the companies wanted it as a single – it was a strong single after the lightweight *Buster* stuff. It's not just a question of money, you have to embarrass and convince governments into doing something and get people to ask questions – in America, for instance, the homeless organizations wanted to play the song to Congress because they thought it said in five minutes what they were trying to get across.'[4] During Phil's solo tour local homeless charities were invited to the shows to collect money from the crowds, donations that were more than matched by Phil himself and his record companies.

The album enabled Phil to redress the balance, taking from himself the unfair 'Mr Entertainment' label with which the press had saddled him after *Buster* and its accompanying hits, a tag which implied all those noxious Tarby, Brucie and Terry connotations. Phil looked at issues which had made an impression on him, dealing with Northern Ireland, inner-city tension, apartheid as well as homelessness. If the album had come from Billy Bragg, the critics would have been lauding it to the skies but from Phil it seemed disgraceful – a millionaire worrying about social issues? What right did he have to worry about anything? Some misguidedly seem to believe that vast wealth equates a lack of humanity, and some politicians do little to correct that view. None the less, people continue to deride Phil's attempts to draw attention to the plight of others, top-trendies Carter USM recently launching an attack on 'Paradise' – two years after its release – presumably from some neurotic fear that he might be jumping alongside them on the caring bandwagon. Everyone encounters the homeless at some time or another, whether it be as 'the people who you step over when you go to the opera' as one Tory politician described them, or in day-to-day life around the nation's towns and cities. Notwithstanding his fame and fortune Phil Collins felt sufficiently moved to bring it to people's attention – surely that's better than espousing what appears currently to be the appalling concensus politics of greed, self-interest and class division? Not only that, but while those artists who are identified as 'political' or 'socially aware' make some good records, they sell in relatively small quantities and preach mainly to the converted. Phil's songs are heard by more people and since those listeners don't feel they're being lectured, maybe they're more open to suggestion.

The message aside, . . .*But Seriously* was certainly Phil's best album to date. Utilizing his familiar strengths, there were the pacy rockers featuring the Phenix Horns such as 'Hang In Long Enough' and 'Something Happened On The Way To Heaven' – originally written for Danny De Vito's movie *The War of the Roses* – the melancholic 'Do You Remember?' and the beautiful ballad 'That's Just The Way It Is'. The most adventurous and intelligent song on view was 'Colours' which dealt at first factually and then emotionally with the plight of black South Africa. At times there is a lack of experimentation, as he tends to steer a course close to the previous musical shoreline, but that is a minor quibble in the face of a very fine album. Its release led Collins into a hectic schedule of press and promotional work across Europe and the States prior to beginning a tour that through 1990 saw him play 127 gigs in front of two million people in fifty-seven cities with a band that included Daryl and Chester from Genesis, the Phenix Horns, Leland Sklar on bass and Brad Cole on keyboards, plus the Seriousettes, three backing singers. The tour was so successful that it stretched beyond its original finishing date, contributing to the delay in Genesis getting back together to write and record.

Even so, Genesis did find time to do a brief thirty-minute set at Knebworth Park at a benefit for the Nordoff-Robbins Music Therapy Centre where they were joined by a star-studded cast including Paul McCartney, Eric Clapton, Mark Knopfler, Elton John and Pink Floyd. Phil played a solo set first, going on to use his band to augment the Genesis sound.

With Phil still busy, Mike and Tony found the time to make further records of their own. Mike and the Mechanics' *Word Of Mouth* was the first to reach the shops in April 1991, just after Genesis had gone back into the studio. This time, to bring in some fresh ideas, Mike drafted in Russ Titelman to co-produce with himself and Chris Neil, but sadly the alliance was unsuccessful. The original release date had been set for September 1990, with an accompanying three-month tour pencilled in, and with hindsight Mike feels he persisted with Titelman longer than perhaps he should, finally dispensing with his services after four months. After a brief break they reconvened in September to continue recording, only for Paul Carrack to be struck with a sinus infection that affected his performance, delaying things yet further.

Word Of Mouth saw the Mechanics taking their foot off the accelerator compared with the previous two records, being rather more laid back than before. Mike's view was 'Part of what I want from the Mechanics is for it to be a little bit loose and a little bit less serious. It's hard because the business itself is getting very

serious which I don't like. If the Mechanics went a couple of rungs
down the ladder it might not be a terrible thing.'[110] It is all the more
strange, therefore, that Titelman should have been employed in
the first place, given his pedigree for producing AOR hits in the
USA. The music was a little disappointing, with too much reliance
on unexceptional ballads, the album having a slightly jaded feel
that betrayed the strains caused by the difficult recording process.
Word Of Mouth was caught between two stools, neither providing
that looser, less polished, less intense feel, nor quite achieving
the mainstream acceptance that some of the tracks were pushed
towards. There was an Americanized edge to the production that
didn't always sit well on material that, on occasion, still stood out
from the crowd – 'Yesterday, Today, Tomorrow' was tight and
punchy, but 'Stop Baby' seemed to plod aimlessly. The album was
full of these ups and downs. It sold respectably, proof that the
group had built up a sizeable following, which gave Mike the
foothold for which he'd been looking, the relaxed atmosphere
among the principals boding well for their future as a group,
despite the glaring inconsistencies on the three albums to date.
When they've succeeded in getting it right, the results have been
spectacular – 'The Living Years', 'All I Need Is A Miracle' or 'Silent
Running' – but Mike and the Mechanics have yet to carve out a
truly distinctive style, something of which they are more than
capable.

The lack of a coherent voice was a problem that continued to
afflict Tony. With *Bankstatement* having done little to boost his
profile, he went back to the 'solo' idea, utilizing four guest vocalists
– Fish and Jayney Klimek from previous projects, plus Nik
Kershaw and Andy Taylor. The result, *Still*, was an astounding
affair – the most astounding aspect being its lack of success. Records of such intelligence and imagination are very rare in popular
music these days and one can only assume that it was this fact
that reduced its sales. 'I Wanna Change The Score' featured Nik
Kershaw and was the first single, an infectious tune and lyric that
had it gone under the Genesis banner would have graced the
higher echelons of the chart, but in Tony's solo guise failed to do
so. The airplay for the album and its singles was minimal as again
the record company marketing machinery failed dismally. While
Tony did hold fire on the instrumentals, possibly to ease the job
of the marketing men, he was not to be denied the opportunity to
experiment and explore some ideas more fully. 'Another Murder
Of A Day' was a full-blown epic, 'Hero For An Hour' was a
supremely assured pop song and 'Back To Back' could well have

been a hit single, as the whole album soared and swooped, encompassing very strong mood changes and allowing Tony to paint quite staggering landscapes with the rich palette of keyboard colours at his disposal.

The production was correspondingly powerful, with Nick Davis as co-producer following his work as engineer on Mike and the Mechanics' *Living Years* album. Tony and Davis created a driving, dynamic sound that put some very good songs in the best possible light. Undoubtedly Tony's finest hour musically, notwithstanding the inventiveness that made *A Curious Feeling* such a delight, *Still* was one of the albums of the year yet its release remained a well-kept secret. Admittedly Tony himself did little in terms of visible promotional work, but Virgin found it difficult to sell the album to a market hungry for the cheap thrills of dance music. Naturally, he was very upset about the album's fate, all the more so since it featured such a lot of material that would have appealed to a wide audience had they been exposed to it. 'I've got a sort of feeling that I won't do it again because it just makes you feel so bad,' he says. 'I love making records but it's always a frustration when you put the things out. I don't think it's worth depressing myself.'[30] He adds, 'If you put out a record that doesn't sell to anyone except those who collect anything by Genesis, it just seems terribly indulgent.'[71]

While musically Tony contributes as much as anyone to the Genesis sound and is as equally adept at turning out soulful ballads – see 'Still It Takes Me By Surprise' – and catchy four-minute pop songs – 'The Gift' – as he is at writing the more taxing pieces for which he's known, as a personality he remains in the background, which is not helped by the variety of singers he has used over the years. Though these others have offered technically better voices, they haven't provided the image so crucial to record sales today – the weakness Tony has suffered from, in comparison with Mike, Phil and indeed Peter Gabriel, is in never having a really *great* or distinctive voice with which to work, those whom he has used were neither as individual, for instance, as Peter Gabriel nor as soulful as Paul Young. *The Fugitive* had garnered some publicity, and in retrospect it may well have been better if Tony had continued as the lead voice on all his future solo albums, giving the public time to get used to his voice and hang their own mental picture on it. With his self-confessed reluctance to be a salesman for his songs, the pathway to acceptance was always likely to be a long and difficult one – a vocal continuity might have helped. In spite of his own doubts, Tony's voice does possess character, his performance on 'Hero For An Hour' not losing in comparison with Fish, Kershaw or Taylor, though again Jayney Klimek might have been given greater scope.

Their solo careers for the moment having run full course Tony, Phil and Mike finally synchronized their watches to go back to Fisher Lane Farm in March 1991 and begin work as Genesis.

CHAPTER TWENTY-ONE

'Always one more tomorrow'

'When you come back together again, you're not quite the same people as when you left and you keep introducing new elements into the group,'[111] is Tony Banks' explanation for the way Genesis maintain their passion for the band while still changing and producing different types of sounds. Even so, a break of five years between leaving the studio following *Invisible Touch* and entering it to make *We Can't Dance* was longer than the norm, leading to questions as to how easy it would be for them to get back in the saddle. As the album has proved, in terms of writing and recording there was no problem. Tony says, 'Once you've been back a few days, you slip into it very fast',[111] the writing from scratch taking just two months. If it offered no practical difficulties in that sense, he does concede, 'There has been a long gap between albums. I'd like them to happen with more frequency, it's good for the momentum.'[4] Having made such a solid album in *Invisible Touch*, then capitalizing on it on the road, it would have been fascinating to have seen the three then go back into the studio together to make a new album that built on the work they'd done over the course of the year.

But that was never an option, the three having long before decided to do solo projects following the end of the tour. As a result, when they did return with *We Can't Dance*, it bore little relation to the sort of album that had preceded it, although in a sense the idea of constant evolution aided and abetted by absence from each other is part and parcel of the enduring appeal of the band. What it does illustrate, however, is the way hardcore Genesis fans seem to see the group – while solo albums are of interest, they really want the opportunity of getting their teeth into a new group LP. There's little doubt that they 'tolerate' the extra-curricular activity rather than warm to it, though Phil and, to a lesser extent, Mike have circumvented that by attracting significantly different audiences for their solo work. It's odd that so many fans take that attitude after such a long time, since it is those very activities away from the band that have kept Genesis fresh and vibrant. Without new avenues to explore, locked into 'Genesisvision' it's unlikely that Genesis would have continued beyond the early eighties, or made such startlingly different and exciting music. Hugh Padgham comments, 'They exist for eighteen months every four or five years, so they don't get stale.'[4]

As they had not released anything for five years, and with a similar period likely to pass before the next record, it was not a surprise that they returned with a double album, as Mike explained: 'Now that CDs are almost the main thing we had extra time on the album, it gave us time to explore one or two areas.'[112] As a result, it's the proverbial curate's egg – there are spine-tingling moments next to meandering ballads, the glorious rush of an irresistible melody sitting next to cloying sentimentality. Some of these inconsistencies lie in the sheer length of the album, a straight seventy-two minutes on CD. It's an enormous amount of new music to take in in one gulp and, top-heavy as the latter stages are on slower songs, the tired mind does wander. As with so many double albums over the years, it was three great sides and one side of lesser tunes – had it been restricted to nine songs, it might well have been one of their very best albums whereas it's merely a very good one with some astonishing moments. Heard individually all the songs stand up perfectly well to the closest scrutiny, but together it's a bridge too far, although that impression recedes a little more on each play as the tunes become familiar.

The flavour of the record is of a youthful vigour, a great enthusiasm generated from simply working together and attempting to do something new as Genesis. Despite achieving so much, they were still keen to change and develop the group's sound. Always looking for new elements, this time they brought in Nick Davis to replace Hugh Padgham as producer, mainly because they felt it was time for a change rather than resulting from any dissatisfaction with Hugh. Tony had already struck up a working relationship with Davis on *Still* so he was very much in the frame when they decided that it was time to try someone new. Davis' input clearly moved things into a different area, most notably in terms of the relationship between guitar and keyboards with Mike taking a more prominent role on a number of tracks, with some very aggressive lead lines (perhaps returning to his Anon roots and their Rolling Stones covers!). Tony was a little more subdued, though he was able to make some telling contributions, even returning to the organ sounds that were so central to the early Genesis records.

All human life was here, the band taking on more of a social perspective than had been the case before. 'No Son of Mine' adeptly handled the sensitive subject of child abuse in its widest sense and boded well for what was to follow. Some of the material was better than even the most ardent Genesis fan could have hoped for, 'Dreaming While You Sleep' creating so strong a mood that it is very difficult to cope with another song following it. A look into the mind of a hit-and-run driver, a man who'd made the unforgivable mistake of refusing to stop at the scene of an accident – shades of Tom Wolfe's *Bonfire Of The Vanities* – it vividly captured his inner turmoil, the loss of his own freedom as his life is over-shadowed by the tragedy, his mind tortured by his guilty secret as his victim lies in a coma. The mesmerizing instrumentation conjures up the necessary pictures to provide a compelling and disturbing few minutes. The song is equalled by the dramatic 'Driving The Last Spike', the lyrics of which Phil pieced together around its working title, 'Irish'. 'The feel of the title and the music led me to improvise some words that would work with an idea from a book I'd got hold of about the building of the railways. The Irish were the workforce, it was amazing the amount of work they did. They had to blast through hills . . . and a lot of people lost their lives because of the appalling safety conditions, people were blown to pieces because of sloppy explosives.'[113] The drama of the story was conveyed in part by Tony's keyboards, using the melodramatic organ sounds of yore to give the song a huge sound, which was further amplified by Mike's stinging guitar contributions and a very powerful vocal from Phil. It typified some of the more advanced areas of Genesis' work with some fine group playing, illustrating their ever-increasing vocabulary of musical dynamics. The three musicians dovetailed superbly here, Tony agreeing that they are very skilled at drawing the best from one another. 'I think the other two are quite good in doing the opposite to me, I may stretch them out a bit, but I think they also condense my ideas quite nicely at times.'[113]

The longer songs worked well, the closing 'Fading Lights' maintaining their tradition of musical innovation, allowing them to settle into a mood and then expand upon it. Tony: 'Historically, our strength has always lain in being able to give ourselves a bit of room to breathe . . . it gives us a chance to do more instrumental work and a chance to tell more of a story with the lyrics.'[111] This was certainly true of the album as the shorter songs such as 'Hold On My Heart' or 'Never A Time', though well realized, were less memorable, purely because so many other people do songs in a similar vein. A couple of other ballads found their way on to the album, 'Since I Lost You', a lyric from Phil written for his great friend Eric Clapton, expressing compassion and sympathy for those who have lost someone close, and 'Tell Me Why', Phil again penning his reaction to the disgraceful desertion of the Kurds in the aftermath of the Gulf War. Phil did indeed write far more lyrics for this than any previous Genesis record, partly a result of circumstances. The normal process had involved the individuals dividing up the music between them, choosing those ideas for which they felt they could most comfortably write lyrics. As Mike and Tony's solo albums were released later than planned, they had to take a break from Genesis to do some promotional duties and returned to find that Phil, with time on his hands, had a sheaf of lyrics ready and waiting. That gave a nice contrast to the album itself and its relationship to their existing body of work. Phil's 'Tell Me Why' was almost directly answered by Mike's 'Way Of The World' – 'It's good to try and put things right, but you shouldn't forget that there will always be a balance of highs and lows in the world.'[112] For each of Phil's conversations such as 'Hold On My Heart', Tony would respond with a story idea, shying away from the personal angle: 'I don't like to express my deepest feelings in a song, I feel self-conscious about it.'[4]

If some of the lyrical ideas were fairly heavy, there was lighter relief in 'I Can't Dance', a swipe at the jeans adverts and the models that populate them. Mike was very pleased with the track saying, 'It's the most radical song . . . if it wasn't Phil that was singing, you'd have to be told it was Genesis.'[112] Written around a Stones-style guitar riff, Phil says, 'The lyrics were set around the scenario of the jeans commercials, just suggesting that some of these hunks may not have too much else going for them apart from the fact that they look great.'[112] While Genesis were striking a blow for the male emancipation movement, they took time out to attack the TV evangelists in the States on 'Jesus He Knows Me', a hangover from watching too much TV on too many American tours! 'You can't change the dial on a Sunday without seeing one, it's just wall to wall,'[112] says Phil. Tony agrees, 'It has a hold over there and as an English person you always feel that these people are charlatans. When we first went there many years ago, I came across one on TV and I thought I was watching a comedy show. It took me half an hour to realize that it was serious!'[112]

After five years and despite the weight of expectations, Genesis were able to release an album that satisfied their audience and picked up new fans. Playing up their anti-fashion stance, the music maintained its own direction and momentum, a message emphasized by the title as Phil explained: 'There is a lot of dance and rap stuff around at the moment, the charts are dominated by it, but it's something that we've never done, probably never will. So we can't dance, but we can do this!'[112] Each piece on the album was a fine song, the instrumental sections kept in check and used only in the service of the overall mood of its master. As if to blast a final convincing hole in the argument to which the desperate clung, namely that Genesis records were all the same, the first three single releases, 'No Son Of Mine', 'I Can't Dance' and 'Hold On My Heart' were all radically different from one another, and in the pop charts of early 1992 that was a blessing indeed, particularly when 90 per cent of the competition were making the same record. This new music illustrated that there was still enough energy and enthusiasm in the group for what they were doing for them to continue indefinitely, though in keeping with earlier pronouncements touring was scaled down, and ran from the beginning of May to early August 1992 after Phil had taken a break in Australia to make a new film, *Frauds*, a black comedy in which he plays a villain, (this time a considerably nastier piece of work than before). As normal, Daryl and Chester joined the band for the gigs, Chester emphasizing just how much things had changed during his fifteen-year tenure with the band: 'Groove is incredibly important with the stuff we're doing with Genesis now . . . it's very much about how it feels.'[33]

Following the conclusion of the tour, Mike returned to the Mechanics while Tony's plans were uncertain. Phil headed for Hollywood to make the much-vaunted film of *The Three Bears* which also stars Bob Hoskins and Danny De Vito. He has said that following that he's looking to do nothing but film for a year to ensure that he's taken seriously as an actor, though he also maintains he wants to do another solo record relatively soon: 'I look forward to Genesis, but there are other things I want to do so it has to be kept in proportion.'[4] Whatever happens, the three do intend to return to work as Genesis again – on the evidence of their latest record, there is still much that they can do and to which their fanatical following can look forward.

CHAPTER TWENTY-TWO

'A living story'

From an album that sells six hundred copies to one that's multi-platinum, from a school group to probably the biggest concert draw in the world is a long and sometimes painful journey. It's one that couldn't have been made without determination, hard work, a sense of humour, luck, and most of all talent. The story of Genesis is the story of a group of individuals with an extraordinary belief in what they were doing, in the music they could create and in what they could go on to achieve, a single-minded passion for a sound that only they could bring to life. It began with a desire to be songwriters, then songwriters with a difference. They were compelled to form a group when they failed to raise any interest in their material. When they were a group, they were forced to grit their teeth and struggle on as a succession of music publishers told them to forget writing. When they got a record contract, they were forced to deal with a press that, with a few notable exceptions, dealt in the currency of fashion rather than that of musical quality and a public that had little knowledge of their existence. When they were beginning to gain an audience they lost the man who was proclaimed as their major asset and were greeted with obituaries. When they overcame that loss, the musical climate shifted further and from being largely ignored they were now abused and derided. Yet today, they stand at the pinnacle of the rock world.

Dedication and persistence have been the foundations of their success – they sacrificed their teenage years and early twenties to the band, not taking any substantial break until 1979, more than ten years after the group's inception. In that time they played countless hundreds of gigs, gradually nurturing an audience for themselves, a loyal following that has continued to grow to this day, one which recognizes the imagination and innovation that is uniquely Genesis and which marks them out from the crowd. That constant evolution, the refusal to peddle pale copies of former glories, is the key to the high regard in which they are held – there may be a recognizable Genesis element in much of their music, but there's always something else there too, an extra ingredient, a new method of preparation, something to add variety and a new slant to the music. The work that they've put in, particularly during the 1970s, was unparalleled – while the fat cats sat back and released a record every three years or so, often without touring or solo activity in the interim, Genesis were remorselessly tracking down new supporters while still able to release an album of new material on an annual basis without any diminution in the quality of the music.

That music is, of course, the central reason for their success. Over some twenty-five years it has changed dramatically, yet it has always been built on contrasts, from the complex to the simple, the romantic to the absurd, soft to aggressive, and it is the adventurous spirit that this has so clearly displayed that has endeared them to their fans – the feeling that there are so many options available, so many surprises to come makes a Genesis record an event.

Times *have* changed, though – no longer is Genesis the only thing on the minds of the individuals in it, others have come and gone. Anthony Phillips, perhaps the driving force in the beginning and responsible for an important input into the initial premise of the band, left early and has consequently been something of an unsung hero – it was his departure, more so than any other, that almost ended the band, so his influence must be apparent. Peter Gabriel has gone on to carve out a solo career built on experimentation, an inquisitive approach to sounds and technology and a sense of humour that has gradually become more evident in his work, while also acting as a guiding light for the 'world music' fraternity. On leaving, his value to Genesis was over-estimated while now, with the passage of time, it's gone to the other extreme where many barely recognize the important contribution he made to the band. His input as a writer steered Genesis into areas of the bizarre, sometimes the macabre, which tickled the sensibilities of those wanting a little more from their music, than was on offer elsewhere, while his concert persona, so at odds with his behaviour off-stage, was crucial in attracting the media and the 'floating voter'. Steve Hackett was important in providing some of the more off-the-wall musical elements in the group, just as the aggression he added to their music was vital in front of a concert audience. Often not given the credit he richly deserves, his guitar sound was a fundamental part of 1970s Genesis and his departure triggered a far more radical musical rethink than that of either Ant or Peter.

As the album said, and then there were three, and they're still together. Solo projects have taken up a greater share of their time, with Phil's career in particular blossoming in as many directions as you care to name, yet Genesis remains unaffected, coming together whenever the opportunity arises to make new music – and there seems little reason to suppose that this will change. The question repeated ad nauseam nowadays is 'Why are they still together?' Phil, Mike and Tony enjoy one another's company – 'We've worked long and hard at it and the fact we're still together is a testament to how well we get on,'[4] says Phil. Mike agrees: 'People think of us as deadly serious, but we have a lot of fun, we laugh a lot, it keeps us going.'[4] In many ways, the loss of key personnel has acted as a spur, according to Mike. 'Five people developing as personalities and expanding as writers and musicians eventually need more room. We could barely contain five, then we were four for a while and that developed so that we could barely contain that. Now there are three of us, there's a lot more room for us to breathe and move which is the secret.'[66] The music has always been the message and it will continue to be so, whether as solo artists or as Genesis, Mike confirming that the solo outlets 'are probably what keep us together.'[4] The other central factor is the extraordinary chemistry within the band, one enhanced by the return to the 'songwriters collective' ethic. 'It's very exciting creating music with other people,' admits Tony. 'You never know quite what will happen.'[4] Phil concurs, 'It's interesting to be able to write with the other two to see how things develop, how we've changed, what they think.'[4]

How long can Genesis go on for? That's rather like asking how long is a piece of string! The only real restriction is one of time – with all their other activities, Genesis has to take its place in the queue, but there seems little reason to suspect that there won't be more from the band in the future. Mike likes 'the idea that one day you suddenly wake up and you think, "Well that's it, we've done it all, we've done the right amount, now we stop." '[107] Fortunately for the fans' peace of mind, however, Genesis always give the impression that there's more they can do. Mike concedes, 'When we started I thought if we could play the Marquee, we'd made it, but then when we got there, it was history, it wasn't important any more, it was on to the next thing. There's always something else.'[4] Tony takes up this theme: 'There's so many things we haven't had yet – a UK number one single, an American number one album – there's something that always stops us being an everywhere group, a bit of complexity that turns some people away. I still think of us as a big underground group really!'[4]

Musically shedding ever-changing colours, Genesis have emerged from the rock and roll circus with their dignity and integrity intact, inspiring respect from an expanding legion of followers, they've kept us guessing, enthralled and entertained right from the start. It's been a long, long time, hasn't it? Happily, the future remains promising. As Mike says, 'We've come away [from the album] thinking there's still a lot to do with Genesis in the future.'[110] In Tony's view, 'When you've been together a long time, you know the sorts of things that work and until you've exhausted the whole supply, there's no reason to stop.'[112] Finally, Phil states, 'As long as I'm proud of what Genesis does, that's good enough for me. *We Can't Dance* isn't the last Genesis album, as far as I'm concerned.'[111]

APPENDIX I

WISE AFTER THE EVENT

ANTHONY PHILLIPS

Private parts and pieces

There is a persistent school of thought within the music industry that says that only music which sells by the truckload is of any value and that consequently the only form of popular music that is valid and relevant is the simple, homogenized three-minute pop tune which encapsulates current fashion. There are, however, those old sages who recall a time when freedom of expression and originality of thought were the important criteria in measuring the quality of a song or piece of music and who, in spite of the derision of the press, have continued to look for those who make music that can stir the heart and move the soul rather than simply shake the feet. For musicians, the problem is inevitably far more frustrating though some have achieved commercial success – Genesis from the old school, or more recent bands such as The Cure and REM, for instance – whereas others have been denied access to the publicity machines that can breathe life into a career. One such musician has been Anthony Phillips.

Leaving Genesis in 1970 for reasons artistic, temperamental, physical and practical, Ant used the immediate period after his departure to re-evaluate his ambitions. His first reaction was to go on to university, but he eventually decided that music was where his aspirations still lay, especially as he had just 'discovered' classical music – 'I found that suddenly my ears were opened to the whole idea.' As a result, he spent the next few years learning to read music, studying piano and orchestration so that in future he would have full control over his music, something that hadn't been the case on *From Genesis To Revelation* where Arthur Greenslade had arranged the strings. Returning to study 'at nineteen was a strange concept and in the more difficult moments I did occasionally look over my shoulder at what the group were doing. I'd have loved to have worked with Phil because he made such a difference musically and must have helped psychologically just because of his personality. But I was very limited as a guitarist – I had some originality, but my ideas were quite narrow. There's no way that I would have progressed as I have done had I stayed with the group – I was and still am perfectly happy that I was doing the right thing for myself.'

His first steps towards returning to the record business came in 1973 when he began writing again with Mike Rutherford, compiling some of the music that was eventually to be released on *The Geese And The Ghost*. Together they wrote a hymn 'Take This Heart' which featured on Charisma's *Beyond An Empty Dream* compilation, some new music for the forthcoming album and also worked with Phil Collins on 'Silver Song'. The song was lined up for single release, but the master tape didn't have the power of the demo and was shelved.

Returning to the project in 1974, Ant continued to work on the music as well as doing some teaching in the interim, as Mike's time was eaten up by the fact that Genesis' new album, *The Lamb Lies Down On Broadway*, had become a double. The writing and recording time they did have available was fraught. 'We decided to go the cheap recording route and initially did a lot of work on two four-track machines. After that, we used Tom Newman's barge in Little Venice where he had a sixteen-track studio. Unfortunately it was early days for the studio and things kept breaking down so recording took longer and longer. Then when they came off the road after 'The Lamb' tour, which was when we were going to finish the record, Gabriel had left and so Mike had to devote his time and thoughts to the band. When they first came off the road he did spend a lot of time working on it, but once they started having to think about Genesis again, the album was lower down his list of priorities than it ideally would have been. I was sympathetic, but naturally anxious and it was very difficult for Mike too. He'd have liked to have played a bigger part but he just didn't have the time.'

The finished music was a beautiful and impressive advance on the initial twelve-string guitar material that the two had pioneered on and around *Trespass*, but it in no way reflected the recording – 'I wanted a smooth run at it which was the one thing we didn't get, yet we had this serene, peaceful music!'

The various delays had conspired against Ant and when he finally had a record ready, the musical climate had changed for good. 'It took ages for it to come out. I carried on teaching and I had the offer of a full-time music course at Trinity in London, then suddenly Passport Records in the United States agreed to release the record. It did well initially over there and I suddenly seemed to have a recording career in front of me. Even then, it was impossible to get it released in the UK simply because punk had taken over so much. Doing my type of music was only feasible if you were already well established with an army of fans who would ignore the press. Starting out was next to impossible and it was finally released by Hit and Run, my management, almost as an afterthought once Passport had taken it up.' Difficult though things were, in retrospect Ant was very lucky that he did actually succeed in getting the record into the shops, because that at least provided him with a foothold which then allowed him to continue to make more records. 'I was lucky to keep recording through the dark days – Passport were happy to put everything out, even if I'd done an album of Swedish cycling songs!'

As he had got in just prior to punk, Ant had the chance to continue making albums. However, his recording career did split into two distinct halves – that which was, in part at least, at the mercy of the vagaries of fashion and the shifting sands of industry wisdom, and that which allowed a more low-key but more personal presentation of his music, known as the *Private Parts And Pieces* albums. Ant is happy to hold up his hands and admit that not all of his output has been entirely to his liking but he has been forced into the inevitable industry compromises to maintain his career. Had he not done so, it is quite possible that he would have been unable to make any records whatsoever, meaning that the many other quite delightful pieces that he has released would have gone unheard. 'Many of my decisions were manipulated by the industry – *The Geese And The Ghost* had its faults, but the two twelve-strings was an interesting throwback to 'Stagnation' and gave it a very strong direction which it would have been nice to continue, but there was immediately that pressure for singles and songs rather than instrumentals. On *Sides*, for instance, the people at Arista kept asking, 'Where's the disco single?' The changes must have seemed bizarre to people who had bought the first record and wanted more in that vein – it was bewildering.' While *Sides* and its predecessor *Wise After The Event* featured many short songs as opposed to the longer pieces on his début opus, there was still a great deal of very appealing and attractive music on show (though it has to be admitted that lyrics, especially an entire album's worth, aren't necessarily Ant's forte!). *Sides* did benefit greatly – artistically if not in sales terms – from an opening market-ing ploy by Arista. Passport had recently issued a collection of acoustic guitar and piano pieces that he'd written over a six-year period under the title *Private Parts And Pieces*. Arista picked up on that and issued it free with the first 5000 copies of *Sides*, so if some of the fans of *The Geese And The Ghost* were disappointed with *Sides*, they had an album of the other material to get their teeth into!

Since that time, Phillips' career has been quite clearly split between the two areas – the intimate conversation, almost a private correspondence, that the *Private Parts* series provides on one hand and the rest of his work where concessions have occasionally had to be made. Ant has, however, followed an admirably principled stance towards advertising himself on the back of his old band, there being almost no mention of it in any promotional material for his records. 'I wanted to avoid that tag. I always felt that it would be cashing in on their success which seemed completely wrong to me. I was very uncomfortable with it and did have to fight it because it would obviously have helped record companies generate interest.' Some compromises were made, however, and on the down side of course there was the Anthony Phillips Band, an attempt at image-mongering used in the promotion of *The Invisible Men* LP. 'It went radically wrong! It began as an idea to do a commercial album which was OK, but I found it very difficult to maintain my interest in something that was so overtly commercial and I just lost it completely!'

Happily, not all of his experiences have been so unfortunate and he has been given opportunities to develop his ideas on a wider scale. Some of this material has featured an increasing use of keyboards, including *1984* – not inspired by the Orwell book – and *Slow Dance*, his most recent album, an extremely powerful work with (though one hesitates to use the term) classical over-tones that provides some very emotional and affecting moments. An ambitious and imaginative piece of music that embraces many themes and mood changes, it illustrates perfectly Ant's ability in the field, the orchestration suggesting that he would be at home working on film soundtracks. As he acknowledges, over the last ten years the records have become less important as he has become more involved in composing TV and library music. 'I didn't find it a compromise because I've always enjoyed working to picture. That's been my main financial support over the period. Now I'm signed to Virgin Publishing as a composer and that sometimes has to take priority over the other things, which makes it difficult to promote any of my other work. I had wondered about touring on my own, doing some acoustic concerts in the same way that Steve Hackett did, but a lot of my guitar things are very complex and it would take a long time to rehearse.'

Touring is one way of getting across to an audience that Ant has considered but not pursued. 'Obviously, I have some fear of it still after my time with Genesis, but the real drawback is that I didn't want to form a group – it always felt as if an album had to take off to give me the backing. Without that, you have to borrow heavily and I felt that by starting from a position of weakness, I might be forced to continue touring for years to pay back the debts.' If touring is out, then radio play seems equally unlikely. 'Radio has become very narrow again, it's polarized between pop and classical, that horrendous divide. I may do some more songs again in future, though I do find I write fewer and fewer now.' Word of mouth is still probably the most important marketing tool and it is worth pointing out that no one who is interested in music of imagination and emotion has ever been disappointed with the *Private Parts And Pieces* albums. Again, as the series has developed, keyboards have taken on an increasingly important role adding a further dimension. There is a nice line in humour in both the music and song titles, the cover artwork is a delight and the recent compact disc reissues have also included versions of some of his earliest songs that were written for Genesis – legendary titles such as 'Let Us Now Make Love.'

In a music world where mindless repetition has become the norm, the individualistic talent can often find it harder to shine through, but when uncovered, they do shine all the brighter for the struggle. Just occasionally, the sages are allowed to give their memories a rest and can bask in the light of a music free of the industry's shackles . . .

PETER GABRIEL

Distinctions are clear

The word paradox in its application to people describes one who exhibits apparently contradictory characteristics. It's a word that could have been invented for Peter Gabriel. Off-stage he can be a shy, awkward, inarticulate figure yet put him before a crowd and it would be hard to imagine a more animated or charismatic frontman. He can be both a very shrewd business operator and yet endearingly vague and absent-minded. Musically, he has been affected by the rhythms of Africa in particular, an ebullient, spontaneous, life-loving sound, yet he can take years over albums, working and refining the smallest of details to get things exactly right. He can release some of the most marketable material around and immediately follow it with the obscure or the bizarre. Embracing the big time with a huge hit album *So*, and a world tour to match, he can then disappear for six years, his only release *Passion*, a fascinating, absorbing instrumental album yet so wilfully uncommercial that it was tantamount to turning his back on the audience he had so successfully built. He has created and unleashed powerful emotions from the horns of his personal dilemmas. If ever anyone danced to the beat of a different drum, it's Peter Gabriel.

It's very difficult to believe that Peter was ever a member of a group, for despite his avowed interest in collaboration, he now does things very definitely his own way in his own time – and gives the impression that he does many things simply because they are so perverse. 'Expect the unexpected' was the banner under which his solo career opened in 1977 and rarely has an advertising by-line been so accurate. On leaving the band he had no real desire to return to the fray, spending a year developing his 'bondage to cabbages'[46] and spending time with his family, during which time Genesis had gone on to greater and greater success. Experimenting with songwriting again – even having one recorded by Charlie Drake – when he did finally decide to put out a new record he chose to go for an interesting mix of styles though, the barbershop quartet of 'Excuse Me' aside, he didn't stray too far from the roots he had already put down. Further down the line, his second album was an altogether darker, denser affair with some genuinely disturbing moments, notably 'Exposure' and 'Home Sweet Home'. Since then his music has been heavily rooted in rhythms rather than the more melodic style of his past and he has become something of a spokesman for the growing world music movement. His work with Youssou N'Dour has been especially exciting and his concert tour of 1986/87 is best remembered for their joining forces on 'In Your Eyes', a heart-warming climax to the shows and a vindication of Peter's diligent studies of other cultures and their music.

His third album was really the first to build songs from rhythmic ideas and was a great artistic and critical success, even if its idiosyncracies did alienate his record company in America so that they dropped him from their roster of artists. History has proved who had the last laugh. If his music has been truly ground-breaking – the unusual sounds that he has used, particularly in the early days of the Fairlight have been adventurous and generally successful – his intellect has at times got in the way of the joyous nature of the music, though again paradoxically it is that same intellect that has made his records so appealing. Indeed, Tony Stratton-Smith was moved to say of Peter after he left Genesis, 'In the long term the only thing Genesis lost was Peter's mind, but I believe that was a very substantial loss and perhaps made the difference between Genesis being a world heavyweight champion for life and just a very good heavyweight champion.'[114]

At times Peter comes across as a very earnest, overly serious individual, but this is mainly a result of his discomfort in interviews and hides a mischievous sense of humour and a very quick mind. He doesn't believe in voicing opinions until he's sure of his ground, so when he does speak it is from a position of knowledge and his opinions are worth listening to. His work for Amnesty International, including the USA 'Conspiracy Of Hope' tour and the global trek for 'Human Rights Now!', is tireless and he is able to speak intelligently on the subject of human rights and its global implications – while his song 'Biko' has become an anthem for the struggle across the world. His championing of this and other causes has tended to put him into the political arena and has at times detracted attention from his musical work, but it's very clear that he is still a potent artistic figure.

His ideas have sometimes been swamped in a clutter of detail but on *So* he was able to strike a happy medium. His humour came through far more strongly – indeed it was a much more playful record than any in his past and there were some very beautiful melodies underpinned by some rhythmic innovation, a delicate balance but one which he accomplished with consummate ease. Working as purely a singer and arranger, he had intended to return to the blues and soul music that had so excited him in the sixties and do a record of cover versions. Shelving that, he did succeed in capturing the feel of those times on two of his own compositions, 'Sledgehammer' and 'Big Time', both massive hit singles.

True to form, Peter chose not to cash in on his newly won eminence, eschewing the opportunity to make *So 2* immediately. Instead he sunk much of his earnings from the album into the construction of a new state of the art studio in Bath, called Real World, also the name of the record company he has pioneered to bring unsung acts to the attention of the Western world. Artists such as Nusrat Fateh Ali Khan have recorded there at very low cost, Real World financing these projects by also allowing other more famous names to use the facility at ordinary commercial rates. The studio environment is particularly important to Gabriel, a legacy of years of recording in dark, dingy urban studios which are often not conducive to good performances. Real World is in a rural area, open to natural light and so a far healthier and more inspirational setting in which artists can work.

Peter's first work there was *Passion*, an extension of the soundtrack he wrote for Martin Scorsese's provocative film *The Last Temptation of Christ*. Having researched the music of the time and location with his customary vigour, Peter found that he had written additional material that didn't suit the movie and wanted to release a full, coherent body of work, not just a simple accompanying soundtrack LP. *Passion* eventually contained twenty-one pieces of music and was released simultaneously with a companion record *Passion Sources*, which gave an indication of his inspirations. While inevitably having a restricted audience, *Passion* was an exciting record of exploration and, to the more esoteric members of his audience, his most rewarding album to date.

There have been other, similarly esoteric side roads that Peter has investigated over the years, one of them being a film version of *The Lamb Lies Down On Broadway*. The idea seemed viable in 1979 and there was talk of the band reforming to record a soundtrack for the film, Peter spending two months working on a script with Jodorowsky, director of *El Topo*. Problems soon arose, particularly when Peter was dropped by Atlantic Records prior to his third album release, leaving his ability to raise capital at an all-time low. There was also a degree of reluctance on the part of the rest of the band to return to past glories and re-work old ideas. If the film had bitten the dust, Peter was slowly laying the foundations for another concept piece, the story of Mozo. Accepting that part of the problem in gaining acceptance for Rael was the amount of new music, Peter had the idea of introducing some songs that featured him on to his albums – songs such as 'On The Air' and 'Here Comes The Flood' though like a number of Peter's ideas, it is far from certain just what future there is, if any, for Mozo.

His latest interests lie around another Real World, one he describes as 'a hybrid mixture of university, holiday camp, theme park and Disneyland. A place where people can go to test themselves, to challenge themselves and entertain themselves, ideally transform certain parts of what they are.'[8] His fascination with technology and how it can interact with the human experience has been central to his work for many years and it clearly will continue to be so.

Nevertheless, music will still be the major source of expression and creativity. 'There's a great similarity between what I do and blues music, almost a cathartic reaction in which I can pour my heart out and feel a lot better at the end of it.'[115] Inside the man and the musician beats a heart irrevocably committed to the honest expression of his feelings, thoughts and ideas, someone drawn to the humanity in himself and in others – an indecently fine song-writer and a very decent man.

Hackett to pieces

'It wasn't an easy birth, far from an immaculate conception and nothing like natural childbirth, but I did manage to bring the child into the world kicking and screaming!' So said Steve Hackett of his 1983 album *Highly Strung*, but he could just as easily have been talking of his career since leaving Genesis. Of the three key departures from the band, Steve's was probably the bravest, Anthony Phillips being simply unable to continue, while Peter Gabriel, if initially leaving to go into retirement, must have been well aware that he had a readily sustainable solo career waiting for him should he ever want it. Steve, on the other hand, faced the problem that all non-singers seem to confront when cut adrift from their erstwhile group – the lack of any real identity, a problem all the more relevant to a refugee from a relatively faceless band such as Genesis who were still not a commercial proposition worldwide.

While major solo success in this country and in America has constantly eluded Steve, he has been very successful across Europe, having at times eclipsed his old group! His records have continued to be interesting adventures, naturally centred around the electric and acoustic guitar far more than was the case in Genesis and he has cornered himself a hardcore of devoted fans who are enthralled by the imaginative ways in which he employs his instrument. There have been dalliances with the mainstream such as 'Cell 151', a single ultimately defeated by record company inactivity, flirtations with the wildly bizarre in the form of 'Ace Of Wands' and a dance with the devil during his time with GTR, but always at the heart of his music has been the acoustic guitar, a love affair fully exposed on 'Bay Of Kings' and 'Momentum'.

His career away from the home that was Genesis began in earnest in 1978 with *Please Don't Touch*, a charming album full of clever ideas and lyrical melodies, a peace disturbed by some powerful intrusions of heavier playing as on the title track. Having left a self-contained unit, Steve spread his wings and recruited a whole range of players and singers to help out, which did give a disorientating impression and did little to set him up as a new artist, a problem exacerbated by his failure to take the music on the road. Rectifying that fault and in order to give the music a sharper focus, he assembled a band for his next album, *Spectral Mornings*, probably the finest of his career, one imbued with a real *joie de vivre* – the band enjoyed each other's company and while the songs were Steve's and he was clearly the ringmaster, a number of ideas were thrown up spontaneously. It was fortunate that the band, which included Dik Cadbury, Nick Magnus, John Shearer and Pete Hicks, got on so well together, for when they came to record in Holland they found themselves knee-deep in snow, marooned in the studio and its environs! It was a period of high confidence for Steve, the title track a mesmerizing piece of guitar work that returned to the grand orchestral, romantic sweep that Genesis had left behind on Steve's departure, while 'Clocks' thundered along showcasing the band to best effect. Album sales were impressive as was the supporting tour, doing especially well at the Reading Festival over the August Bank Holiday in 1979. The band continued to grow and develop its own style, though they were sometimes diffident, reining back when they could have stamped their own imprint on the music. The *Defector* album in 1980 showed a solid growth musically if not reaching the heights of *Spectral Mornings*, though the ensuing tour was stunning.

By this juncture, Hackett was beginning to carve out his own niche in the rock world, his popularity seemingly ensured, consistently playing to packed houses and making albums that achieved steady sales and good chart placings and yet allowed him the freedom of expression to attempt more intricate instrumentals such as 'Jacuzzi' and to employ the acoustic guitar to exhilarating effect, as on 'Two Vamps As Guests'. The band approach was central to this advance since it afforded the opportunity of extensive touring – always a good way of attracting an audience – giving the records a pugnacious cutting edge that a solo venture would have lacked. The interaction and strong personal relationships in a band set-up provided a healthy input to the music. Unfortunately, bands that operate on behalf of a leader do have their problems: 'I ran into Bill Bruford around 1980 when he had a group as well and he said, 'My band are driving me to the poorhouse – how about you?' It was very much the same thing, I don't know how I found the wages every week and unfortunately I had to split the band up which was a shame.'

Deprived of the gathering momentum, *Cured* was a workman-like response which featured some nice ideas – 'The Air-Conditioned Nightmare', in particular – but lacked consistency, recorded as it was around a nucleus of Steve and keyboard wizard Nick Magnus. The drums came courtesy of a machine and the whole thing lacked impact. Steve also had to handle all the vocals rather than just those which suited his range and that told on the finished product too. He was still able to assemble a band to tour which helped the record, but it was time for a period of re-assessment. When *Highly Strung* was released eighteen months later, Hackett returned to a group line-up, using the musicians who had worked on his previous tour, the results being far more satisfactory. The advance single, 'Cell 151', was a radio hit that just narrowly missed the charts, partly as a result of poor promotion from Charisma which was in a state of some turmoil, just before Virgin took control of its operations. That apart, the LP represented a return to the inquisitive stance he had taken since leaving Genesis, questioning the limits of conventional rock guitar and quietly extending those boundaries. Similarly, his next record *Bay Of Kings* repeated the process but in terms of acoustic guitar. 'I like to find the point at which it sounds like other instruments – there are areas of shading which are immense. I like to create "optical" illusions with it.'

Married to Kim Poor, a Brazilian artist, it seemed a matter of time before Hackett utilized the percussion and rhythmic ideas from that country and *Till We Have Faces* was the record to do that. It suffered very badly, however, from the lack of a support tour, in part impossible because of the awesome range of percussion that the new music used and which could not realistically be reproduced live. There were financial difficulties too, one of the reasons for Steve's involvement in the glossy world of American AOR with GTR. Its advance press stated that GTR intended to establish the guitar as the premier rock instrument, taking it into the nineties and it promised much with Hackett alongside Steve Howe from Yes, a very talented musician in his own right. When the record came out though, it was something entirely different: 'I always saw it in terms of a one-off. We both went in with our eyes open, it wasn't the most subtle thing we'd ever done, but it was a huge success in the States which filled the coffers and allowed me to make another record and tour with it.' *Momentum* was Steve's second acoustic album and was another delightful selection adding weight to his claims that 'I think the idea is to maintain a level of diversity and cross-over. I would like to continue to work at both ends of the music spectrum, though whether the rock and the acoustic things remain separate for ever I can't say.'

More than twenty years after advertising himself as a musician who was 'determined to strive beyond existing stagnant music forms,' Steve's greatest virtue is still his all-consuming passion for making music and discovering new ideas. 'It is a compulsion, an obsession. There's always so much ground to cover – when I started out, it was wonderful whenever I managed to find another chord, like another world! I've always felt that there are many victories ahead if you just keep going.'

APPENDIX II

PUT ANOTHER RECORD ON

GENESIS UK DISCOGRAPHY

'A living story'

ALBUMS

From Genesis To Revelation

Where The Sour Turns To Sweet; In The Beginning; Fireside Song; The Serpent; Am I Very Wrong?; In The Wilderness; The Conqueror; In Hiding; One Day; Window; In Limbo; Silent Sun; A Place To Call My Own.
Produced by Jonathan King. March 1969. Decca.

Trespass

Looking For Someone; White Mountain; Visions Of Angels; Stagnation; Dusk; The Knife.
Produced by John Anthony. October 1970. Charisma.
(Reached number ninety-eight on reissue in 1984.)

Nursery Cryme

The Musical Box; For Absent Friends; The Return Of The Giant Hogweed; Seven Stones; Harold The Barrel; Harlequin; The Fountain of Salmacis.
Produced by John Anthony. November 1971. Charisma.
(Reached number thirty-nine in 1974 and number sixty-eight on reissue in 1984.)

Foxtrot

Watcher Of The Skies; Time Table; Get 'Em Out By Friday; Can-Utility And The Coastliners; Horizons; Supper's Ready: (i) Lover's Leap, (ii) The Guaranteed Eternal Sanctuary Man, (iii) Ikhnaton And Itsacon And Their Band Of Merry Men, (iv) How Dare I Be So Beautiful?, (v) Willow Farm, (vi) Apocalypse In 9/8 (Co-starring The Delicious Talents Of Gabble Ratchet), (vii) As Sure As Eggs Is Eggs (Aching Men's Feet).
Produced by David Hitchcock and Genesis. October 1972. Charisma.
Chart: 12.

Live

Watcher Of The Skies; Get 'Em Out By Friday; The Return Of The Giant Hogweed; The Musical Box; The Knife.
Produced by John Burns and Genesis. August 1973. Charisma.
Chart: 9.

Selling England By The Pound

Dancing With The Moonlit Knight; I Know What I Like (In Your Wardrobe); Firth of Fifth; More Fool Me; The Battle Of Epping Forest; After The Ordeal; The Cinema Show; Aisle Of Plenty.
Produced by John Burns and Genesis. October 1973. Charisma.
Chart: 3.

The Lamb Lies Down On Broadway

The Lamb Lies Down On Broadway; Fly On A Windshield; Broadway Melody Of 1974; Cuckoo Cocoon; In The Cage; The Grand Parade Of Lifeless Packaging; Back in N.Y.C.; Hairless Heart; Counting Out Time; Carpet Crawl; The Chamber Of 32 Doors; Lilywhite Lilith; The Waiting Room; Anyway; Here Comes The Supernatural Anaesthetist; The Lamia; Silent Sorrow In Empty Boats; The Colony Of Slippermen: (i) Arrival, (ii) A Visit To The Doktor, (iii) Raven; Ravine; The Light Dies Down On Broadway; Riding The Scree; In the Rapids; It.
Produced by John Burns and Genesis. November 1974. Charisma.
Chart: 10.

A Trick Of The Tail

Dance On A Volcano; Entangled (Hackett/Banks); Squonk (Rutherford/Banks); Mad Man Moon (Banks); Robbery, Assault and Battery (Banks/

Collins); Ripples (Rutherford/Banks); A Trick Of The Tail (Banks); Los Endos.
Produced by David Hentschel and Genesis. February 1976. Charisma. Chart: 3.

Wind And Wuthering

Eleventh Earl Of Mar (Banks/Hackett/Rutherford); One For The Vine (Banks); Your Own Special Way (Rutherford); Wot Gorilla? (Collins/ Banks); All In A Mouse's Night (Banks); Blood On The Rooftops (Hackett/ Collins); Unquiet Slumbers For The Sleepers . . . (Hackett/Rutherford); . . . In That Quiet Earth; Afterglow (Banks).
Produced by David Hentschel and Genesis. January 1977. Charisma. Chart: 7.

Seconds Out

Squonk; The Carpet Crawl; Robbery, Assault and Battery; Afterglow; Firth Of Fifth; I Know What I Like; The Lamb Lies Down On Broadway; The Musical Box (Closing Section); Supper's Ready; The Cinema Show; Dance On A Volcano; Los Endos.
Produced by David Hentschel and Genesis, assisted by Neil Ross. October 1977. Charisma.
Chart: 4.

. . . And Then There Were Three . . .

Down And Out; Undertow (Banks); Ballad Of Big; Snowbound (Rutherford); Burning Rope (Banks); Deep In The Motherlode (Rutherford); Many Too Many (Banks); Scenes From A Night's Dream (Collins/Banks); Say It's Alright Joe (Rutherford); The Lady Lies (Banks); Follow You Follow Me.
Produced by David Hentschel and Genesis. April 1978. Charisma. Chart: 3.

Duke

Behind The Lines; Duchess; Guide Vocal (Banks); Man Of Our Times (Rutherford); Misunderstanding (Collins); Heathaze (Banks); Turn It On Again; Alone Tonight (Rutherford); Cul-De-Sac (Banks); Please Don't Ask (Collins); Duke's Travels; Duke's End.
Produced by David Hentschel and Genesis. March 1980. Charisma. Chart: 1.

Abacab

Abacab; No Reply At All; Me And Sarah Jane (Banks); Keep It Dark; Dodo; Lurker; Who Dunnit?; Man On The Corner (Collins); Like It Or Not (Rutherford); Another Record.
Produced by Genesis. September 1981. Charisma.
Chart: 1.

Three Sides Live

Turn It On Again; Dodo; Abacab; Behind The Lines; Duchess; Me And Sarah Jane; Follow You Follow Me; Misunderstanding; In The Cage (Medley – The Cinema Show, Slippermen); Afterglow; One For The Vine; Fountain Of Salmacis; It/Watcher Of The Skies.
Produced by Genesis. June 1982. Charisma.
Chart: 2.

Genesis

Mama; That's All; Home By The Sea; Second Home By The Sea; Illegal Alien; Taking It All Too Hard; Just A Job To Do; Silver Rainbow; It's Gonna Get Better.
Produced by Genesis with Hugh Padgham. October 1983. Charisma.
Chart: 1.

Invisible Touch

Invisible Touch; Tonight, Tonight, Tonight; Land Of Confusion; In Too Deep; Anything She Does; Domino: (i) In The Glow Of The Night, (ii) The Last Domino; Throwing It All Away; The Brazilian.
Produced by Genesis and Hugh Padgham. June 1986. Virgin.
Chart: 1.

We Can't Dance

No Son Of Mine; Jesus He Knows Me; Driving The Last Spike; I Can't Dance; Never A Time; Dreaming While You Sleep; Tell Me Why; Living Forever; Hold On My Heart; Way Of The World; Since I Lost You; Fading Lights.
Produced by Genesis and Nick Davis. November 1991. Virgin.
Chart: 1.

SINGLES

The Silent Sun/That's Me. February 1968.

A Winter's Tale/One Eyed Hound. May 1968.

Where The Sour Turns To Sweet/In Hiding. June 1969.

The Knife (Part 1)/*The Knife* (Part 2). May 1971.

Happy The Man/Seven Stones. October 1972.

I Know What I Like (In Your Wardrobe)/Twilight Alehouse. February 1974.
Chart: 21.

Counting Out Time/Riding The Scree. November 1974.

The Carpet Crawlers/Evil Jam (The Waiting Room Live). April 1975.

A Trick Of The Tail/Ripples. March 1976.

Your Own Special Way/It's Yourself. February 1977. Chart: 43.

Spot The Pigeon EP: Match Of The Day (Banks/Collins/Rutherford);
Pigeons (Banks/Collins/Rutherford); Inside And Out. May 1977.
Chart: 14.

Follow You Follow Me/Ballad Of Big. March 1978. Chart: 7.

Many, Too Many/The Day The Light Went Out (Banks)/Vancouver
(Collins/Rutherford). June 1978. Chart: 43.

Turn It On Again/Behind The Lines Part 2. March 1980. Chart: 8.

Duchess/Open Door (Rutherford). May 1980. Chart: 46.

Misunderstanding/Evidence Of Autumn (Banks). August 1980. Chart: 42.

Abacab/Another Record. August 1981. Chart: 9.

Keep It Dark/Naminanu. October 1981. Chart: 33.
12": As 7" plus Abacab (long version).

Man On The Corner/Submarine. March 1982. Chart: 41.

3 × 3 EP: Paperlate/You Might Recall/Me And Virgil. May 1982. Chart: 10.
7" picture disc: As 7".

Mama/It's Gonna Get Better. August 1983. Chart: 4.
12": Mama (ext.)/It's Gonna Get Better (ext.)
Later released as CD as per 12" release.

That's All/Taking It All Too Hard. November 1983. Chart: 16.
7" shaped picture disc: As 7".
12": As 7" plus Firth Of Fifth (live).

Illegal Alien/Turn It On Again (live). January 1984. Chart: 46.
7" shaped picture disc: As 7".
12": Illegal Alien/Turn It On Again (specially ext. live version).

Invisible Touch/The Last Domino. May 1986. Chart: 15.
7" clear vinyl fold-out sleeve: As 7".
12": As 7" with Invisible Touch (ext.).

In Too Deep (edit)/Do The Neurotic (edit). August 1986. Chart: 19.
    12": In Too Deep/Do The Neurotic.
    12" picture disc: In Too Deep/Do the Neurotic.
Land Of Confusion/Feeding The Fire. November 1986. Chart: 14.
    12": As 7" plus Land Of Confusion (ext.).
    CD: As 7" plus Land Of Confusion (ext.) and Do The Neurotic.
Tonight, Tonight, Tonight (remix edit)/In The Glow Of The Night. March
    1987. Chart: 18.
    12": Tonight, Tonight, Tonight (remix edit)/In The Glow Of The Night/
    Paperlate/Tonight, Tonight, Tonight (12" remix).
    12" gatefold sleeve: Tonight, Tonight, Tonight, (remix edit)/In The
    Glow Of The Night/Tonight, Tonight, Tonight (12" remix).
    CD: Tonight, Tonight, Tonight (remix edit)/In The Glow Of The Night/
    Invisible Touch (12" remix)/Tonight, Tonight, Tonight (12" remix).
    CD: Tonight, Tonight, Tonight (remix edit)/In The Glow Of The Night/
    Paperlate/Tonight, Tonight, Tonight (12" remix).
Throwing It All Away/I'd Rather Be You. June 1987. Chart: 22.
    Cassette: Throwing It All Away (live)/I'd Rather Be You/Invisible Touch
    (live).
    12": Throwing It all Away (live)/I'd Rather Be You/Invisible Touch
    (live).
No Son Of Mine/Living Forever. October 1991. Chart: 6.
    Cassette: As 7".
    12" gatefold and print: As 7" plus Invisible Touch (live).
    CD: As 7" plus Invisible Touch (live).
I Can't Dance/On The Shoreline. December 1991. Chart: 7.
    Cassette: As 7".
    CD: I Can't Dance/On The Shoreline/I Can't Dance (Sex Mix).
    CD and band history booklet: I Can't Dance/On The Shoreline/In Too
    Deep (live)/That's All (live).
Hold On My Heart/Way Of The World. April 1992. Chart: 16.
    Cassette: As 7".
    CD: Hold On My Heart/Way Of The World/Home By The Sea (live).
    CD and postcards: Hold On My Heart/Way Of The World/Your Own
    Special Way (live).
Jesus He Knows Me/Hearts On Fire. July 1992. Chart: 20.
    Cassette: As 7".
    CD: Jesus He Knows Me/Hearts On Fire/I Can't Dance (The Other
    Mix).
    CD and Collector's Box: Jesus He Knows Me/Hearts On Fire/Land Of
    Confusion (Rehearsal Version).

VIDEOS

Three Sides Live

Recorded in November and December 1981 at Long Island Nassau Coliseum, New York Savoy Theatre and Birmingham NEC: Behind The Lines; Duchess; Misunderstanding; Dodo; Abacab; No Reply At All; Who Dunnit?; In The Cage (Medley – Cinema Show/Slippermen); Afterglow; Me And Sarah Jane; Man On The Corner; Turn It On Again.
Released 1982. Wienerworld.

Live – The Mama Tour

Recorded in February 1984 at Birmingham NEC: Abacab; That's All; Mama; Illegal Alien; Home By The Sea; Second Home By The Sea; Keep It Dark; It's Gonna Get Better; In The Cage; Cinema Show; Afterglow; Turn It On Again; Final Medley.
Released 1985. Virgin Video.

Visible Touch

Anything She Does; Throwing It All Away; Tonight, Tonight, Tonight; Land of Confusion; In Too Deep; Invisible Touch; Tour Documentary.
Released 1987. Virgin Video.

Videos Volume 1

Mama; No Reply At All; Land Of Confusion; That's All; Tonight, Tonight, Tonight; Duchess; Anything She Does; Robbery, Assault and Battery; In Too Deep; Abacab; Follow You Follow Me.
Released 1988. Virgin Video.

Videos Volume 2

Illegal Alien; Throwing It All Away; Misunderstanding; Ripples; Keep It Dark; A Trick Of The Tail; Home By The Sea; Second Home By The Sea; Man On The Corner; Turn It On Again; Many Too Many; Invisible Touch.
Released 1988. Virgin Video.

Invisible Touch Tour

Recorded at Wembley Stadium, July 1987: Mama; Abacab; Domino; That's All; Brazilian; Land Of Confusion; Tonight, Tonight, Tonight;

Throwing It All Away; Home By The Sea; Invisible Touch; Drum Duet;
Los Endos; Turn It On Again (medley); Do The Neurotic.
Released 1988. Virgin Video. (Initial copies included free CD: Domino
live).

Genesis – A History

Released 1991. Virgin Video.

Knebworth – The Event

Recorded at Knebworth Park, 30 June 1990: Mama; Throwing It All Away;
Turn It On Again medley.
Released 1991. Castle Music Pictures.

BOOKS

Fielder, Hugh, *The Book of Genesis*, Sidgwick & Jackson, London, 1984
Gallo, Armando, *Genesis – The Evolution of a Rock Band*, Sidgwick &
    Jackson, London, 1978
    Genesis – I Know What I Like, DIY Books, Los Angeles, 1980
    Genesis – From One Fan To Another, Omnibus Press, London, 1984
Kamin, Philip, and Peter Goddard, *Genesis – Peter Gabriel, Phil Collins and
    Beyond*, Sidgwick & Jackson, London, 1984
Parkyn, Geoff, *Genesis – The Illustrated Discography*, Omnibus Press,
    London, 1983. Reprinted in 1984 as *Turn It On Again*.
Poor, Kim (illustrator), *Genesis Lyrics*, Sidgwick & Jackson, London, 1979.

INFORMATION

Genesis Information Service: PO Box 107, London, N6 5RU.

TONY BANKS UK DISCOGRAPHY

'The power to move and satisfy'

ALBUMS

A Curious Feeling

From The Undertow; Lucky Me; The Lie; After The Lie; A Curious Feeling; Forever Morning; You; Somebody Else's Dream; The Waters Of Lethe; For A While; In The Dark.
Produced by David Hentschel and Tony Banks. October 1979. Charisma.
Chart: 21.

The Wicked Lady – Original Soundtrack

The Wicked Lady; Spring; The Chase; Caroline; Jerry Jackson; Repentance; Kit; Barbara; *Prelude To The Wicked Lady; *Caroline's Theme; *Scherzo; *Pastorale; *The Wicked Lady; *Kit's Theme; *Finale.
*Played by National Philharmonic Orchestra of London. Other music recorded by Tony Banks. April 1983. Atlantic.

The Fugitive

This Is Love; Man Of Spells; And The Wheels Keep Turning; Say You'll Never Leave Me; Thirty-Threes; By You; At The Edge Of The Night; Charm; Moving Under; K2; Sometime Never.
Produced by Tony Banks assisted by Stephen Short. June 1983. Charisma.
Chart: 50.

Soundtracks

*Shortcut To Somewhere (Banks/Fish); Smilin' Jack Casey; Quicksilver Suite; †You Call This Victory (Banks/Diamond); †Lion Of Symmetry (Banks/Wilcox); Redwing Suite.
Produced by Tony Banks, except * by Richard Burgess; † by Tony Banks and John Eden. May 1986. Charisma.

Still

Red Day On Blue Street (Banks/Kershaw); Angel Face; The Gift; Still It Takes Me By Surprise; Hero For An Hour; I Wanna Change The Score (Banks/Kershaw); Water Out Of Wine; Another Murder Of A Day (Banks/Fish); Back To Back; The Final Curtain.
Produced by Tony Banks and Nick Davis. May 1991. Virgin.

WITH BANKSTATEMENT

Bankstatement

Throwback; I'll Be Waiting; Queen Of Darkness; That Night; Raincloud; The Border; Big Man; A House Needs A Roof; The More I Hide It; Diamonds Aren't So Hard; Thursday The Twelfth.
Produced by Steve Hillage and Tony Banks. August 1989. Virgin.

SINGLES

For A While/From The Undertow. October 1979.
For A While (remix)/A Curious Feeling. July 1980.
The Wicked Lady/The Wicked Lady (played by the National Philharmonic Orchestra Of London). April 1983.
This Is Love/Charm. May 1983.
    12": This Is Love (ext.)/Charm (ext.)
And The Wheels Keep Turning/Man Of Spells. August 1983.
Lorca And The Outlaws EP: You Call This Victory; Redwing; Lion Of Symmetry. 1985.
Shortcut To Somewhere/Smilin' Jack Casey. September 1986. Chart: 75.
    12": Shortcut To Somewhere/Smilin' Jack Casey/K2.
    (Billed as Fish and Tony Banks.)

I Wanna Change The Score/Hero For An Hour. May 1991.
    Cassette: As 7".
    12": As 7" plus Big Man.
    CD: As 7" plus Big Man and The Waters Of Lethe.
The Gift/Back to Back. July 1991.
    Cassette: As 7".
    12": As 7" plus A House Needs A Roof.
    CD: As 7" plus A House Needs A Roof and Redwing.
Still It Takes Me By Surprise (edit)/The Final Curtain. February 1992.
    CD: As 7" plus Still It Takes Me By Surprise (full-length version).

WITH BANKSTATEMENT

Throwback/Thursday The Twelfth. 1989.
    12": As 7" plus This Is Love.
    CD: As 7" plus This Is Love.
I'll Be Waiting/Diamonds Aren't So Hard. 1989.
    12": As 7" plus And The Wheels Keep Turning.
    CD: As 7" plus And The Wheels Keep Turning.
NB. Tony Banks' specially commissioned soundtracks can be heard on
    the video releases of *The Wicked Lady, Lorca And The Outlaws, Quick-
    silver* and *The Shout* (co-written with Mike Rutherford).

PHIL COLLINS UK DISCOGRAPHY

'All of my life'

ALBUMS

Face Value

In The Air Tonight; This Must Be Love; Behind The Lines (Banks/Collins/ Rutherford); The Roof is Leaking; Droned; Hand In Hand; I Missed Again; You Know What I Mean; Thunder And Lightning; I'm Not Moving; If Leaving Me Is Easy; Tomorrow Never Knows (Lennon/ McCartney); Over The Rainbow (Harburg/Arlen).
Produced by Phil Collins, assisted by Hugh Padgham. February 1981.
Virgin.
Chart: 1.

Hello, I Must Be Going

I Don't Care Anymore; I Cannot Believe It's True; Like China; Do You Know, Do You Care?; You Can't Hurry Love (Holland/Dozier/Holland); It Don't Matter To Me; Thru These Walls; Don't Let Him Steal Your Heart Away; The West Side; Why Can't It Wait 'Til Morning?
Produced by Phil Collins, assisted by Hugh Padgham. November 1982.
Virgin.
Chart: 2.

No Jacket Required

Sussudio; Only You Know And I Know (Collins/Stuermer); Long Long Way To Go; I Don't Wanna Know (Collins/Stuermer); One More Night; Don't Lose My Number; Who Said I Would?; Doesn't Anybody Stay

Together Anymore? (Collins/Stuermer); Inside Out; Take Me Home; We Said Hello Goodbye.
Produced by Phil Collins and Hugh Padgham. February 1985. Virgin. Chart: 1.

. . .But Seriously

Hang In Long Enough; That's Just The Way It Is; Do You Remember?; Something Happened On The Way To Heaven (Collins/Stuermer); Colours; I Wish It Would Rain Down; Another Day In Paradise; Heat On The Street; All Of My Life; Saturday Night And Sunday Morning (Collins/ Washington); Father To Son; Find A Way To My Heart.
Produced by Phil Collins and Hugh Padgham. November 1989. Virgin. Chart: 1.

Serious Hits . . . Live!

Something Happened On The Way To Heaven; Against All Odds; Who Said I Would?; One More Night; Don't Lose My Number; Do You Remember; Another Day In Paradise; Separate Lives (Bishop); In The Air Tonight; You Can't Hurry Love; Two Hearts (Collins/Dozier); Sussudio; Groovy Kind Of Love (Bayer Sager/Wine); Easy Lover (Collins/East/ Bailey); Take Me Home.
Produced by Phil Collins and Robert Colby. November 1990. Virgin. Chart: 2.

WITH FLAMING YOUTH

Ark II

Guide Me Orion (Smith); Earthglow (Smith/Chatton); The Planets (Chatton/Collins/Smith/Caryl); Changes (Smith/Collins); Pulsar (Smith/ Chatton); Space Child (Collins); In The Light Of Love (Smith/Collins/ Chatton/Caryl); From Now On (Immortal Invisible) (Chatton).
Produced by Barry Ainsworth. November 1969. Fontana.

With Brand X

Unorthodox Behaviour

Nuclear Burn; Euthanasia Waltz; Born Ugly; Smacks Of Euphoric Hysteria; Unorthodox Behaviour; Running On Three; Touch Wood.
All songs by Collins/Goodsall/Lumley/Jones.
Produced by Brand X and Dennis Mackay. July 1976. Charisma.

Moroccan Roll

Sun In The Night (Goodsall); Why Should I Lend You Mine (When You've Broken Yours Off Already) . . . into Maybe I'll Lend You Mine After All (Collins); Hate Zone (Goodsall); Collapsar (Lumley); Disco Suicide (Lumley); Orbits (Jones); Malaga Virgen (Jones); Macrocosm (Goodsall).
Produced by Dennis Mackay and Brand X. April 1977. Charisma.
Chart: 37.

Livestock

Nightmare Patrol (Goodsall/Dennard); -Ish (Goodsall/Lumley/Jones/Pert/ Collins); Euthanasia Waltz; Isis Morning: (i) (Goodsall/Jones/Lumley/ Pert/Collins), (ii) (Collins); Malaga Virgen.
Produced by Brand X. November 1977. Charisma.

Product

Don't Make Waves (Goodsall); Dance Of The Illegal Aliens (Jones); Soho (Goodsall/Collins); Not Good Enough – See Me! (Jones/Robinson); Algon (Where An Ordinary Cup Of Drinking Chocolate Costs £8,000,000,000) (Lumley); Rhesus Perplexus (Giblin); Wal to Wal (Jones/ Giblin); . . . And So To F . . . (Collins); April (Giblin).
Produced by Brand X with Colin Green and Neil Kernon. September 1979. Charisma.

Do They Hurt?

Noddy Goes To Sweden (Jones); Voidarama (Goodsall); Act Of will (Goodsall); Fragile! (Jones/Robinson); Cambodia (Goodsall); Triumphant Limp (Goodsall/Giblin/Lumley/Collins); D.M.Z. (Jones).
Produced by Brand X and Neil Kernon. May 1980. Charisma.

Is There Anything About?

Ipanaemia (Goodsall); A Longer April (Giblin); Modern, Noisy And Effective (Goodsall/Lumley/Short); Swan Song (Collins/Lumley/Giblin/Short); Is There Anything About? (Jones/Goodsall/Lumley/Collins); TMIU-ATGA (Giblin/Robinson/Lumley).
Produced by Robin Lumley and Steven Short. September 1982. CBS.
Chart: 93.

SINGLES

In the Air Tonight/The Roof Is Leaking. January 1981. Chart: 2.
   7" cartoon booklet: As 7".
I Missed Again/I'm Not Moving. March 1981. Chart: 14.
   12": As 7".
If Leaving Me Is Easy/In The Air Tonight (demo)/I Missed Again (demo)/If Leaving Me Is Easy (demo). May 1981. Chart: 17.
   7" poster sleeve: As 7".
Thru These Walls/Do You Know, Do You Care? October 1982. Chart: 56.
   7" picture disc: As 7".
You Can't Hurry Love/I Cannot Believe It's True. November 1982. Chart: 1.
   7" picture disc: As 7".
   12": As 7" plus Oddball.
   Later released as CD as per 12" release.
Don't Let Him Steal Your Heart Away/Thunder And Lightning. March 1983. Chart: 45.
   12": Don't Let Him Steal Your Heart Away/ . . . And So To F . . . (live).
Why Can't It Wait 'Til Morning/Like China. May 1983.
Against All Odds (Take A Look At Me Now)/Making A Big Mistake (written and performed by Mike Rutherford). April 1984. Chart: 2.
   7" picture disc: As 7".
Sussudio/The Man With The Horn. January 1985. Chart: 12.
   12": As 7" plus Sussudio (ext. remix).
   12" picture disc: As 7" plus Sussudio (ext. remix).
One More Night/I Like The Way (Collins/Stuermer). April 1985. Chart: 4.
   7" shaped picture disc. As 7".
   12": One More Night (ext. mix)/I Like The Way.
Take Me Home/We Said Hello Goodbye. July 1985. Chart: 19.
   12": As 7" plus Take Me Home (ext. remix).
   12" gatefold: As 7" plus Take Me Home (ext. remix).

In The Air Tonight (88 Remix)/I Missed Again. June 1988. Chart: 4.
    12": As 7" plus In The Air Tonight (ext.).
    CD: As 7" plus In The Air Tonight (ext.).
A Groovy Kind Of Love (Big Noise (Collins/Dozier). August 1988.
    Chart: 1.
    12": As 7".
    12" gatefold: As 7".
    CD: As 7" plus Will You Be Waiting? (written and performed by Anne
    Dudley).
Two Hearts/The Robbery (written and performed by Anne Dudley).
    November 1988. Chart: 6.
    12": As 7".
    12" & postcards: As 7".
    CD in heart-shaped box: As 7".
Another Day In Paradise/Heat On The Street. October 1989. Chart: 2.
    Cassette: As 7".
    12": As 7" plus Saturday Night And Sunday Morning.
    CD: As 7" plus Saturday Night And Sunday Morning.
I Wish It Would Rain Down/Homeless. January 1990. Chart: 7.
    Cassette: As 7".
    12": As 7" plus You've Been In Love (That Little Bit Too Long).
    12" & lyric sheet: As 7" plus You've Been In Love (That Little Bit Too
    Long).
    CD: As 7" plus You've Been In Love (That Little Bit Too Long).
Something Happened On The Way To Heaven/I wish It Would Rain Down
    (demo). April 1990. Chart: 15.
    7" booklet sleeve: As 7".
    Cassette: As 7".
    12": As 7" plus Something Happened On The Way To Heaven (one
    world remix).
    CD: As 7" plus Something Happened On The Way To Heaven (one
    world remix).
That's Just The Way It Is/Broadway Chorus. July 1990. Chart: 26.
    Cassette: As 7".
    12": As 7" plus In The Air Tonight (ext.).
    CD: As 7" plus In The Air Tonight (ext.).
Hang In Long Enough/Around The World in 80 Presets. October 1990.
    Chart: 34.
    Cassette: As 7".
    12": Hang In Long Enough (Pettibone 12" mix)/Hang In Long Enough
    (7")/Hang In Long Enough (Pettibone dub mix).
    CD: Hang In Long Enough/Around The World in 80 Presets/Hang In
    Long Enough (Pettibone 12" mix).

CD picture disc numbered edition: Hang In Long Enough/That's How I Feel/Hang In Long Enough (Pettibone dub mix).

Do You Remember? (Live)/Against All Odds (live). December 1990. Chart: 57.
12": As 7" plus Doesn't Anybody Stay Together Anymore? (live).
CD: As 7" plus Doesn't Anybody Stay Together Anymore? (live)/Inside Out (live).
CD picture disc in carousel: Do You Remember? (live)/Doesn't Anybody Stay Together Anymore? (live)/The Roof is Leaking (live).

PHIL COLLINS AND MARILYN MARTIN

Separate Lives (Bishop)/Only You Know And I Know. November 1985. Chart: 4.
7" white vinyl and poster: As 7".
7" × 2 interlocking picture discs: As 7".
12": Separate Lives/Only You Know And I Know (ext. remix).

PHILIP BAILEY AND PHIL COLLINS

Easy Lover (Bailey/Collins/East)/Woman (written and performed by Philip Bailey). March 1985. Chart: 1.
12": Easy Lover. (ext. remix)/Woman.

WITH FLAMING YOUTH

Guide Me Orion/From Now On (Immortal Invisible). November 1969.

WITH BRAND X

Soho/Dance Of The Illegal Aliens. September 1979.
12": Soho/Noddy Goes To Sweden/Pool Room Blues (Brand X).

VIDEOS

Video EP

In The Air Tonight; I Missed Again; Thru These Walls; You Can't Hurry Love.
Released 1983. Picture Music International.

Live At Perkins Palace

Live In California, 1983: I Don't Care Anymore; I Cannot Believe It's True; Thru These Walls; I Missed Again; Behind The Lines; The Roof Is Leaking; The West Side; In The Air Tonight; You Can't Hurry Love; It Don't Matter To Me; People Get Ready.
Released 1983. Picture Music International.

No Jacket Required EP

Sussudio; One More Night; Who Said I Would?; Don't Lose My Number; Take Me Home.
Released 1985. Virgin Video.

No Ticket Required

Live At Reunion Arena, Dallas, Texas, 1985: Only You Know And I Know; Against All Odds; Who Said I Would?; Sussudio; Behind The Lines; The West Side; One More Night; In The Air Tonight; Like China; You Can't Hurry Love; It Don't Matter To Me; Hand In Hand; Take Me Home; It's Alright; Droned.
Released 1985. Virgin Video.

Gold Rushes

You Can't Hurry Love; One More Night.
Released 1987. Wienerworld.

Phil Collins Is Buster (The Making Of The Movie)

A Groovy Kind Of Love; Two Hearts.
Released 1988. Vestron Video.

The Singles Collection

Don't Lose My Number; I Missed Again; A Groovy Kind Of Love; Who Said I Would?; You Can't Hurry Love; Thru These Walls; Sussudio; One More Night; Two Hearts; In The Air Tonight; Easy Lover; Against All Odds; Take Me Home.
Released 1989. Virgin Video.

Buster

Released 1990. Vestron Video.

Seriously Live In Berlin

Live In Berlin, 1990: Hand In Hand; Hang In Long Enough; Against All Odds; Don't Lose My Number; Inside Out; Do You Remember?; Who Said I Would?; Another Day In Paradise; Separate Lives; Saturday Night And Sunday Morning; The West Side; That's Just The Way It Is; Something Happened On The Way To Heaven; Doesn't Anybody Stay Together Anymore?; One More Night; Colours; In The Air Tonight; You Can't Hurry Love; Two Hearts; Sussudio; A Groovy Kind Of Love; Easy Lover; Always; Take Me Home.
Released 1990. Virgin Video.

Knebworth – The Event

Recorded at Knebworth Park, 30 June 1990: In The Air Tonight; Sussudio.
Released 1991. Castle Music Pictures.

. . .But Seriously, The Videos

Hang In Long Enough; Another Day In Paradise; Do You Remember?; Colours; Something Happened On The Way To Heaven; All Of My Life; Heat On The Street; That's Just The Way It Is; Saturday Night And Sunday Morning; Father To Son; Find A Way To My Heart; Around The World In Eighty Presets.
Released May 1992. Virgin Video.

BOOKS

Waller, Johnny, *The Phil Collins Story*, Zomba Books, London, 1985.

INFORMATION

Information Service: PO Box 107, London N6 5RU.

MIKE RUTHERFORD UK DISCOGRAPHY

'Everybody gets a second chance'

ALBUMS

Smallcreep's Day

Smallcreep's Day – Between The Tick And The Tock, Working In Line, After Hours, Cats And Rats (In This Neighbourhood), Smallcreep Alone, Out Into The Daylight, At The End Of The Day; Moonshine; Time And Time Again; Romani; Every Road; Overnight Job.
Produced by David Hentschel. January 1980. Charisma.
Chart: 13.

Acting Very Strange

Acting Very Strange; A Day To Remember; Maxine (Rutherford/Bellotte); Halfway There (Rutherford/Palmer); Who's Fooling Who (Rutherford/Palmer); Couldn't Get Arrested (Rutherford/Bellotte); I Don't Wanna Know; Hideaway.
Produced by Mike Rutherford, assisted by Nick Launay. September 1982. WEA.
Chart: 23.

WITH MIKE AND THE MECHANICS

Mike And The Mechanics

Silent Running (On Dangerous Ground) (Rutherford/Robertson); All I Need Is A Miracle (Rutherford/Neil); Par Avion (Rutherford/Neil);

Hanging By A Thread (Rutherford/Neil/Robertson); I Get The Feeling (Rutherford/Neil); Take The Reins (Rutherford/Neil/Robertson); You Are The One (Rutherford/Neil); A Call To Arms (Banks/Collins/Rutherford/ Neil/Robertson); Taken In (Rutherford/Neil).
Produced by Christopher Neil. November 1985. WEA.
Chart: 78.

Living Years

Nobody's Perfect (Rutherford/Robertson); The Living Years (Rutherford/ Robertson); Seeing Is Believing (Rutherford/Robertson); Nobody Knows (Rutherford/Neil); Poor Boy Down (Rutherford/Neil); Blame (Rutherford/ Neil); Don't (Rutherford/Neil); Black & Blue (Rutherford/Robertson/ Young); Beautiful Day (Rutherford/Neil/Young); Why Me? (Rutherford/ Robertson).
Produced by Christopher Neil and Mike Rutherford. October 1988. WEA.
Chart: 2.

Word Of Mouth

Get Up (Rutherford/Carrack); *Word of Mouth (Rutherford/Neil); A Time And Place (Rutherford/Robertson); *Yesterday, Today, Tomorrow (Rutherford/Robertson); The Way You Look At Me (Rutherford/ Carrack); *Everybody Gets A Second Chance (Rutherford/Robertson); *Stop Baby (Neil/Rutherford); My Crime Of Passion (Rutherford/Carrack/Lee); Let's Pretend It Didn't Happen (Rutherford/Robertson); Before (The Next Heartache Falls) (Rutherford/Carrack).
Produced by Christopher Neil, Mike Rutherford and Russ Titelman, except * by Christopher Neil and Mike Rutherford. April 1991. Virgin.
Chart: 11.

SINGLES

Working In Line/Compression. January 1980.
Time And Time Again/At The End Of The Day. July 1980.
    Also mispressed with Overnight Job as the B-side.
Halfway There/A Day To Remember. August 1982.
Acting Very Strange/Couldn't Get Arrested (nix mix). October 1982.
    12": Acting Very Strange (ext.)/Couldn't Get Arrested (ext. nix mix).
Hideaway/Calypso. January 1983.
    NB. Mike Rutherford's song 'Making A Big Mistake' forms the B-side
    to Phil Collins' 'Against All Odds (Take A Look At Me Now)'.

With Mike and the Mechanics

Silent Running/I Get The Feeling. October 1985 and February 1986.
Chart: 21.
 7" shaped picture disc: As 7".
 12": As 7" plus Too Far Gone.
All I Need Is A Miracle (remix)/You Are The One. May 1986. Chart: 53.
 7" double pack: included Silent Running 7".
 12": as 7" plus A Call To Arms.
 12" picture disc: As 7" plus A Call To Arms.
Nobody's Perfect/Nobody Knows. October 1988.
 12": Nobody's Perfect (ext.)/Nobody Knows/All I Need Is A Miracle.
 CD: Nobody's Perfect/Nobody's Perfect (ext.)/Nobody Knows.
Living Years/Too Many Friends (Rutherford/Neil). January 1989. Chart: 2.
 12": As 7" plus I Get The Feeling (live).
 CD: As 7" plus I Get The Feeling (live).
Nobody Knows (edit)/Why Me? April 1989.
 Cassette: As 7".
 12": As 7" plus Nobody Knows (full version).
 CD: As 7" plus Nobody Knows (full version).
Word Of Mouth/Let's Pretend It Didn't Happen. March 1991. Chart: 13.
 Cassette: As 7".
 12" gatefold: As 7".
 CD: As 7".
 CD individually numbered edition: As 7" plus Taken In (live).
A Time And Place/Yesterday, Today, Tomorrow. May 1991. Chart: 58.
 Cassette: As 7".
 12": As 7" plus Word Of Mouth (east west mix).
 CD: As 7" plus Word Of Mouth (east west mix).
 CD with photo wallet: As 7" plus Word Of Mouth (east west mix).
Stop Baby/Get Up. October 1991.
 CD: As 7" plus Before (The Next Heartache Falls).
 CD: As 7" plus I Think I've Got The Message (Rutherford/Robertson)
 and My Crime Of Passion (acoustic version).
Everybody Gets A Second Chance/The Way You Look At Me. January 1992.
 Chart: 62.
 Cassette: As 7".
 CD: As 7" plus At The End Of The Day.

VIDEO

With Mike and the Mechanics

A Closer Look

Silent Running; All I Need Is A Miracle; Taken In; Nobody's Perfect;
Nobody Knows;
Released 1991. Warner Music Vision.
Seeing Is Believing; The Living Years.
NB. Mike Rutherford's specially commissioned soundtrack, written with
Tony Banks, can be heard on the video of *The Shout*.

ANTHONY PHILLIPS UK DISCOGRAPHY

'Back to the pavilion'

ALBUMS

The Geese And The Ghost

Wind – Tales; Which Way The Wind Blows; Henry – Portraits From
Tudor Times (Phillips/Rutherford): (i) Fanfare, (ii) Lutes' Chorus, (iii)
Misty Battlements, (iv) Henry Goes to War, (v) Death of A Knight, (vi)
Triumphant Return; God If I Saw Her Now; Chinese Mushroom Cloud
(Phillips/Rutherford); The Geese And The Ghost (Phillips/Rutherford);
Collections; Sleepfall; The Geese Fly West.
Produced by Simon Heyworth, Anthony Phillips and Michael
Rutherford. March 1977. Hit & Run Music.
Reissued on CD in 1990 by Virgin Records, including 'Master Of Time
(demo)'.

Wise After The Event

We're All As We Lie; Birdsong; Moonshooter; Wise After The Event;
Pulling Faces; Regrets; Greenhouse (Gilbert/Phillips); Paperchase; Now
What (Are They Doing To My Little Friends?).
Produced by Rupert Hine. June 1978. Arista Records.
Reissued on CD in 1990 by Virgin Records, including 'Squirrel'.

Sides

Um & Aargh; I Want Your Love; Lucy Will; Side Door; Holy Deadlock
(Phillips/Hall); Sisters Of Remindum; Bleak House; Magdalen;
Nightmare.

Produced by Rupert Hine. March 1979. Arista Records.
Reissued on CD in 1990 by Virgin Records, including 'Souvenirs' and 'Magdalen'.

Private Parts And Pieces

Beauty And The Beast; Field Of Eternity (Phillips/Rutherford); *Tibetan Yak-Music; Lullaby – Old Father Time; Harmonium In The Dust (Or Harmonious Stratosphere); Tregenna Afternoons; Reaper; Autumnal; Flamingo; Seven Long Years.
Produced by Anthony Phillips, except * Harry Williamson. March 1979. Arista Records. (Issued free with first 5000 copies of *Sides*.)
Reissued on CD in 1990 by Virgin Records, including 'Stranger' and 'Silver Song' (demo) (Phillips/Rutherford).

1984

Prelude '84; 1984 Part 1; 1984 Part 2; Anthem 1984.
Produced by Anthony Phillips, assisted by Richard Scott. July 1981. RCA Records.

Antiques: Private Parts And Pieces III (With Enrique Berro Garcia)

Motherforest; Hurlingham Suite: (i) Ivied Castles (Phillips), (ii) Frosted Windows, (iii) Bandido, (iv) Church Bells At Sunset; Suite In D Minor: (i) Whirlpools, (ii) Cobblestones, (iii) Catacombs; Danse Nude; Esperansa; Elegy; Otto's Face; Sand Dunes; Old Wives Tale (Phillips).
Produced by Anthony Phillips. March 1982. RCA Records.
All songs by Phillips and Berro Garcia unless stated.

Harvest Of The Heart

Esperanza; Salmon Leap; Flapjack; Bouncer; Beauty And The Beast; Amorphous, Cadaverous And Nebulous; Salmon's Last Sleepwalk; Bandido; Sistine; Lindsay; Over The Gate; The Sea And The Armadillo; Lights On The Hill; Trail Of Tears; Erotic Strings.
September 1985. Cherry Records. (Compilation – credits as per original album.)

Missing Links Volume 1 – Finger Painting

Force Majeure; Mountain Voices; Lord Of The Smoking Mirror; Sea Horses; Dungeons; Between The Rings; Evening Ascent; Streamer; After

The Rain; Rottweiler; Sad Fish; A Song; God's Chosen Car Park Suite: (i) Professional, (ii) Meditation, (iii) Cave Painting; Tropical Moon Over Dorking Suite: (i) Estrangement, (ii) Myra's Dream, (iii) Reconciliation; Fountain Pool; CQ; Three Piece Suite: (i) To The Shrine, (ii) Through The Forest, (iii) Towards The Light; Boulevard Of Fallen Angels; Land Of Dragons Suite: (i) Land Of Dragons Part 1, (ii) Kites, (iii) The Harbour At Sunset, (iv) Dance Of The Crabs, (v) Sand Octopus And The King Crabs, (vi) Do The Shrimps Know They're Chinese?, (vii) Land Of Dragons Part 2; And A Prayer; Terra Del Fuego; Paradise Found.
Produced by Anthony Phillips. 1989. Cassette only. Reissued on CD in 1992 by Brainworks Records.

Slow Dance

Slow Dance (Part 1); Slow Dance (Part 2).
Produced by Anthony Phillips and Simon Heyworth. September 1990. Virgin Records.

Back To The Pavilion: Private Parts And Pieces II

†Scottish Suite: (i) Salmon Leap, (ii) Parting Thistle, (iii) Electric Reaper, (iv) Amorphous, Cadaverous And Nebulous, (v) Salmons' Last Sleepwalk; Lindsay; *K2; *Postlude – End Of The Season; Heavens; *Spring Meeting; Romany's Aria; *Chinaman; Nocturne; Magic Garden; Von Runkel's Yorker Music; Will O' The Wisp; Tremulous; I Saw You Today; Back To The Pavilion; Lucy: An Illusion.
Produced by Anthony Phillips, except * by Rupert Hine and † by Anthony Phillips and Anton Matthews. February 1991. Virgin Records.
(Originally released in the USA in 1980.)

A Catch At The Tables: Private Parts And Pieces IV

Arboretum Suite: (i) Set Piece, (ii) Over The Gate, (iii) Flapjack, (iv) Lights Of The Hill; Earth Man; Dawn Over The Lake; Bouncer; Eduardo; Heart Of Darkness; The Sea And The Armadillo; *Sistine; Erotic Strings; A Catch At The Tables.
Produced by Anthony Phillips, except * by Anthony Phillips, Richard Scott and Trevor Vallis. February 1991. Virgin Records.
(Originally released in the USA in 1984.)

Twelve: Private Parts And Pieces V

January; February; March; April; May; June; July; August; September; October; November; December.
Produced by Anthony Phillips. 1991. Virgin Records.
(Originally released in the USA in 1985.)

Ivory Moon: Private Parts And Pieces VI

Suite – Sea-Dogs Motoring: (i) Sunrise Over Sienna, (ii) Basking Shark, (iii) Sea-dogs' Air, (iv) Safe Havens; Tara's Theme (From Masquerade); Winter's Thaw; The Old House; Moonfall (From Masquerade) (Phillips/Hine); Rapids; Let Us Now Make Love.
Produced by Anthony Phillips. 1991. Virgin Records.
(Originally released overseas in 1987.)

Slow Waves, Soft Stars: Private Parts And Pieces VII

Ice Flight: (i) Flight Of The Snow Petrel: Glacier Bay, (ii) Flight Of The Whale Birds: Blizzard Mountain, (iii) Flight Of The Albatross: Ice Island, (iv) White Heaven, (v) Cathedral Of Ice; Beachrunner (Phillips/Berro Garcia); End Of The Affair (Phillips/Berro Garcia); The Golden Pathway; Behind The Waterfall; Carnival; Through The Black Hole; Pluto Garden; Sospirando; Elevenses; Goodbye Serenade; Bubble And Squeak; Vanishing Streets; Slow Waves, Soft Stars.
Produced by Anthony Phillips. 1991. Virgin Records.
(Originally released overseas in 1987.)

WITH THE ANTHONY PHILLIPS BAND

Invisible Men

Sally (Phillips); Golden Bodies; Going For Broke; It's Not Easy (Phillips); Love In A Hot Air Balloon; Traces; I Want Your Heart; Falling For Love; Guru (Phillips); The Women Were Watching; My Time Has Come (Phillips).
Produced by Anthony Phillips and Richard Scott. March 1984. Street Tunes.
All songs written by Phillips and Scott unless stated.
Reissued on CD in 1990 by Virgin Records including Alex (Phillips); Ballad Of Penlee (Phillips); Trail Of Tears (Phillips).

With Harry Williamson

Tarka

Movement I (Williamson/Phillips); Movement II (Williamson); Movement III (Phillips); The Anthem (Phillips/Heyworth).
Produced by Simon Heyworth. 1988. Precision Records.

SINGLES

We're All As We Lie/Squirrel/Sitars and Nebulous. June 1978.
Um & Aargh/Souvenirs. April 1979.
Prelude '84/Anthem '84. July 1981.

With the Anthony Phillips Band

Sally/Women Were Waiting/Exocet. 1984.
Released as 12" only.

With Harry Williamson

The Anthem From Tarka/The Rising Spring. 1988.
CD: *The Anthem From Tarka* (single mix)/The Rising Spring (Williamson)/
Excerpt From Tarka – Movement I Part I/Excerp, From Tarka – Movement
III/The Anthem From Tarka (single mix extended version).

INFORMATION

Information Service: 174 Salisbury Road, Everton, Liverpool, L5 6RU.

PETER GABRIEL UK DISCOGRAPHY

'A different drum'

ALBUMS

Peter Gabriel

Moribund The Burgermeister; Solsbury Hill; Modern Love; Excuse Me
(Gabriel/Hall); Humdrum; Slowburn; Waiting For The Big One; Down
The Dolce Vita; Here Comes The Flood.
Produced by Bob Ezrin. February 1977. Charisma.
Chart: 7.

Peter Gabriel

On The Air; DIY; Mother Of Violence (P. Gabriel/J. Gabriel); A Wonderful
Day In A One Way World; White Shadow; Indigo; Animal Magic;
Exposure (Gabriel/Fripp); Flotsam And Jetsam; Perspective; Home Sweet
Home.
Produced by Robert Fripp. June 1978. Charisma.
Chart: 10.

Peter Gabriel

Intruder; No Self Control; Start; I Don't Remember; Family Snapshot;
And Through The Wire; Games Without Frontiers; Not One Of Us; Lead
A Normal Life; Biko.
Produced by Steve Lillywhite. June 1980. Charisma.
Chart: 1.

Peter Gabriel

The Rhythm Of The Heat; San Jacinto; I Have The Touch; The Family
And The Fishing Net; Shock The Monkey; Lay Your Hands On Me;
Wallflower; Kiss Of Life.
Produced by David Lord and Peter Gabriel. September 1982. Charisma.
Chart: 6.

Peter Gabriel Plays Live

The Rhythm Of The Heat; I Have The Touch; Not One Of Us; Family
Snapshot; DIY; The Family And The Fishing Net; Intruder; I Go Swim-
ming; San Jacinto; Solsbury Hill; No Self Control; I Don't Remember;
Shock The Monkey; Humdrum; On The Air; Biko.
Produced by Peter Walsh and Peter Gabriel. May 1983. Charisma.
Chart: 8.

Birdy

At Night; Floating Dogs; Quiet And Alone; Close Up; Slow Water;
Dressing The Wound; Birdy's Flight; Slow Marimbas; The Heat; Sketch-
pad With Trumpet And Voice; Under Lock And Key; Powerhouse At
The Foot Of The Mountain.
Produced by Peter Gabriel and Daniel Lanois. March 1985. Charisma.
Chart: 51.

So

Red Rain; Sledgehammer; Don't Give Up; That Voice Again (Gabriel/
Rhodes); In Your Eyes; Mercy Street; Big Time; We Do What We're Told;
This Is The Picture (Anderson/Gabriel).
Produced by Daniel Lanois and Peter Gabriel. May 1986. Virgin.
Chart: 1.

Passion

The Feeling Begins; Gethsemane; Of These, Hope; Lazarus Raised; Of
These, Hope – Reprise; In Doubt; A Different Drum; Zaar; Troubled;
Open (Gabriel/Shankar); Before Night Falls; With This Love; Sandstorm;
Stigmata (Gabriel/Mahmoud Tabrizi Zadeh); Passion; With This Love
– Choir; Wall Of Breath; The Promise Of Shadows; Disturbed; It Is
Accomplished; Bread And Wine.
Produced by Peter Gabriel. June 1989. Real World.
Chart: 29.

Shaking The Tree – Sixteen Golden Greats

Solsbury Hill; I Don't Remember; Sledgehammer; Family Snapshot; Mercy Street; Shaking The Tree (Gabriel/N'Dour); Don't Give Up; San Jacinto; Here Comes The Flood; Red Rain; Games Without Frontiers; Shock The Monkey; I Have The Touch; Big Time; Zaar; Biko.
November 1990. Virgin.
Chart: 11

SINGLES

Solsbury Hill/Moribund The Burgermeister. March 1977. Chart: 13.
   Later released as CD with Solsbury Hill (full-length live version).
Modern Love/Slowburn. June 1977.
DIY/Perspective. May 1978.
DIY (remix)/Mother Of Violence/Me And My Teddy Bear (Coots/ Winters). September 1978.
Games Without Frontiers/The Start/I Don't Remember. February 1980. Chart: 4.
No Self Control/Lead A Normal Life. May 1980. Chart: 33.
Biko/Shosholoza (Traditional)/Jetzt Kommt Die Flut. August 1980. Chart: 38.
   12": As 7".
Shock The Monkey/Soft Dog. September 1982. Chart: 58.
   7" picture disc: As 7".
   12": As 7".
I have The Touch/Across The River (Gabriel/Shankar/Rhodes/Copeland). December 1982.
I Don't Remember (live)/Solsbury Hill (live). July 1983. Chart: 62.
   12": As 7" plus Kiss Of Life (live).
   12": As 12" plus free white label 12" of Games Without Frontiers and Schnappschuss.
Walk Through The Fire/The Race (written and performed by Larry Carlton). May 1984. Chart: 69.
   12": As 7" plus I Have The Touch.
Sledgehammer/Don't Break This Rhythm. April 1986. Chart: 4.
   Cassette: As 7".
   12": As 7" plus I Have The Touch 85 remix.
   12": Sledgehammer Dance Mix/Don't Break This Rhythm/I Have The Touch 85 remix/Biko (ext.).
   Later released on CD as per 1st 12" single.

Don't Give Up (with Kate Bush)/In Your Eyes (special mix). October 1986.
  Chart: 9.
  7" with poster: As 7".
  12": As 7" plus This is The Picture.
Big Time/Curtains. March 1987. Chart: 13.
  Cassette: As 7".
  12": Big Time (ext.)/Big Time (7")/Curtains.
  CD: Big Time (ext.)/Big Time (7")/Curtains/Across The River/No Self
  Control.
Red Rain/Ga-ga. July 1987. Chart: 46.
  Cassette: As 7".
  12": As 7" plus Walk Through The Fire.
Biko (live)/No More Apartheid (Little Steven). November 1987. Chart: 49.
  12": as 7".
  CD: As 7" plus I Have The Touch 85 remix.
Solsbury Hill/Shaking The Tree. December 1990. Chart: 57.
  Cassette: As 7".
  12": As 7" plus Games Without Frontiers (live).
  CD: As 7" plus Games Without Frontiers (live).

WITH YOUSSOU N'DOUR

Shaking The Tree/Old Tucson. May 1989. Chart: 61.
  12": As 7" with Sweeping The Leaves.
  CD: As 7" with Sweeping The Leaves.
NB. Tracks other than Shaking The Tree were Youssou N'Dour songs
  from his album *The Lion*.

VIDEOS

CV

Big Time; Don't Give Up; Shock The Monkey; Mercy Street; Sledgehammer; I Don't Remember; Red Rain; Don't Give Up.
Released 1987. Virgin Music Video.

POV

Recorded in Athens, 1987: This Is The Picture; San Jacinto; Shock The Monkey; Games Without Frontiers; No Self Control; Mercy Street; Sledgehammer; Solsbury Hill; Lay Your Hands On Me; Don't Give Up; In Your Eyes; Biko.
Released 1990. Virgin Music Video.

The Desert And Her Daughters (with Jon Hassell)

Released 1990. Hendring Video.

NB. Peter Gabriel's specially commissioned soundtracks are also featured on the video releases of *Birdy* and *The Last Temptation Of Christ*.

BOOKS

Bright, Spencer, *Peter Gabriel – An Authorized Biography*, Sidgwick & Jackson, London, 1988.
Gallo, Armando, *Peter Gabriel*, Omnibus Press, London, 1986.

STEVE HACKETT UK DISCOGRAPHY

'People dream in colour here'

ALBUMS

Voyage Of The Acolyte

Ace Of Wands; Hands Of The Priestess Part I; A Tower Struck Down
(S. Hackett/J. Hackett); Hands Of The Priestess Part II; The Hermit; Star
Of Sirius; The Lovers; Shadow Of The Hierophant (Hackett/Rutherford).
Produced by Steve Hackett and John Acock. October 1975. Charisma.
Chart: 26.

Please Don't Touch

Narnia; Carry On Up The Vicarage; Racing In A; Kim; How Can I?;
Hoping Love Will Last; Land Of A Thousand Autumns; Please Don't
Touch; The Voice of Necam; Icarus Ascending.
Produced by John Acock and Steve Hackett. April 1978. Charisma.
Chart: 38.

Spectral Mornings

Every Day; The Virgin And The Gypsy; The Red Flower Of Tachai
Blooms Everywhere; Clocks – The Angel Of Mons; The Ballad Of The
Decomposing Man; Lost Time In Cordoba; Tigermoth; Spectral
Mornings.
Produced by John Acock and Steve Hackett. May 1979. Charisma.
Chart: 22.

Defector

The Steppes; Time To Get Out; Slogans; Leaving; Two Vamps As Guests; Jacuzzi; Hammer In The Sand; The Toast; The Show; Sentimental Institution (Hackett/Hicks).
Produced by Steve Hackett and John Acock. June 1980. Charisma.
Chart: 9.

Cured

Hope I Don't Wake; Picture Postcard; Can't Let Go; The Air-Conditioned Nightmare; Funny Feeling (Hackett/Magnus); A Cradle Of Swans; Overnight Sleeper (Hackett/Poor); Turn Back Time.
Produced by Steve Hackett, John Acock, Nick Magnus. August 1981. Charisma.
Chart: 15.

Highly Strung

Camino Royale (Hackett/Magnus); Cell 151; Always Somewhere Else; Walking Through Walls; Give It Away; Weightless; Group Therapy; India Rubber Man; Hackett to Pieces (Hackett/Magnus).
Produced by Steve Hackett and John Acock. March 1983. Charisma.
Chart: 16.

Bay Of Kings

Bay Of Kings; The Journey; Kim; Marigold; St Elmo's Fire; Petropolis; Second Chance; Cast Adrift; Horizons; Black Light; The Barren Land; Calmaria.
Produced by Steve Hackett and John Acock. November 1983. Lamborghini.
Chart: 70.

Till We Have Faces

Duel; Matilda Smith-Williams Home For The Aged (Hackett/Magnus); Let Me Count The Ways; A Doll That's Made In Japan; Myopia (Hackett/Magnus); What's My Name (Hackett/Magnus); The Rio Connection; Taking The Easy Way Out; When You Wish Upon A Star (Harina/Washington).
Produced by Steve Hackett. Co-produced by John Acock, Nick Magnus and Waldemar Falcao. September 1984. Lamborghini.
Chart: 54.

Momentum

Cavalcanti; The Sleeping Sea; Portrait Of A Brazilian Lady; When The Bell Breaks; A Bed, A Chair And A Guitar (Trad.); Concert For Munich; Last Rites Of Innocence; Troubled Spirit; Variation On Theme By Chopin; Pierrot; Momentum.
Produced by Steve Hackett and John Acock. April 1988. Start.

WITH QUIET WORLD

The Road

The Great Birth; Theme; First Light; Theme; Star; Theme; Loneliness; Theme; Change Of Age; Christ One; Hang On; Christ Continued; Body To The Mind; Traveller; Let Everybody Sing; Theme; Children Of The World; Change Of Age; Love Is Walking.
1970. Dawn Records.

WITH GTR

GTR

When The Heart Rules The Mind (Hackett/Howe); The Hunter (Downes); Here I Wait (Hackett/Howe); Sketches In The Sun (Howe); Jekyll And Hyde (Hackett/Howe/Bacon); You Can Still Get Through (Hackett/ Howe); Reach Out (Never Say No) (Hackett/Howe/Spalding); Toe The Line (Hackett/Howe); Hackett To Bits; Imagining (Hackett/Howe/Mover).
Produced by Geoff Downes. June 1986. Arista.
Chart: 41.

SINGLES

How Can I? (featuring Richie Havens)/Kim. May 1978.
Narnia (remix)/Please Don't Touch. October 1978.
Every Day (re-recorded)/Lost Time In Cordoba. June 1979.
Clocks – The Angel Of Mons (remix)/Acoustic Set (live). September 1979.
    12″: As 7″ plus Tigermoth (live).
The Show/Hercules Unchained (Hackett/Hicks). March 1980.
Sentimental Institution/The Toast. August 1980.
Hope I Don't Wake/Tales Of The Riverbank (anon.). August 1981.

Picture Postcard/Theme from *Second Chance*. October 1981.

Cell 151/Time Lapse At Milton Keynes. March 1983. Chart: 66.
   12": As 7" plus Air-Conditioned Nightmare (live).
   12": As 12" plus free white label of Clocks 12" release.

A Doll That's Made In Japan/A Doll That's Made In Japan (instr.). August 1984.
   12": A Doll That's Made In Japan/Just The Bones.

With Quiet World

Love Is Walking/Children Of The World. 1970.

With GTR

When The Heart Rules The Mind/Reach Out (Never Say No). May 1986.
   7" shaped picture disc: As 7".
   12": As 7" plus Sketches In The Sun and Hackett To Bits.

NB. Steve Hackett also organized and produced the Rock Against Repatriation single 'Sailing'. Released on 7" and CD in 1990 on IRS.

VIDEO

Steve Hackett – Live

Recorded at Central Studios, Nottingham 1990: Camino Royale; Please Don't Touch; Every Day; In That Quiet Earth; Depth Charge; Wonderpatch; In The Heart Of The City; Black Light; Horizons; Jacuzzi; Theatre Of Sleep; Jazz Jam; Spectral Mornings; Clocks.
Released 1992. Castle Music Pictures.

WAS IT A OR WAS IT B OR WAS IT X OR Z?

Sources

Some of the material in the book comes directly from interviews that we have carried out with members of the group. Where this is not the case, the quotes are given a superscript number which relates to the list of sources below.

1   Piccadilly Radio, Manchester, September 1982
2   'The Angel Gabriel' by Penny Vincenzi, *Options*, July 1987
3   *Moondogs*, Dutch Radio, 3 June 1986
4   BBC Scotland
5   *Genesis – I Know What I Like* by Armando Gallo, Omnibus Press, 1987
6   Interview by Geoff Parkyn, *Genesis Information 24*, 1982
7   *From Genesis To Revelation* LP review by Mark Williams, *International Times* 57, 23 May 1969
8   *Peter Gabriel – An Authorized Biography* by Spencer Bright, Sidgwick & Jackson, 1988
9   'Blind Date' review by Roger Waters, *Melody Maker*, 10 January 1970
10 *The Phil Collins Story* by Johnny Waller, Zomba Books, 1985
11 *Trespass* LP review by Jerry Gilbert, *Sounds*, 14 November 1970
12 *Trespass* LP review by Michael Watts, *Melody Maker*, 12 December 1970
13 Concert review Godalming Gin Mill (20 December 1970), by Jerry Gilbert, *Sounds*, 26 December 1970
14 Concert review London Lyceum (24 January 1971), by Michael Watts, *Melody Maker*, January 1971
15 'The Charterhouse Boys' by Steve Clarke, *New Musical Express*, 1 June 1974
16 'The Genesis Guide to Genesis' by Steve Clarke, *New Musical Express*, 4 December 1976
17 *Nursery Cryme* LP review by Jerry Gilbert, *Sounds*, 4 December 1971
18 'The Spaghetti Scene' by Tony Tyler, *New Musical Express*, 22 April 1972
19 'Talking with Genesis', *Zig Zag*, 29 June 1973
20 *The Book of Genesis* by Hugh Fielder, Sidgwick & Jackson, 1984
21 Quote from March 1973. Source unknown. Printed in *Genesis Information* 12, July 1979

22   *Electronics and Music Maker*, November 1983
23   *Nursery Cryme* LP review by Richard Cromelin, *Rolling Stone*, 26 October 1972
24   '$16,000 Debut' by Jerry Gilbert, *Sounds*, 23 December 1972
25   'Genesis: Monster Smash' by Chris Welch, *Melody Maker*, 17 February 1973
26   'What Genesis Did On Their Holidays' by Chris Welch, *Melody Maker*, 28 July 1973
27   'Genesis: A Live Treat' by Chris Welch, *Melody Maker*, 4 August 1973
28   'Genesis Play the West End' by Michael Wale, *The Times*, 15 January 1974
29   Review by Robin Denselow, *Guardian*, 17 January 1974
30   'We Can't Dance' by Martin Townsend, *Vox*, December 1991
31   'Genesis, A Revelation: No "Pale" Imitation' by John Swenson, *Crawdaddy*, March 1974
32   'Masked Idol' by Chris Welch, *Melody Maker*, 19 January 1974
33   'The Drums of Genesis' by Robin Tolleson, *Drums and Drumming*, summer 1987
34   *Peter Gabriel* by Armando Gallo, Omnibus Press, 1986
35   'Public School Boy Reprimands Critics' by Neil Spencer, *New Musical Express*, 2 November 1974
36   *Andy Peebles Show*, Piccadilly Radio, Manchester, 28 April 1975
37   'Mickey Mouse Lies Down On Broadway' by Barbara Charone, *Sounds*, 26 October 1974
38   'Plodding Genesis' by Chris Welch, *Melody Maker*, 23 November 1974
39   'Lamb Like A Polished Diamond' by Barbara Charone, *Sounds*, 23 November 1974
40   *Text from 'The Lamb Lies Down On Broadway'* by Peter Gabriel
41   'Gabriel's Cosmic Juice' by Max Bell, *New Musical Express*, 15 March 1975
42   'Peter Gabriel', *Beat Instrumental*, April 1977
43   'Gabriel's Ladder' by Chris Welch, *Melody Maker*, 15 March 1975
44   'Backseat Driver' by Chris Welch, *Melody Maker*, 26 April 1975
45   'Behind Peter Gabriel's Mask' by Chris Welch, *Melody Maker*, December 1975
46   Letter from Peter Gabriel to the music press, September 1975
47   'Genesis Post Gabriel' by Jim Farber, *International Musician and Recording World*, June 1976
48   'Genesis' by Barbara Charone, *Zig Zag* 53, June 1975
49   *Mummy's Weekly* with Nicky Horne, Capital Radio, London, 11 July 1979
50   'The Lamb Lies Down But Genesis Carry On' by Barbara Charone, *Sounds*, 13 September 1975
51   'Where In Hell's Name We Gonna Rake Up Another Guy With A Mush Like That?' by Tony Tyler, *New Musical Express*, 13 September 1975
52   'Genesis After Gabriel: How Will They Survive?' by Mick Houghton, Circus, 1976
53   *Andy Peebles Show*, Capital Radio, London, 25 June 1977
54   'Genesis: Supper Is Definitely Ready' by Barbara Charone, *Sounds*, 15 May 1976
55   'Genesis: Chapter II' by Barbara Charone, *Sounds*, 14 February 1976
56   *Perspective* with Pat Sharp, BRMB Radio, 3 March 1989
57   'Genesis' Night To Remember' by Chris Welch, *Melody Maker*, 19 June 1976
58   *Tim Lyons Show*, Piccadilly Radio, Manchester, October 1979

59   Interview by Roger Newell, *Genesis Information* 51, 1990
60   'Britain's Premier Drummer', *International Musician and Recording World*, March 1978
61   'Cold Genesis' by Chris Welch, *Melody Maker*, 8 January 1977
62   'Then There Were Three' by Hugh Fielder, *Sounds*, 22 October 1977
63   'A Solo Voyage' by Peter Douglas, *Beat International*, June 1978
64   Hallam FM, Sheffield, 11 March 1980
65   'Genesis: A Return To The Roots' by Karl Dallas, *Melody Maker*, 11 March 1978
66   *Genesis in Liverpool*, Granada TV, 1980
67   'Game for a Laugh' by Andy Hughes, *Zig Zag*, October 1982
68   *Tom Russell Show*, Clyde 1 FM, Glasgow, 24 September 1982
69   '12–45, 50% Female' by David Hepworth, *Q*, September 1982
70   'The Shocking Truth About Genesis in America' by Hugh Fielder, *Sounds*, 22 April 1978
71   'Banks Account' by Paul Colbert, *Making Music*, September 1989
72   'Phil Collins and His Groovy Kind of Love' by Ian Woodward, *Me*, 6 November 1989
73   'The Genesis Phenomenon' by Lynden Barber, *International Musician and Recording World*, May 1980
74   *Smallcreep's Day* LP review by Hugh Fielder, *Sounds*, 9 February 1980
75   John Martyn 'Piece by Piece' Tour Programme by Brendan Quayle
76   'Facing Up To New Values' by Lynden Barber, *Melody Maker*, 7 February 1981
77   BBC Radio 1 Interview with Kid Jensen, 12 March 1980
78   'Musicianship Over Personalities Over Fashion Equals Genesis' by Ray Coleman, *Melody Maker*, 4 October 1980
79   'Duke of Hazard' by Hugh Fielder, *Sounds*, 10 May 1980
80   'Power Pomp Supremos' by Hugh Fielder, *Sounds*, 5 April 1980
81   *Robin Valk Show*, BRMB Radio, Birmingham, 1 February 1981
82   'Face the Press' by Steve Lake, *Melody Maker*, 30 March 1985
83   BBC Radio 1 Interview with Mike Smith, 6 June 1986
84   BBC Radio 1 Interview with Richard Skinner, 12 September 1981
85   Hallam FM, Sheffield, 28 September 1981
86   'Face the Music' by Allan Jones, *Melody Maker*, 7 February 1981
87   BBC Radio 1 Interview with Andy Peebles, May 1982
88   *Robin Valk Show*, BRMB Radio, Birmingham, January 1982
89   'Why I Had To Leave The Nest' by Hugh Fielder, *Sounds*, 7 February 1981
90   'The Great Escape' by Hugh Fielder, *Sounds*, 26 September 1981
91   'Three Wise Men' by Cathi Wheatley, *Sounds*, 26 September 1981
92   Concert review, New York Savoy Theatre (November 1981) by Hugh Fielder, *Sounds*, December 1981
93   *Three Sides Live* LP review by Hugh Fielder, *Sounds*, June 1982
94   'The Lamb Wakes Up' by Paul Strange, *Melody Maker*, 9 October 1982
95   'A Tale Told By An Idiot' by Amrik Rai, *New Musical Express*, 9 October 1982
96   *Acting Very Strange* LP review by Paul Strange, *Melody Maker*, September 1982
97   'Italian Inferno' by Hugh Fielder, *Sounds*, 26 September 1982

98   'From Genesis To Revelation' by Tony Goodman, *Soundmaker*, 5 February
      1983
99   'Phil Collins Goes Into Overdrive' by Steve Gett, *Kerrang*, 16 October 1982
100   'Mothercare' by Bill Black, *Sounds*, 17 September 1983
101   'Brum Punch' by Chris Welch, *Kerrang*, 23 February 1984
102   'Mama Mia' by Chris Welch, *Kerrang*, 6 October 1983
103   'Mama From Heaven' by Hugh Fielder, *Sounds*, 1 October 1983
104   BBC Radio 1 *Saturday Sequence* with Johnnie Walker, 13 June 1987
105   Interview by Geoff Parkyn, *Genesis Information* 38, Winter 85/86
106   *Tonight, Tonight, Tonight* promotional LP, Atlantic Records, USA
107   BBC Radio 1 *Classic Albums* with Roger Scott, 3 June 1989
108   Giants Stadium New York Press Conference, May 1987, reported by Geoff
      Parkyn, *Genesis Information* 44, 1987
109   Interview by Geoff Parkyn, *Genesis Information* 48, 1989
110   Interview by Geoff Parkyn, *Genesis Information* 52, 1991
111   Virgin Records press release, 1991
112   BBC Radio 1 *Gary Davies Show*, November 1991
113   BBC Radio 1 *Saturday Sequence* with Johnnie Walker, November 1991
114   'Faultless Phil' by Michael Watts, *Options*, May 1987
115   'The Ever Changing Face of Peter Gabriel', *Melody Maker*, 14 February 1981.

Index